SOVEREIGN
RARITIES

MORE THAN A CENTURY *of* COLLECTIVE EXPERIENCE in NUMISMATICS

SOVEREIGN RARITIES LTD IS A SPECIALIST TEAM OF EXPERIENCED NUMISMATISTS WITH A WORLD-CLASS REPUTATION FOR OFFERING COLLECTORS THE HIGHEST QUALITY RARE COINS. CONTACT US TODAY TO START OR ADD TO YOUR COLLECTION.

17 - 19 MADDOX STREET, LONDON, W1S 2QH
TEL +44 (0)20 3019 1185
FAX +44 (0)33 0119 3730
INFO@SOVR.CO.UK
WWW.SOVR.CO.UK

HERITAGE AUCTIONS
The World's Largest Numismatic Auctioneer

Great Britain: Edward VIII gold Proof Pattern 5 Pounds 1937
PR67 Ultra Cameo NGC
Realised $2,280,000
Perhaps the Finest Known

1787 New York-Style Brasher Doubloon
MS65★ NGC. CAC
Realised $9,360,000
The Finest-Known Example

Jewish War (66-70 AD). AR Shekel
Realised $1,105,375
Prototype Year One Shekel
One of Two Known Specimens

Accepting consignments year-round for Select, Showcase, and Signature® Auctions. Contact a Heritage Consignment Director today for a free appraisal of your collection.

Cole Schenewerk | Managing Director, Heritage London
+44 (0)207 493 0498 | UK@HA.com

HERITAGE
AUCTIONS
THE WORLD'S LARGEST NUMISMATIC AUCTIONEER

DALLAS | NEW YORK | BEVERLY HILLS | CHICAGO | PALM BEACH
LONDON | PARIS | GENEVA | BRUSSELS | AMSTERDAM | HONG KONG

BP 20%; see HA.com. 64275

ECOINOMICS

Your Guide to the Global Numismatic Market

世界のレアコイン市場へのガイド

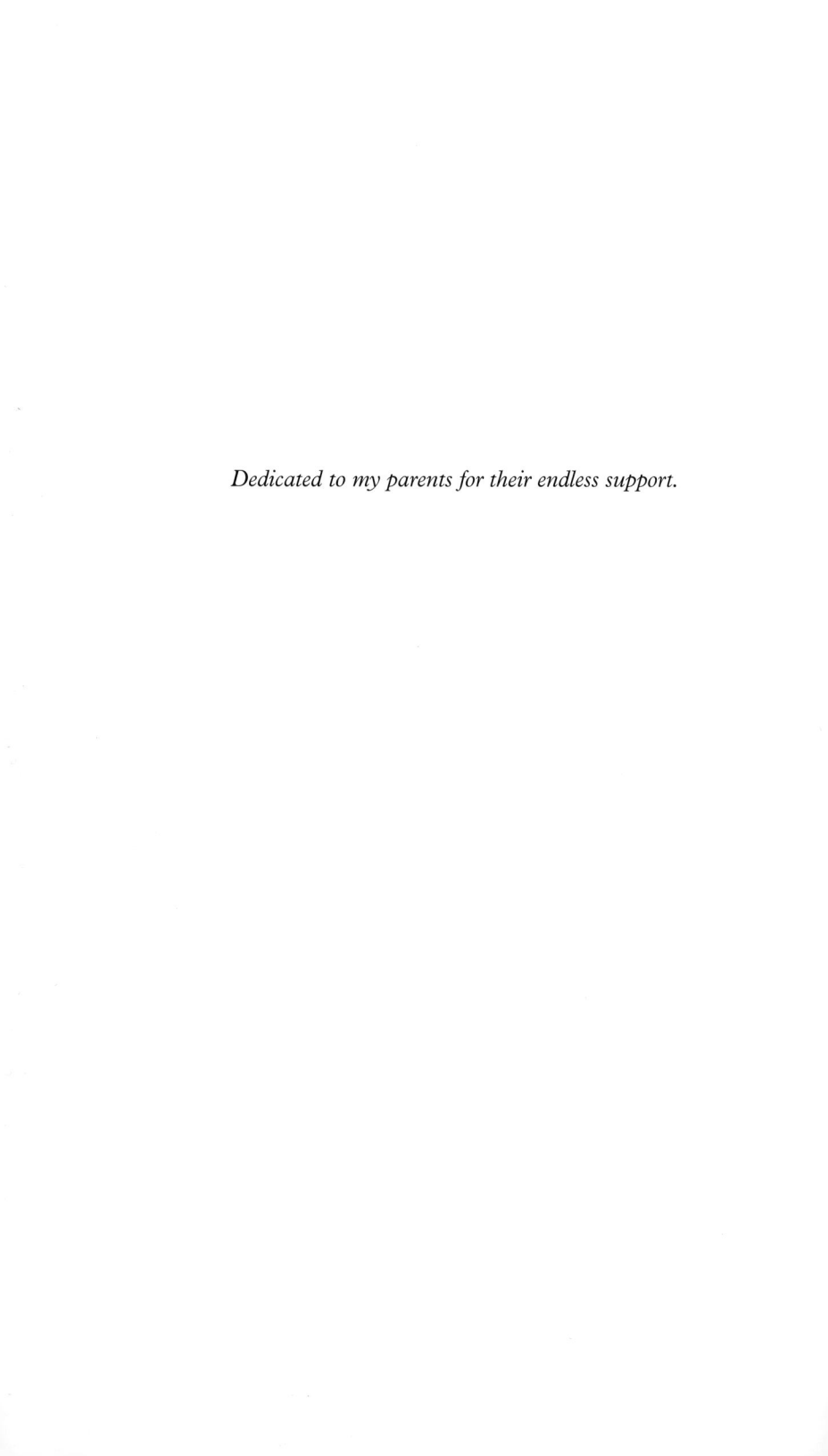

Dedicated to my parents for their endless support.

ECOINOMICS

Your Guide to the Global Numismatic Market

世界のレアコイン市場へのガイド

ROBERT PARKINSON

SPINK

First published in 2022 by Spink and Son Ltd

Copyright © 2022 Robert Parkinson

The moral right of Robert Parkinson to be identified as the author of this work has been asserted by him in accordance with the Copyright, Designs and Patents Act of 1988.

All rights reserved. No part of this publication may be reproduced, stored in a retrieval system or transmitted in any form or by any means, electronic, mechanical, photocopying, recording or otherwise, without the prior permission of both the copyright owner and the above publisher of this book.

A CIP catalogue record for this book is available from the British Library.

ISBN 978-1-912667-78-9

Typeset by Russ Whittle, Litmus Graphics

Printed and bound by Gutenberg Press Ltd, Malta

Spink and Son Ltd
69 Southampton Row
London WC1B 4ET

www.spinkbooks.com

Contents

Acknowledgements vi

My Two Cents 2

Section 1: The Numismatic Market

1.1. History of Numismatics 10

1.2. What Makes a Coin Valuable? 28

1.3. Third-Party Grading 69

1.4. Global Markets 83

1.5. Market Participants..98

Section 2: Coins as an Asset Class

2.1. Knowledge is Power 120

2.2. Putting Cash into Cash 131

2.3. Market Dynamics 151

2.4. Costs, Fees and Taxation 178

2.5. Coins in Context 188

Section 3: Trading Coins

3.1. Conducting Research 213

3.2. Quality and Authenticity 227

3.3. Buying 259

3.4. Selling 275

Heads or Tails...292

Bibliography...297

Index 299

Acknowledgements

I wish to acknowledge the valuable contribution of the following who have provided information or submitted images to enhance this book.

Kevin Clancy, Royal Mint
Max Spiegel, NGC
Ann Laffeaty
Brian Parkinson
Leonard Louloudis
Christian Winge
Diego Rodriguez
Cale Meier
Zachary Beasley
Steve Hill
Sovereign Rarities Ltd
Spink & Son Ltd
Heritage Auctions
Baldwin's
St James's Auctions
Classical Numismatic Group
Dix Noonan Webb
Numismatica Ars Classica
Stack's Bowers
Coutts & Co
Ira and Larry Goldberg
Rex Rarities
Roma Numismatics
Noble Numismatics
Joseph McGregor
Ian Russell, Great Collections
The British Museum
Eric Guinther
John Loffredo, former Managing Director and Co-Head, Municipal Portfolio Management Group, BlackRock

SOVEREIGN RARITIES LTD

MORE THAN A CENTURY *of* COLLECTIVE EXPERIENCE *in the* HIGHEST QUALITY NUMISMATICS

CONTACT THE AUTHOR OF ECOINOMICS TO SELL YOUR COINS AT AUCTION

GEORGE IV (1820-30), GOLD PROOF FIVE POUNDS, 1826, ENGRAVED BY WILLIAM WYON, GRADED BY NGC AS PF63 SOLD BY SOVEREIGN RARITIES LTD AT AUCTION FOR £148,800 INCLUDING BUYER'S PREMIUM.

THE AUTHOR OF THIS BOOK IS A SENIOR NUMISMATIST AT SOVEREIGN RARITIES LTD, A LEADING NUMISMATIC DEALERSHIP AND AUCTION HOUSE WITH A WORLD-CLASS REPUTATION FOR SPECIALISING IN THE RAREST AND HIGHEST QUALITY COINS. CONTACT ROBERT PARKINSON TO DISCUSS COMPETITIVE RATES AND INCENTIVES FOR SELLING INDIVIDUAL COINS OR AN ENTIRE COLLECTION WITH SOVEREIGN RARITIES LTD.

17 - 19 MADDOX STREET, LONDON, W1S 2QH
TEL +44 (0)20 3019 1185
FAX +44 (0)33 0119 3730
INFO@SOVR.CO.UK
WWW.SOVR.CO.UK

My Two Cents

Picture the scene. It is May 2020 and the coronavirus pandemic has plunged the global capital markets into chaos. The FTSE 100 and Dow Jones are both down 20% from their January levels and the world economy is hurtling towards recession. Over 30 million Americans have filed for unemployment claims so far, with some economists predicting that this number could reach 28% of the US workforce before the month is out. On the other side of the world, China's economy has shrunk for the first time in four decades while Japan - which already reported its own economy shrinking by 6.3% year over year in the three months to December 2019 – has had to cancel the 32nd Olympic Games, a further blow to its economy. Everywhere one looks there is economic turmoil.

Yet in an auction house in Tokyo, bidders are competing fiercely for a prized item. Paddles are raised in the room while bids come in from Europe, the US and elsewhere in Asia via phone and the internet. When the dust settles and all but one bidder is defeated, the price stands at an incredible ¥99,475,000, equivalent to more than $930,000. The item? A coin, a British Five Pounds struck in 1839. It is not even a unique work of art since at least 400 examples were produced - most of which survive to this day. The price attained by this coin is not an anomaly, either. In April 2020 a British Triple Unite struck in 1642 sold for $360,000 in Dallas, Texas while in March a US Dollar from 1804 realised $1.8 million in Santa Ana, California. The question is, why would anyone spend this much money on coins during such troubled times?

Regular reporting of such immense prices has led to a widespread popular awareness that coins can often command significant value. Tabloids vie for our attention with stories of modern circulating coins selling for hundreds online while newspapers tell tales of auctions in which hundreds of thousands are paid for a single coin. As a result, many of us nowadays hold a perception of coins beyond their simple use as a method of payment. We look twice at that interesting penny in our change, we casually research that inherited silver dollar from a junk box in the attic because we feel that we could be holding a real piece of treasure.

"The Current State of the Coin Market" – Unknown Artist, March 2020

The true extent of the numismatic market is even more astounding. Literally billions of dollars change hands every year for rare coins in even the hardest of times. This is because coins occupy a unique niche in the alternative asset market, being bought not only as luxury collectables but also as safe haven investments as a form of hedging. The drive to buy coins is fuelled by collector interest but stabilised by a perception of intrinsic value. So, despite being affected by the same uncertainty that sweeps every other sector, coins are able to weather the storm for three main reasons; they represent a tangible asset, they are seen as a constantly appreciating commodity, and the market is fuelled by both collectors and investors. This means that within a relatively short time, coin values can experience explosive growth. Twenty years ago, that same 1839 Five Pounds that sold in Tokyo in May for $930,000 would have traded hands for $20,000. Additionally, since it is still considered legal tender, if sold by a British collector it would not be subject to any capital gains tax. By investing $20,000 in the year 2000, the owner would have netted more than $900,000 completely tax-free.

However, the new would-be investor is naturally hesitant to dip a toe into the numismatic market as there is so much to learn. The fuel behind any financial market is belief and trust. Buyers need to believe that a transaction will be profitable for them and simultaneously trust the system, platform or individual through which they are transacting. This can be simplified as confidence. Confidence can be gained through a variety of avenues, be it monkey-see-monkey-do, research, advice or experience, but in its absence buyers would never part with their capital and the concept of 'value' would cease to have any meaning.

Within numismatics it can be unclear what to believe or who to trust, and even with proper research we worry that the coin we purchase for $100 might actually be worth just $1. There is plenty of literature available detailing coin varieties, history and a rough idea of values, but the aim of this book is to educate you the reader - whether you are a novice or an industry professional - in the intricacies of numismatics and the market itself. Over the course of this book, I will seek to address the many factors that determine coin value; the range of participants and platforms in the global market and how collector mentality differs from country to country; the performance of coins as assets plus their risk/return profile; and finally the specifics of how one buys and sells.

The majority of my numismatic career has been specifically as a British coin specialist, and so throughout this book the reader will find more references to coins struck in the UK than in other countries. Be this as it may, these coins have been merely selected from my own experience as examples that I feel to be illustrative of wider market and collector trends within numismatics, and can be applied to any and all coin types from every country and era. The purpose of this narrative is to give a truly global perspective of the coin market, from the bazaar in central Asia to the auction houses of the US.

Additionally, in some cases, I am bound by confidentiality to not give identifying details of a client or case. In these instances I will simply refer to the vague themes involved and rough description of locations or sums.

Whether you are aiming to buy coins purely for profit, to build an interesting collection, or a combination of both, this book will educate you on the ins-and-outs of numismatics and equip you with the knowledge to buy wisely and to participate in the market with confidence.

Robert Parkinson, London, 2022

Section 1
The Numismatic Market

CONSIGN NOW

THE GLOBAL COLLECTABLES AUCTION HOUSE

LONDON | NEW YORK | HONG KONG | SINGAPORE | SWITZERLAND

SPINK
Where History is Valued

Follow us on social media

WWW.SPINK.COM

The 'numismatic market' is the blanket term for every exchange of capital for coins, from the small booth in a local market to the most valuable and rare pieces selling at national auctions. For as long as coins have existed their owners have made efforts to establish their values, but without giving much thought to the reasons behind these values. When confronted with an unfamiliar coin, the most common urge is to ask "What is this worth?", when the more important question is "*Why* is this worth that much?".

It is generally well-known that the value of a coin comes down to elements such as its age, rarity, material, condition and collector base. However, the processes and factors which ultimately decide the value of a single coin have their roots in a vast global market with a range of geographical, historical and economic influences. A particular coin may be identical to its counterparts yet feature a rarer mintmark or a minute striking error that immediately increases its value by a multiple of ten. Equally, a coin may have been previously worth tens of thousands, but if the country by which it was made has encountered recent economic hardship its value may suddenly plummet. It is only through understanding factors such as these that the collector or investor can buy wisely in the hope of a profitable resale.

This first section will delve into the ins-and-outs of the hobby as a whole, beginning with its background. Numismatics has an extensive and illustrious history which plays an important part in the mind-set and habits of many collectors today. I will then detail the numerous elements which govern coin value, the different grading standards and procedures practised by regional markets, how collecting trends differ from country to country, and the range of participants in the market from collectors to auction houses.

Listed below is a comprehensive list of appropriate terms, some of which will be used throughout the book and some included for the sake of completeness:

Term	Meaning
Adjustment marks	Filing marks on the face of a coin to remove excess metal, applied before striking
Ancient	Used to describe ancient Greek, Roman and Byzantine coinage, a distinct market from world coins
Cleaned	Improperly wiped, brushed or polished leaving unnatural surfaces or hairlines
Date	The year and sometimes month of production featured on a coin
Denomination	The accepted currency value of a coin, e.g. one Dollar, Five Pounds etc.
Devices	Raised designs on a coin (with a small minority rendered incuse)
Dies	Production elements, pair of metallic stamps on which the designs to be struck on a coin are engraved in reverse and incuse
Edge	Edge of the coin, often bearing reeding or lettering
Engraving	The applying of the design to the dies by the 'engraver'
Field	Empty space between the devices on a coin
Filing	Scraping of metal from the edges of a coin after striking
Hairlines	Fine scratches to a coin's surfaces, generally from friction or cleaning
Hallmark	Small mark or symbol denoting the origin of a coin's metal
Hammered	Early production method in which thin metal blanks were placed between dies and struck with a hammer by hand, generally producing crude coins
Legend	Writing on the face or edge of a coin
Lustre	Desirable original sheen on a coin's surface, microscopic metal striations caused by act of striking
Matte/Matt	Describes devices struck with sandblasted dies to reduce the sheen, giving a 'frosted' look
Milled	Production of coins by machine giving round and even planchets and a more uniform strike, the replacement to hammering as production method
Mintmark	Small mark or symbol denoting the production location of a coin

Mirrored	Surfaces which strongly reflect light, generally associated with proofs
Moneyer	The inclusion of the name of the person who produced the coin, a feature of some early medieval coinage
Mount mark	Evidence of a coin having been previously soldered as a piece of jewellery, most often found on the edge
Obverse	'Heads' side of the coin, often considered the front
Off-Metal	Producing a coin in a metal other than its usual form
Overdate	The punching of a number in the date over an earlier number
Pattern	Trial for a new coin design, sometimes privately produced
Planchet	Intrinsic fabric of a coin (generally metal) on which the designs have been struck; used interchangeably with 'blank' or 'flan'
Portrait	Depiction of a monarch or other figure on the obverse of a coin
Proof	A coin produced as a presentation piece often with reflective fields and matte devices, not intended for circulation
Piedfort	A coin struck to double its weight and thickness
Provenance	Ownership history of a coin including past auctions and collections
Reeding	Also called 'milling', the parallel lines rendered around the edge of some coins
Reverse	'Tails' side of the coin
Rim	Sharp lip where a coin's surfaces meet its edge, most common area to encounter dents or bruises
Specimen	A specially-produced example of a circulating coin, similar to a proof or pattern
Strike	Describes the extent to which the devices have been rendered on the coin, considered weak if the upper elements lack detail
Surfaces	Texture and appearance of the coin itself, combining lustre, patina and strike quality
Tone/Patina	Colouration of a coin from chemical interaction with the environment, often a desirable element

Chapter 1.1.
The History of Numismatics

1. The Coinage Revolution

"The thing that differentiates man from animals is money."
Gertrude Stein

Two and a half thousand years ago in Lydia (modern-day Turkey) the first coins were struck, and global economics was transformed forever. These early metal ingots were produced from electrum - a naturally occurring alloy of gold and silver - and bore the symbol of a lion in representation of the Lydian king Alyattes. Irregular in both appearance and in proportion of gold to silver, the buying power of these first coins was hard to regulate. However, their production represented the final stage of a process ongoing in human society for nearly 10,000 years: the drive to consolidate wealth.

12,000 BC saw the beginning of the Neolithic period and the development of agriculture in the Levant, allowing humans to shift from their nomadic hunter-gatherer lifestyle into a sedentary existence for the first time. Crops were cultivated and animals domesticated, allowing populations to grow and put down roots, the foundations of the first cities. Farming brought stability, society, sedentism – and a hitherto unprecedented surplus of food. This was what first amounted to 'wealth' in human society, the knowledge that one would be provided for throughout the next winter or two, making the society with the biggest surplus the richest. As the millennia passed, this form of wealth evolved. No longer were those in charge of this food surplus satisfied with the expiration date their riches carried. The presence of excess food allowed trade, and trade helped assign value to non-consumable objects such as animal hides, horns, bones and shells; wealth was able to find a new form in substances which could not be consumed. The longer lasting the asset the more desirable it was, and thus the inevitable terminus of this abstract concept of value was a finite, non-spoilable, universally appreciated and stable commodity in which wealth could be stored: metal.

Alyattes's son and successor Croesus took the Lydian coinage one step further than his father, separating electrum into its component metals to create the first bi-metallic gold and silver coins of regular weight and purity in around 550 BC. The societal impact of this 'Croeseid' coinage was instantaneous. The standardised monetary system meant the speculative 'bartering' aspect was removed from transactions and anyone could make their fortune despite their ancestors or resources. Trade blossomed, cementing the Lydians as the first peoples to sell goods by retail, opening shops and markets in the capital city Sardis. Women were able to save up their own dowry and choose their husbands for the first time, and gambling came into being (Lydians, alongside coins, also being credited with inventing the first dice). The ancient Greek historian Herodotus remarked of the Lydians that they were a nation of *kapeloi*, or "merchants".

The wealth that coins helped bring to Lydia fostered considerable arrogance in Croesus and led him to attempt war with the far larger Achaemenid (Persian) Empire. Within just one year his forces were defeated and Sardis was sacked. Despite this, his legacy lived on; the sprawling and discordant Persian Empire recognised the value of the innovative Croeseid coins which had so united Lydia in commerce and introduced their own Daric coinage in response. Lydia's closest neighbour Greece quickly followed suit, their various states producing a range of distinctive coins. Within a century, coins had spread through the Mediterranean, India and southern Asia, copper coins appearing simultaneously in China in the 4th century BC. Coins came to be seen as a societal constant with every kingdom, state and ruler vying to strike their own, their production seen as not only the lifeblood of trade but as a consolidation and demonstration of power. As the Roman Empire was born and expanded out of Italy in the late 2nd century BC, its string of victories were each marked with the production of celebratory coin designs, its generals rewarded with gold medallions. Unscrupulous acts by individuals and usurpers heralded a similar response – on the assassination of Julius Caesar in 44 BC, his murderer Brutus produced a coin bearing two daggers and the date "EID . MAR" for the Ides of March, the date of the act.

Rome, Marcus Junius Brutus "Assassin of Caesar and Imperator" Denarius, 44-42 BC

Besides being a requirement for standardised trade, coins had become a medium for cultural transmission and a celebration of artistic prowess, a handful of different metals struck in a million different designs all across the world. A thousand years on from the first electrum prototypes it seemed as if the role coins played in society would be eternal – but this was not to be.

Precious metals - being held in high regard by almost every culture - had become the standard by which most judged wealth. As such, the use of gold and silver coins meant that civilians were picking directly from the exposed vein of global finance, and what ran through people's hands on a day-to-day basis was the lifeblood of economics, the foundation of entire financial systems. This put society in a vulnerable position. Ultimately, the downfall of coins eventually arose from what was their original intrinsic benefit – their production from a finite resource. In some sense every citizen had become a bullion trader, exploiting arbitrage and even selling their coins at a profit abroad, and naturally coins trickled away to where they received the best price for their metal. By the 9th century AD, the demand for gold and silver in the strong commercial centres of the Islamic Empire led to a dearth of coinage in Western Europe, meaning that many states were unable to produce their own coins; the Islamic Dinar became the only major circulating gold coin, and some early British issues even took to imitating these types to ensure they were accepted by sellers. Distrust grew around unfamiliar coins, of which there were many. While the symbol of Alyattes on Lydia's coinage may have been sufficient to inspire trust amongst his subjects, the range of foreign coin types circulating by the turn of the 1st millennium meant that sellers were often forced to accept currency with no 'backing' as it were, further hindering transactions. Society, now dependent on coinage to function, experienced significantly stunted growth at its loss. The wealth of metal which had underpinned human civilisation for over a thousand years had become an anchor dragging it down.

With the Eastern Mediterranean crusades of 1096-1271, some balance was restored; not merely a religious mission, these conflicts allowed specie to be recovered for Western society. This influx of metal saw a flood of new coin denominations produced in Europe, with problems immediately arising regarding exchange rates. Purity of gold and silver coinage would vary from country to country, and some coin denominations were simply abandoned shortly after invention as they did not divide well into foreign standards. The confusion of interlocking values brought issues with tax and long-distance trade, and these issues fostered innovation. In 14th century Florence, Italy, a vital step was taken towards modern banking and away from the use of coins in finance: the establishment of the Medici Bank by Giovanni de Bicci de' Medici. Money lending had been a practise for millennia but Giovanni used his already-established reputation as a currency trader to remove the barriers of denomination in transactions, the papacy serving as a perfect client due to the range of different currencies flowing in and out of the Vatican. Through addressing the issue of currency, the Medici Bank grew to be a multi-generational line of moneylenders and the largest bank in Europe in the 15th century until its fall in 1494.

Despite its eventual collapse, the Medici model of banking served as foundation for the British, Dutch and Swedish financial systems in the 17th century. Banks became more accustomed to holding balances in multiple currencies, systems of cheques and debits allowing transactions to take place without coins physically changing hands. The ratio of precious metal reserves to deposits held in banks began to be gradually reduced, the concept of 'credit' grew and wealth began its slow detach from gold and silver. Meanwhile, the Spanish Price Revolution saw large quantities of New World-mined precious metals enter Western Europe producing significant inflation, and the effects of coin counterfeiting, clipping and excessive circulation wear cast more and more scrutiny on this physical system of exchange.

> *"In Consequence of the Vitiating, Diminishing and Counterfeiting of the Currant Moneys, it is come to pass, that great Consequences do daily arise amongst the King's subjects, in Fairs, Markets, Shops, and other Places throughout the Kingdom, about the Passing or Refusing of the same, to the disturbance of the Publick Peace; many Bargains, Doings and Dealings are totally prevented and laid aside, which lessens Trade in general; Persons before they conclude in any Bargains, are necessitated first to settle the Price or Value of the very Money they are to Receive for their Goods; and if it be in Guineas at a High Rate, or in Clipt or Bad Moneys, they set the Price of their Goods accordingly, which I think has been One great Cause of Raising the Price not only of Merchandizes, but even of Edibles, and other Necessaries for the sustenance of the Common People, to their great Grievance."*
>
> -A Report Containing an Essay for the Amendment of the Silver Coins, Charles Bill, London, 1695

By the end of the 17th century, older coins in circulation were seen as nuisances, unreliable, adulterated and prone to losses of value. Whether it was an excess or dearth of silver and gold, trade was affected either way and a need for a new economic system became starkly apparent.

1695 saw a 'Great Recoinage' occur in Britain - where older currency was withdrawn and struck as new coins - but in this same year the newly-established Bank of England released some of the first permanent issue banknotes into circulation. This new paper currency proved highly popular, initially intended to be traded for a set amount of specie if taken to a bank but eventually exchanged as money in itself. Crucially, bankers were able to issue more banknotes than they had reserves of precious metals on the assumption that not every bearer would choose to withdraw simultaneously, vastly expanding the monetary supply and furthering credit. These notes were also able to assist in further monetary shortages, such as the significant lack of circulating silver coinage in Britain throughout the 18th century. In many ways, a paper commitment to a set amount of currency had immediately become more reliable than the currency itself.

An early banknote issued by Taunton Bank, UK, for Ten Pounds, Ten Shillings (10 Guineas) in 1787

Even with the innovations of paper currency and credit, some traditionalists still clung to the idea that precious metals equalled money and chose to adhere to the Gold Standard (a monetary system where paper notes are inextricably linked to gold) in the 19th and early 20th centuries. WWI shook the gold standard to its core; but it took the 1929 Wall Street Crash to finally sever this link between circulating currency and gold, when financial uncertainty in the stock market led to a run on the banks, investors rushing to cash in their banknotes and withdraw their gold. The ensuing Great Depression forced an end to the gold standard in the British Empire, whilst in the United States the Gold Reserve Act of 1934 outlawed circulating gold and deemed it no longer legal tender. Silver coinage followed suit, being withdrawn from circulation in the mid-20th century onwards. Today we use a universally accepted 'fiat' coinage – that is, coins without intrinsic metal value, their tradability resulting from confidence in their backing authority.

As finance evolved, the concept of money outpaced the need for physical metal coins, 'wealth' exploded and took on a new form: that of theory. Just as our ancestors traded food - a commodity with actual intrinsic value to survival – for stable yet useless precious metals, we in turn traded these for numbers on a screen. Money has become an electrical current of agreements and futures and obligations able to root itself in the human psyche in a way mere metal could not. Real wealth is now no longer found in the coffers of a precious metal-based economy but instead within the effective sharing and circulation of obligation in a credit-based financial system.

2. The Hobby of Kings

As pieces of medallic art and a tangible link to both the past and foreign cultures, coins have always been highly effective at capturing the imagination. The slow divorce of coins from money eventually allowed an entirely new phenomenon to emerge – the collecting of coins for enjoyment. However, for the majority of modern history the nature of wealth and metal were too interlinked for much of society to comfortably retain their coins as curiosities. Before the 18th century there were only a few forerunners able to collect coins in this manner and not risk bankrupting themselves in the process: the nobility, the elite, and monarchs.

The earliest recorded coin collector was Caesar Augustus, Rome's first emperor between 27 BC and 14 AD. Roman culture had absorbed and continued the artistic style of ancient Greece, and there was a widespread appreciation and respect for the history and imagery of Greek culture. Augustus is said to have maintained a collection of coinage bearing great generals from history including Alexander the Great, and according to the contemporary historian Suetonius he gave "coins of every device, including old pieces of the kings and foreign money" as Saturnalia gifts (a festival of Saturn held in December). Augustus may have been one of the few known numismatists of the ancient world, but there is an abundance of evidence that coins held status beyond that of mere currency even at this early stage. In ancient Greece, Alexander the Great is purported to have personally issued a limited number of ceremonial silver 'Decadrachms' - equivalent to 10 Attic Drachms in value - to Macedonian officers in 324 BC, and there is a well-documented practice of Roman emperors issuing large gold medallions as honorary gifts to neighbouring peoples and victorious generals. In the ancient world coins were highly respected and treasured, but were only able to be retained by the rich and powerful while the majority of society would need to cash in on their value sooner or later.

Beside their use as currency and occasionally as presentation pieces, coins represented perhaps the best-known and most widely circulated form of art in the Roman Empire. Even after the empire itself fell in the 5th century BC a widespread appreciation of classical coinage remained. Charlemagne, king of the Franks, introduced a series of coins closely resembling Roman imperial issues in the early 9th century BC; this imitative Roman style was also seen on 12th and 13th century coins of Mesopotamia (today Iraq, Syria and Turkey). However, only a small number of ancient coin collections are known to have existed during this period, and it was not until a major upheaval of Western culture that the collecting of antique coins began to pick up pace.

Portrait of a Man with a Roman Medal – Hans Memling, German-Flemish, c.1480

Between the 14th and 16th centuries, the Renaissance blossomed out from Italy and spread throughout Europe, affecting every aspect of society it touched. The heart of this movement was a rediscovery of classicism, with a return to classical philosophies and learnings and a revival of ancient technologies and artistic styles. Architecture and sculpture took the form of Greco-Roman temples and statues, and with this vogue came a renewed appreciation for that most persistent form of ancient art: coins.

This era saw some of the first dedicated collections of coins begin to be formed. Petrarch (1304-1374), a renowned Italian scholar during the Renaissance, is widely credited as curating one of the first scientific and artistic collections of ancient coins; it is no coincidence that Petrarch was also one of the first humanists, a term for a revival of the study of classical antiquity. The sharp rise in the popularity of coins brought with it a corresponding rise in price, and the majority of collectors from this period were all united through their wealth and status. Pope Boniface VIII and Pope Paul II both kept assemblages of ancient coins; at least two Holy Roman Emperors, Maximilian I and Ferdinand I, were also collectors. Henry IV and Louis XIV of France followed suit, as well as Catherine Parr, King Henry VIII's sixth wife. Between the 14th and 16th centuries a long list of Archdukes, Princes and monarchs all were considered coin collectors, cementing the reputation of numismatics as the "hobby of kings".

As this hobby was essentially just a fad to these wealthy collectors, comparatively little research or study was conducted and coins were often treated as simply alternative forms of art or as historical curiosities. It was not until much later that numismatics began to take proper form, when coins began to become accessible to the wider public.

3. The Numismatic Revolution

"When this Book was first publish'd in the Year 1726, our English Coins had been very much neglected; there were but few Collections, and the Author (then a young Member of the Society of Antiquaries) could offer very little from his own Observation. His principal View was, to excite others to a Search into this Branch of English Antiquities; and considering how eagerly our English Coins have been sought after, how

much the Value of them has been inhanced (sic), and how many curious Collections have been made since that Time, it seems to have had the desired Effect."

-An Historical Account of English Money, Stephen Martin-Leake Esq, London, 1745

Up until the 17th and early 18th centuries, coin collecting was still not widely practised outside of noble families. Coins were still heavily relied upon for their place in day-to-day exchange; this dependence took its toll on circulating coinage. In Britain for example, decades of circulation had reduced many of the coins in circulation to blank or worn disks weighing far below what they should, which significantly hindered everyday transactions. This was partially addressed through the Great Recoinage of 1695 where older silver coins were recalled and struck anew, but Gresham's Law[1], a monetary principle stating that 'bad money drives out good', meant that inferior coins still remained in circulation whilst those seen as more valuable or higher quality were hoarded. Many arbitraged between the British and European markets as the latter gave a higher price for silver than domestically in Britain, leading to a mass export of newer coins. By the mid-18th century hardly any new silver coins were in production in Britain, and large quantities of coins had disappeared from the country altogether. The reliance on precious metals in trade meant that for the most part, one could simply not afford to keep coins as anything more than savings intended to be eventually spent. These metal shortages brought with them invention, however, and by 1745 standardised banknotes had begun to be printed in Britain for denominations ranging anywhere from £20 to £1,000, building on the success of the 1695 Bank of England issue. For the first time, one was able to trade effectively without sums of precious metals actually manifesting themselves. With the average family income significantly below £50, these banknotes represented wealth beyond the reach of the majority of the population at the time. Fortunately the 18th century also saw an event which allowed many to generate previously unimaginable

---

1   Named for Thomas Gresham (1519-1579), a financier during the English Tudor dynasty.

riches – namely the Industrial Revolution.

Beginning in Britain in the mid-18th century and spreading throughout Europe and the United States, the Industrial Revolution was just that - a revolution. Manufacturing processes in many core industries switched from labour to machine production and significantly increased efficiency. Steam power was developed and implemented, and the face of the iron production, textile production, chemical manufacturing and machine industries were transformed. Even coin production was affected, the firm Boulton & Watt producing the first steam-powered coin presses in the 1790s. The Industrial Revolution brought with it an unprecedented rise in average income and produced a wealthy middle class of businessmen, engineers and foremen able to spend money on non-essentials for the first time.

The driving force behind this industrialisation of industry was partially that of another revolution which had begun centuries beforehand: the Scientific Revolution. Initially a 16th century effort to recover the knowledge of the classical world, the Scientific Revolution evolved into a revaluation of nature and the forces within it. Followers attempted to abandon assumption and to see the world with an open mind, gather data and develop a scientific method. This approach permeated all of society, prompting the new mathematical, physical, and chemical discoveries underpinning the Industrial Revolution, but also creating a new scientific perspective on the arts and antiques. This period of scientific and philosophical discovery is referred to as the Age of Enlightenment.

Enlightenment brought with it a renewed appreciation for history and especially historical artefacts. Just as the Renaissance had fostered a return to Greco-Roman ideals, neoclassicism once again entered European culture and influenced contemporary arts and architecture. Objects from the past were examined and studied anew, and some of the first antiquarians began amassing collections of foreign and ancient 'curiosities' to display. It was collections such as these that represented the origins of modern archaeology and the foundations of many museum collections today. Naturally this appreciation of the past led to coins once again being widely collected, but there was a notable difference between the effect of the Age of Enlightenment and the Renaissance on coin collecting. Rather than solely focussing on ancient coins, Enlightenment led to even modern coins becoming the subject of attention; in 1746, the British Royal Mint produced the first-ever set of proof coins for collectors representing the newfound fondness for them. Alongside the collecting of coins for amusement, scientific method was applied to their study for the first time. Books and reference guides on coin types started to become more common, museum collections were put together and curated, and the science of numismatics was born.

The Scientific Revolution did not just lead to the academic study of coins, but can ultimately be said to have created the coin market itself. Alongside the Age of Enlightenment creating a fascination for coins, the impact of the Industrial Revolution on the spread of wealth meant that coins were affordable to far more collectors than ever before. These factors, coupled with the issue of banknotes, meant that within a short period of time coins had been transformed from exclusively a medium of day-to-day exchange to a highly collectable commodity with a reasonably standardised value: in a sense, a Numismatic Revolution had taken place.

In the mid-18th century, some of the first auction houses opened their doors offering artworks, rare books and antiquities. Coins were offered publicly almost as early as these other collectables, and certainly brought comparable sums. A catalogue I once read for a noteworthy auction held in London in 1787 described a 1651 pattern Halfcrown selling for an immense sum of £30, equivalent then to a year and a half's wages for seaman in the East India Company - and for a coin then barely a century old.

England, Commonwealth pattern Halfcrown 1651, by David Ramage

By the 19th century, coin auctions had become a regular occurrence, and dealerships began to be established trading in rare coins. Coin societies were founded and began producing their own academic journals postulating theories and announcing prominent discoveries or auctions. The swift rise in public interest in coins was met by an increasing number of proof sets being struck by Mints for collectors or as presentation sets for issue[2]. The quality of coin engraving markedly increased, and a greater abundance of patterns were produced for new issues or trial coins. More attention was given to the style and quality of a country's coinage both by those producing the coins and by those spending them. Over the course of the next century the depth and spread of the marketplace markedly grew and some of the most famous collections were assembled, and by the 20th century coins had become one of the core components of the collectables market with an immensely strong financial backing.

4. The Bubble Bursts

It has been arguably since the mid-20th century that the most significant developments in the numismatic market have taken place. In 1962, 40,000 numismatists attended the first international numismatic convention held in Detroit, Michigan, sponsored by the American Numismatic Association (ANA) and Royal Canadian Numismatic Association. Such assemblages were soon to become a regular occurrence. The 1970s saw several numismatic dealers switch from a retail to an auction format while many entirely new auction houses emerged, allowing collectors themselves to decide what to pay instead of buying at dealers' prices. In the 1980s, third-party coin certification came into being; this was performed by companies who would examine coins, determine their quality and encapsulate them with a numerical 'score'. Grading began to be standardised across the trade and coin price guides were widely published allowing a more systematic approach to collecting. The pace of growth within numismatics saw no sign of slowing.

But pride comes before a fall, and two centuries of numismatic markets could not escape the attention of those who had no interest in

---

[2] Some of the most valuable coins on the market today formed part of these sets, including the rare 1804 US Dollar which can trade for over $3 million.

coins but nonetheless sought to profit. The introduction of innovative new grading practices and accompanying price standardisation allowed unexperienced investors to gain a foothold in the market for the first time. By buying solely to generate wealth with little knowledge of what they were doing or the true extent of market demand, these investors caused prices to rise to unprecedented levels until the market simply could not cope and the bubble burst, triggering the 1989 Coin Market Collapse.

In the late 1980s, the US economy was heading towards a recession; interest rates were high and the US dollar very weak. Investors sought safe haven in alternative assets and alongside price rises for other collectable categories, coins began to experience their own rapid jumps in price. Third party grading, the professional evaluation and numerical 'scoring' of coins by quality, was still a relatively new and poorly understood practice. However, the assigning of grades allowed even the inexperienced to assess coin quality, and unfortunately this half-understanding was worse than none and meant that the market ultimately lost out on both sides of the equation. Investors began to pay extraordinary prices for the highest numerically graded coins, while grading for uncertified coins remained subjective and with considerable arbitrage. Telemarketers advertised numismatic investments to wealthy buyers, and even major investment firms such as Merrill Lynch established their own rare coin funds. When Wall Street began participating in the numismatic market, prices climbed further.

As investor participation increased, actual collectors lost their confidence in the numismatic market. Coins had never been in such demand and yet so unwanted. Prices had exceeded what actual collectors would pay while speculators had stopped trading coins among themselves. Values began to falter as investors sought to cash out and were unable to find a market for their coins. The mythical collector base that was supposed to reward speculators failed to appear, and the market began to haemorrhage money. Those same innovations which began to standardise numismatic markets ultimately led to their downfall.

Some pinpoint the collapse of the coin market to the ANA convention in Pittsburgh, August 1989. In the months leading up to the show, rumours had spread that a major brokerage firm intended to buy up third party-graded coins for long term investment. The market breathed a sigh of relief and certified coins were once again bought up en mass in anticipation of this buyout, accelerating as the convention approached. One dealer later commented that while in the air on the way to Pittsburgh he pulled out his briefcase and managed to sell $35,000 worth of coins to a dealer sitting next to him on the plane. Two days later, word came through that the brokerage firm was officially out. The bubble burst, and the US coin market collapsed, sending shockwaves throughout numismatics worldwide.

At this point, coins had built up their reputation as an academic hobby for centuries and had only just come to be regarded as a viable investment. This surge of investor interest without proper standardisation and transparency had inflated prices beyond their stable levels and led to their ruin. Despite their few years of commoditisation, coins declined simultaneously with every other class of subjective alternate asset: art, cars, real estate all dipped in the late 80s and early 90s. It would take a miracle to repair the numismatic market's shattered reputation; and fortunately, a miracle is precisely what appeared.

5. The King of Hobbies

Salvation arrived in the mid-1990s: the introduction of the internet. The revival of the coin market was both dramatic and instantaneous. The internet formed the other half of the process that third party grading had begun; not only could coins be precisely ordered by grade, but now their actual market values could be instantly researched and established. Suddenly, collectors were able to access the coins they sought in the click of a button and immediately consult the results of previous auctions for price comparisons. Through market transparency, coins finally began to perform effectively as commodities as well as a hobby, and the market grew exponentially in response.

It was this new means of global connectivity that truly injected liquidity into the trade. Market prices for coins had been subjective for decades and the investment efforts of the late 80s were based on a flimsy foundation of academia and subjectivity. The impact of the internet allowed for far healthier and more organic growth and the market resurged. Since 1995 coin values have almost exclusively risen year-on-year[3] and have shown no immediate signs of slowing even through the 2008 global financial crisis. Numismatics remains one of the world's most prevalent hobbies and its breadth of material offers almost limitless opportunities to the collector. Beginning as the hobby of kings, the widespread popularity and illustrious past of coin collecting has led to its being referred to today as the "king of hobbies".

Coins are still being struck as we speak, millions upon millions of them in all shapes and sizes and by every major mint on the planet. Most are intended for circulation but many more are produced for collectors and commemorate events or historical figures. More coins are available to collectors than ever before – and yet there is a belief held by some that the slow move away from using cash in everyday transactions will negatively affect the numismatic market. Nowadays, even those with an interest in coins are using them less in payments. Indeed, if I myself had a penny for every time I chose to use contactless payment instead of coins then I would probably not need to make contactless payments all the time. Many collectors today gained their interest from examining the coins in their change as children, and followers of this theory say that the reduction in coin use will consequently produce fewer collectors than in previous generations. Part of the driving force behind this thought process is the swift decline in value for rare stamps; once a wide and diverse marketplace, the drop in stamp usage over the last few decades has correlated with a dramatic fall in collectable stamp values.

The reality is that coins almost needed to be liberated from their purpose in order to be collected by a wide market, just as they were in the Numismatic Revolution. If regarded as necessary and solely functional, coins become mere tools designed to be traded away as opposed to objects in their own right. The British Royal Mint has said it will continue producing one and two pence coins for years to come despite their limited spending power. Even when they are of lower value or

---

3   A prominent client of mine began collecting coins in 1997 and was told that he had 'missed the real bargains by a couple of years'. Considering how low coin prices in 1997 now seem, this is rather ironic.

reduced significance nobody throws coins away, and circulating coinage still offers an accessible route into numismatics for many. Indeed, a vast proportion of numismatists in the UK and US collect exclusively modern coins. Whereas stamps have only a two-hundred-year long memory and are vulnerable to damp, heat, improper handling and tearing, coins rank among the most hard-wearing and expressive of all historical objects and have proved time and again throughout history to be a perpetual source of fascination. Two and a half thousand years of ingrained knowledge that coins represent money, value, a link to different cultures and an artistic medium cannot be shaken. Many collect coins purely for this historical and cultural intrigue.

On the other hand, coins are still linked with the world of investments. The same motivations that fuelled investor demand prior to the 1989 collapse still remain strong today. This investment mindset is partially fuelled through the trade of bullion; a very large proportion of investors store some percentage of their value in precious metals, and much modern bullion is struck in the form of coins. It is only a small leap from accruing bullion coins to adding one or two collectable coins to your portfolio, and before you know it you are an ardent numismatist. Additionally, the introduction and proliferation of third party grading, despite the problems it caused initially, has now allowed coins to grow as a commodity – a subject which remains controversial in numismatics. In many ways, the coin market does mirror that of a financial market, and offers the potential to make a handsome profit when you come to resell your coins.

The numismatic trade is split between those collectors and professionals who are comfortable categorising coins as investments and those who see them exclusively as a hobby. Regardless of which camp you are in, numismatics is almost guaranteed to be a more profitable pastime than any other you might choose. Even if you collect coins for 20 years, come to resell and achieve 70 per cent of what you paid, you have still netted a far greater return than you would had you spent 20 years golfing, and you would also boast a much better chance of retaining full use of your knees. However, no matter what your reasons and motivations are for collecting coins, you will surely have a vested interest in your return being as high as possible. It is vital for anyone with an interest in numismatics to have a working knowledge of the intricacies of the coin market, and how to evaluate a coin's quality in order to buy and sell wisely. The next chapter will cover just that: the different aspects which determine what exactly makes a coin valuable in the first place.

Chapter 1.2.
What Makes a Coin Valuable?

1. Supply and Demand

"That every thing having any Value or Worth whatsoever, when it becomes Scarce grows Dear, or (which is the same thing) it Rises in Price, and consequently it will serve to pay more Debt, or it will buy greater Quantities of other Goods of Value, or in any thing else it will go further than it did before."

-*A Report Containing an Essay for the Amendment of the Silver Coins*, Charles Bill, London, 1695

In the course of my career I have been asked several times by potential clients to give them a list of coins that 'collectors are looking for'. This is presumably so that they can sort through their pile of change and try to match up what they have with what people want. Unfortunately for them, collectors seek an extremely wide range of coins from across every country and time period and a list of them all would require several inconveniently large buildings to carry it around in. In the pursuit of these coins, various factors come into play governing what people will pay for them: the age of the coin, its appearance, how it fits into their collection, how well it has been preserved and more besides. Nevertheless when discussing coins, perhaps the most ubiquitous term used interchangeably with valuable is 'rare'.

Rarity is, undeniably, the predominant influence driving what a coin will sell for. The fewer examples of a particular type there are available to commerce, the higher price collectors will have to pay to obtain one for themselves. Coins often have well-recorded mintage figures and excellent auction records that allow for quick study of which types are less commonly seen as well as the prices they tend to sell for. Notably, the most famous coin rarities can exhibit tremendous and disproportionate leaps in value due to the mentality of the very wealthiest collectors. Much of the enjoyment of collecting is saving up and completing an impressive collection, but if you boast a substantial income then the majority of collectable items lie within your price range. The perception of achievement and value is somewhat diminished when money is no object. Rarity represents a new limiting factor preventing the rich collector from simply buying what they want instantly. The rarer the item the harder it is to obtain for any sum and the greater the sense of accomplishment and prestige if you are one of the few to own an example. This is the case in all alternative asset classes – art, cars, watches, books, records, etc. Many notable coin collections have been formed with the intention of buying only the very best and rarest of coins, including the impressive US-based Tyrant Collection which currently has a total market value of over $300 million. When a coin is rare, it has a limited supply. However, this is only half of the equation as a coin can be rare and yet still worthless. For it to have significant value, it also must have significant demand.

It seems an obvious statement that without demand coins cease to have value, but the inexperienced appear to think that there exists a vast, endless collector market for coins of every age and type – which to some extent was the cause of the 1989 collapse. I have had many conversations with frustrated clients who do not understand, for example, why their uncommon Sixpence die variety is not worthy of placing in auction. The truth is that a coin could be one of just 50 examples known worldwide but if nobody collects that type then the coin has no value. Even if there were 100 collectors, each would need not wait too long before a specimen entered the market and prices would still stay low. Additionally, if ten of those collectors die or lose interest and move away from collecting, then 20 per cent of the collector base has just vanished in an instant and prices will drop further. A coin cannot simply be produced in limited numbers but must also have a significant number of collectors for its price to stay strong and consistent. The go-to phrase for supply and demand in numismatics is "if the collector is rarer than the coin, then the coin is worthless".

Most importantly, the proportion of supply to demand does not simply determine whether or not a coin will be purchased, but for what amount it will be purchased. Coins do not have an intrinsic and known 'price' which collectors can either pay or not pay; as many higher value coins sell at auction, the market ultimately decides their value and this amount is fluid. Wherever supply fails to meet demand the price will rise, and consequently a more common coin can be worth far more than its rarer equivalents if it has a larger collector base.

This can be put simply in the form of an illustrative equation:

Coin Value = *(Number of collectors / number of surviving examples) x Grade*

Using this equation, the collector bases of particular coins can be compared based on their results. For example, in late 2018 an extremely rare Mexican 'Rincon' 8 Reales from 1536 sold for $528,000 in a US auction. Just three examples of this type are known, of which this was the finest. That same auction house later sold an example of the Una and the Lion Five Pounds in January 2020 for $690,000; one of 400 examples struck, but only 12 of which were of the same technical grade. Collectors can be capricious and 'grade' is a complex issue which can heavily influence the price coins sell for (which will be discussed in more detail later on), but it is clear from these results that the collector base for the British Five Pound coin is far more strong than that of the Rincon 8 Reales - despite the latter being much rarer.

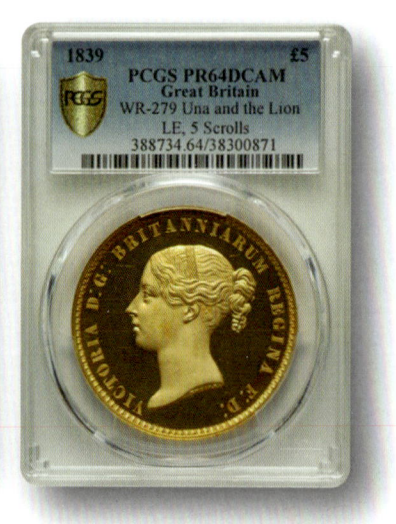

Left: Mexico Rincon 8 Reales, 1536-8. Right: Una and the Lion Five Pounds, 1839

What these results emphasise is another aspect of supply and demand affecting coin value – the wealth of any one given market. Demand for a coin can be strong, but this does not necessarily make a coin valuable, simply of proportionally greater value. The collector base for the Rincon 8 Reales may actually be as large of that for the Una and the Lion, but the results suggest it does not have anywhere near the spending power. Many factors determine the capital behind a given market, but generally those coins struck by countries with a higher GDP attract stronger results due to their greater quantity of disposable income. Returning to the example discussed earlier, a coin may number just 50 examples and have a collector base of 10,000, but if each of these collectors have only $1,000 to their name the coin will undoubtedly be worth little. However if those collectors each have $1,000,000, the coin's value may well be in the hundreds of thousands. This effect is consistently seen in US coins, arguably the world's strongest numismatic market. Ten thousand American collectors will create a significantly higher price than ten thousand Developing Nation collectors, and accordingly more common US coins can sell for many multiples of rarer coins in weaker markets.

What collectors seek is not necessarily fixed, and some coin types enjoy periods of vastly increased collector demand regardless of their country of origin or age. These 'vogues' can be due to world events - such as a rise in value for coins of King Richard III after the monarch's skeleton was discovered underneath a Leicester car park in 2012 – but are largely fuelled by the activities of collectors, dealers and investors. Similar to a stock market, when collectors and dealers see that demand for a coin type is rising they react quickly and attempt to jump on the bandwagon to either a) purchase an example for their collection while the price is low, or b) to purchase an example as an investment. This creates a sudden rise in value. Often these vogues transcend national borders; for instance, recent years have shown massively increased investment in British gold Five Guineas and Five Pounds from collectors in China and Japan. The auction prices for these types still remain extremely high. On the other hand, the value of some coins have spiked in value over the last few years and then dropped off sharply once again. It is important to be able to identify the difference between these 'bubbles' and long-term market trends.

No matter how rare a coin or its perceived significance, it will not be valuable unless collector demand considerably outstrips its supply and as long as that demand is backed up by a strong capital base. As we will go on to cover, many factors can help to determine coin value, but in conjunction with these it is imperative to always remain conscious of the supply and collector demand.

2. History and Provenance

The first coin to ever capture my imagination as a child was an extremely worn Halfpenny struck during the reign of King George III. At the time I was unaware of the denomination of the coin or whose head was on it, but I became fixated on its date: 1799. A coin struck in the 18th century that had somehow survived more than 200 years of circulation and was only costing me 25 pence - surely I had just found a bargain!

When holding an unfamiliar coin, the question that immediately follows "how much is this worth?" is "how old is it?" – and so one of the very first things we look for is the date. For the last 500 years most coins produced have advertised their year of production, allowing the inexperienced to gain a handle on what they are holding even without being able to read the legend or identify the ruler. As a result, without any other information being provided, many have come to assume that the earlier the date the more desirable the coin - as surely an older coin must always be rarer and more historically important.

The perception of this link between the age of a coin and its value has created one of the most common misconceptions held by the layman – that age always equals value. However, a coin that is several hundred years old will not necessarily be worth any more than a coin produced in the last decade. Indeed, many of the most valuable coins today were produced relatively recently. Some major markets – such as China – place a particular emphasis on modern coins because they tend to be made to a higher standard than antique coins. In late 2017, more than $400,000 was paid for a proof 200 Yuan struck in 1989, one of the highest prices ever achieved for a Chinese coin at auction.

For a more everyday example, in 2009 the British Royal Mint produced a new 50 Pence piece commemorating the 250th anniversary of Kew

Gardens in London. The Treasury requested a smaller number of these coins than usual leading to an unusually low mintage of 211,000 pieces. The collector base for British 50 Pence pieces is large and these coins now enjoy online fame, selling for anywhere upwards of £120 each (240 times their face value) while a Farthing struck in the mid-18th century will rarely sell for even half that figure. Once again, it all boils down to supply and demand: the number of examples that are available and the number of collectors who are actively buying.

Since it is a fascination with history that first inspires so many to begin collecting, it is true that an interest in older coins does remain a core part of many people's collecting habits. Antique coins do tend to have a very large and stable collector base, but a correct link between coin age and collector interest is not simply the number of years the coin has existed, but rather its historical significance. As became clear during the Renaissance and Age of Enlightenment, numismatics is at its core a study of the history of civilisation alongside an interest in artistry and different cultures. As such, while there is no direct linear correlation between the age of a coin and its value, when it is struck in an important year or with the portrait of a significant ruler demand for that coin will sharply increase. For example, American collectors may often favour a coin struck in 1776 – when the Declaration of Independence was issued - over an older coin struck in the less significant year of 1766. Additionally, through standardised education in classical and modern history, widespread fascination has been generated for the same historical figures (Alexander the Great, Julius Caesar, Queen Elizabeth I, George Washington etc.), creating heavy interest in any coins with a connection to these leaders.

In addition, the more historically significant the coin, the greater the chance it has of also appealing to non-numismatists as a historical curiosity. Consequently these coins often have a much wider collector base than any other type[4]. Due to many of these coins existing in very large quantities, their value may be proportionally high compared to similar types but their actual monetary value remains relatively low. Bronze Roman coins, for example, exist in numbers equal or greater to many low-value circulating coins and yet each one will sell for $5-10

---

4   This being said, there is often a cap to what these non-numismatists will spend which will be covered later.

minimum – proportionally huge but still a very small sum of money. The perception of coins as pieces of history provides a colossal motivation behind collecting, but this demand does not necessarily bring with it a significant rise in price.

This appreciation of history among numismatists does not apply solely to the age of a coin itself, but also to its ownership history (known as provenance). The value of any given coin can vastly increase when it has a long sale record and a history of being in several notable collections. Collectors love to ponder over all of the hands that previously held their coins, and a well-recorded provenance allows a factual record of exactly who those hands belonged to – and the older they were, the better. The influx of sophisticated modern coin forgeries has meant that the longer a coin has been known to numismatics the higher its chance of being genuine. For example, while working for a previous auction house, my colleagues and I initially estimated a hammered penny of Aethelred I (865-871) would sell for between £400 and £500 ($540-670). By chance, we then found a turn-of-the-century text showing a photo of that same coin which completed its provenance and allowed us to trace it back to a hoard of coins found in 1774. This provenance very likely contributed to its sale price of £2,100 ($2,800), more than four times its top estimate.

England, Kings of Wessex, Aethelred I (865-71) Penny

Provenance also plays a vital part in the trade of ancient coins. Laws on the discovery and exchange of ancient coins are extremely strict in Italy and Greece and the market is heavily policed. Additionally, recent conflict in the Middle East has led to increased concerns over the looting and selling of artefacts from protected archaeological sites, leading to restrictions on the import of antiquities to the US and Europe. Without a provenance, ancient coins have to be assumed to have been dug up illegally. The only means of selling ancient coins legally is when they can be proven to have either been exported with permission or have been within collections for a considerable period of time.

Provenance can also contribute to a coin's value due to a minor celebrity worship tied to some of the most exalted collections. Many collectors were known for their discerning eye, meaning that any coin from their collection has their 'stamp of approval'. The Louis E Eliasburg collection assembled in the 20th century is widely considered to be the most comprehensive and best-quality type collection of US coins ever assembled, and accordingly an Eliasburg provenance will hugely contribute to a coin's selling price. This effect is echoed in various other notable collections stretching back hundreds of years. Provenance is often recorded by paper tickets with handwritten notes bearing price and sale date and these should be retained with the coin. In my first numismatic position I was not aware of these tickets, accidentally threw a number away and then had to search through my bin to retrieve them.

The appreciation of antique coins has undoubtedly played a key role in the foundations of numismatics and remains a core principle of the hobby as a whole. However, 'antique' is such an arbitrary term and one that applies to so many coins that it is ultimately impossible to connect age with value in any meaningful way. As discussed, it is only the historical significance of the coin itself and its collecting history which can contribute to its value, and even then modern coins and antique coins alike will still achieve similar prices. The main contributing factor will always be collector supply and demand.

Despite this, there is one key difference between antique and modern coins that can dramatically alter the price they achieve. Most modern coins are well made and are often found without any wear or damage, an aspect which partially drives their appeal. This quality is thus considered 'normal' for a modern coin. To find an antique coin in similar condition can be extremely rare. If a discerning collector wants to buy only the best of the best (as so many of them do), attractive modern coins are plentiful. However, to find pristine coins above a certain age is near impossible.

Even if a considerable number of a coin's original mintage have survived, many of these will have been produced to a poor standard and will have since encountered considerable circulation. Additionally, those coins that have managed to avoid circulation will often exhibit heavy cleaning or marks from being set in jewellery, leaving them visually unappealing. As such it is less the age of antique coins, but rather the rarity of finding them in a perfect grade that dictates their value – and this touches upon the most important aspects driving coin value, the three Ps: Production, Preservation and Presentation.

3. Production

The first of the three Ps concerns coin production. Production covers every aspect of the manufacture of a coin itself, from its metal fabric to the engraving of its designs. Throughout numismatic history, standards of production have varied significantly from country to country and era to era. Sometimes coins resembled nothing more than crudely cut chunks of silver while sometimes their appearance came close to that of sculpted art. However, even coins of the same type can wildly differ in quality. Many things could go wrong when a coin was struck and even if the process was performed perfectly the moneyer would rarely produce an immaculate end result. It is certainly not every example that boasts sharp details all the way to the highest points of the design (ie the deepest points of the die). As such, even if a coin is subsequently circulated or damaged in some way numismatists will always note how well it was made when analysing its value. The three main factors to look for are the overall standard of production (I), whether the coin features a desirable error or variety (II), and whether the coin has been produced as a proof or pattern (III).

I. Production Standard

The basics of coin production can be split into a) metal and planchet quality, b) die engraving and arrangement, c) strength and position of strike and d) method of manufacture. Remember: for the most part the quality of production is a better determiner of value when comparing coins of the same type as opposed to coins of different series.

   a) **Metal and planchet quality.** The fabric of a coin is integral to its appearance. Firstly, the choice of metal itself affects its appeal; as one would expect, gold coins tend to be the most popular, followed by silver, bronze, brass etc. Silver and gold are less reactive than other metals which mean that coins struck from these materials show less corrosion or unsightly patina over time. Secondly, the proportions of the alloy heavily contribute to the quality of a coin. Should a coin be heavily debased, it will appear porous and discoloured on the higher points. During the 1540s, King Henry VIII of England ordered a mass debasement (reduction and replacement of precious metal content with copper) of the coinage to fund his wars against France and Scotland, aptly named the Great Debasement. Accordingly many of his later coins dropped in silver content, initially from 92.5 per cent down to 50 per cent but dropping once more by the end of his reign to just 33 per cent silver. Depending on how the copper and silver are dispersed throughout the metal these coins vary dramatically in quality, and only moderate wear exposes the underlying copper on Henry's protruding nose earning him the nickname "Old Coppernose". Those coins with a higher silver content generally exhibit a sharper appearance and carry a significant premium over more debased specimens.

England, Henry VIII (1509-47) Testoons, 1544-47. The topmost example shows typical crudeness of production while the bottom piece is far superior.

Besides the choice of metal itself, the way in which it is processed into a 'blank' for production can have an impact on the finished product. If a coin's planchet is incorrectly annealed it can show a scattering of surface cracks that interrupt the designs and distract from the aesthetic effect. Additionally, the manufacture of hammered coins focused heavily on planchets containing strictly regulated amounts of precious metal. As a result the correct weight of these coins was often prioritised over their shape, meaning that many of these earlier types have oddly-shaped flans bearing incomplete designs. The strike was also improperly applied and incomplete if the blanks were cut to irregular levels or heavily adjustment marked. Many hammered coins show edge splits or cracks due to the metal of the planchet being irregularly distributed. A coin with a round flan of good quality metal will always attract a higher price than one with ragged edges and irregular surfaces.

b) **Die engraving and arrangement.** This concerns the preparation of the designs intended to be applied to the blank. An appreciation of medallic art is a strong component of numismatics, and many of the most popular coins today are lauded primarily for the artistic talent of their designs. The work of some particular medallic artists are currently in vogue. William Wyon (1795-1851), Chief Engraver at the Royal Mint until his death, engraved the dies for some of the most beloved British coins in numismatics today including the 1817 'Three Graces' Crown, the 1839 'Una and the Lion' Five Pounds and the 1847 'Gothic' Crown. All of these types now attract extremely high premiums.

From left to right: 'Three Graces' Crown, 1817, sold for $204,000; 'Una and the Lion' Five Pounds, 1839, sold for $690,000; 'Gothic' Crown, 1847, sold for $66,000

Vogues aside, any coins with especially well-engraved dies attract attention and this factor can often determine the most valuable coins of a series.

Since the 18th century, most coins have been produced with essentially identical dies. This means it is less useful to compare the engraving quality between coins of the same type as their appearance is typically uniform. However, earlier hammered and ancient coins feature a variety of portrait styles depending on the skill of their engraver and a variety of legends depending on the literacy of the die-sinker (the operative who arranges the die ready for striking). Collectors are more likely to favour those coins that are engraved to a higher standard with the most crisp and well-set legends.

c) **Strength and position of strike**. The strength of a coin's strike determines the extent to which the details are rendered in the metal. It requires a good deal of force to encourage a flat piece of metal to flow into the depth of an engraved die, so the quality of the strike is of the most common areas where production can differ from coin to coin. A weak strike will only show the shallowest points of the design on the coin and leave the centres 'flat', whereas a very firm strike will stand a better chance of imparting sharp detail to the very highest points[5]. Strike can be very quickly assessed through examining the high points of the design and then comparing with other examples of the type. Slight variations in the thickness and composition of the planchet can result in greater or lesser sharpness, and collectors will always prefer coins with a fuller strike.

Amongst hammered and ancient coins, another common production issue is that of the strike's position on the coin – also known as its 'centring'. In these older coins with irregularly prepared flans, it is often the case that the surface area of the metal blank is not sufficient to receive a full impression of the dies. In the 5th century BC, ancient Athens produced a very widespread coinage of Tetradrachms which survive in extremely high numbers today. Their price varies significantly, however, based on how much of Athena's helmet crest is represented and whether or not her nose is on the flan.

---

5   The highest points are also the first to exhibit wear, and if a coin is not only sharply struck but also without wear it can dramatically influence its appeal to collectors.

Two Athenian Tetradrachms (c. 440-404 BC) both sold in the same month in 2020. Despite their similar appearance, the left-hand example realised $2,040 and the right-hand example just $552 due to the off-centre strike.

A more recent example of this effect is seen on the various 'cob' 8 Reales issued by Spain and her colonies between the 16th and 18th centuries. Spanish demand for coinage was so great that millions of irregular coins were struck swiftly in the most bizarre shapes, their weight correct but their appearance unsightly. These types are very common, but so rarely encountered with a decent strike that examples with even moderate distinguishing details can fetch heavy premiums.

Even if a coin blank was correctly made, sometimes the moneyer would incorrectly position the dies when striking, leaving an off-centre coin with an exposed crescent of blank metal and a corresponding loss of design on the other side. This effect is fairly common in hammered coins and for the most part diminishes its value. Double-striking, either by mistake or in order to rectify an earlier positioning error, is also often seen in hammered coins (and more rarely in later milled coins) and is considered to be unappealing since it results in a blurred design.

Lastly, an earlier strike is always favoured to a later strike. Younger dies with fresh engraving have sharper details which allows for a more pleasing finished product. Additionally, dies degrade. If they do not eventually split from overuse leaving unsightly raised cracks on the coin, then they can rust over time exhibiting unappealing blotchy lumps. As die imperfections are still 'as made' elements of coins, they are not as detrimental to value as other more off-putting factors, but collectors may still seek the earliest examples they can when any flaws are at an earlier and less obtrusive stage.

d) **Method of manufacture.** As the previous three factors have suggested, many of the earlier variations in coin quality ceased to be common after the introduction of more sophisticated methods of manufacture. All coin production was originally undertaken by hammering a blank between two dies by hand, a practice inherited from ancient Greece. In the 16th and 17th centuries, in order to combat counterfeiting and clipping the majority of coin production transitioned to a 'milled' method using machines. The earliest of these was a 'screw press' used to add increased downward pressure by the tightening of a coarse screw driven by water-power or horses. 'Milling' resulted in coins of uniform thickness and a perfectly round shape, often with an inscription or pattern applied to the edge to prevent the removal of precious metal. Contemporary rocker presses - where dies were engraved on curved rollers and sheets of metal fed between them - produced coins of a similarly superior quality. By the late 18th century steam-powered presses were introduced capable of producing even finer coins, and nowadays all coin production is undertaken through electricity.

These technological innovations meant that coins developed a consistently high quality and helped to limit variation between examples of the same type. Accordingly values for modern coins are easier to standardise, contributing to the confidence of buyers. In effect, as most collectors are chiefly concerned with the appearance of their coins, probably the highest prices paid today are for these later higher quality issues rather than earlier crude coins. However, despite the fact that it is hammered and ancient coins which vary most significantly from example to example, even modern milled coins can differ in strike strength and metal quality. For this reason, careful in-hand examination is always wise.

After milled coins became the norm and their quality standardised, those mistakes exhibited by some hammered coins (off-centre strikes, double-striking, incorrect planchets, badly-arranged legends) actually became *desirable* to collectors. This has led to one of the areas of numismatics that is best known to the layman: production errors.

II. Mint Errors and Varieties

One of the most commonly recognised but most poorly understood collectable groups of coins are those struck with errors. These accidental flaws manifest themselves in a multitude of ways; some coins have a new date struck over an earlier one (not an error per se but merely the work of a lazy or efficient die-cutter), some have misspelt legends, some have incorrect die pairings or doubled designs and some have even been struck in an incorrect metal. Alongside coin age, errors tend to be the first element that novices look for in their change. As a result, many believe there to be some vast market for coins that have even the slightest production quirk, aided by countless bogus articles and newspaper reports reporting on coins with supposed errors selling for handsome sums online.

Within numismatics, coin errors are a relatively new area of collector interest and one that applies only to coins of comparatively recent production. Poor education and a somewhat abstract approach to spelling means that older hammered coins frequently exhibit blunders in their legends, but are rarely encountered with significant production errors (eg being struck on an incorrect planchet). This is due to the fact that they were produced individually by hand. If a significant mistake were made, the moneyer would immediately realise their error and the coin would not be allowed to circulate, whereas minor issues of die arrangement were rarely noticed. Due to their frequency, hammered coins bearing these syntax errors do not generally have a significant value premium over those with correct legends.

As time went on, the rise of industrialised coin manufacture corresponded with improvements in education. This meant that far more effort was expended in the initial die-preparation stages of coin production than in the actual striking, which was left to machines. As a result, spelling errors began to quickly decrease in occurrence whilst dramatic fabric issues become more often seen. Nowadays a misspelt coin would be extremely unusual and rare, whilst a planchet flaw would be merely scarce. Machine errors are quite common, but human errors are far rarer.

Coin errors do not often produce extremely valuable coins but they do have a significant collector base which divides into roughly two factions. The first focuses on true production errors, moments of mechanical failure immortalised in metal. These are defined by types such as 'broadstruck' coins, where the collar fails and the planchet is spread too thinly, or coins struck significantly off-centre. Some of the most valuable errors are 'brockages', a phenomenon which occurs when a coin from an earlier striking remains stuck to either the upper or lower die. When a new blank is placed between the dies and struck, the new coin is left with one regular face and one with an incuse impression of the stuck coin. The higher the grade of these brockages the more valuable they can be; two notable examples in the Bentley Collection sold in 2012, a South African gold Pond and Victoria 1856 Sovereign, both brought more than $20,000 apiece.

South Africa Pond Brockage, c.1898-1900. Realised £13,000 ($21,000) hammer at the 2012 Bentley Sale

Part of the reason why these two coins commanded such high prices was the fact that they were made of gold; production standards for gold coinage are so high that errors tend to be extremely rare. It is unusual for mechanical errors in non-gold coinage to generate similarly lofty sums, but sometimes an example simply takes a collector's fancy and the price skyrockets. In January 2016, a US-auction house sold a modern Dime struck on a nail for an unbelievable $42,000.

Error collectors authenticate mechanical error coins by asking themselves at which point in the production process that mishap could have possibly occurred. In many ways, mechanical errors in coins fall into their own category of numismatics as a minor form of art. The products collected are so unique that their value cannot be standardised, and the prices paid for them are far more subjective. However, for the most part the market has an upper limit beyond which prices for errors rarely rise as the wealthiest collectors are unlikely to want badly made coins.

The other major motivator in the collecting of error coins is a concentration on varieties and variety collecting. Varieties are essentially seen as rarer versions of accepted issues, such as overdates, rare die pairings and incorrect letter use in legends. Varieties can command higher prices in general than true-blue mechanical errors as the coins themselves have developed a strong collector following as 'types'. Rather than being seen as oddities of production, they are considered to be valid parts of a series which must be obtained before a collection can be considered complete. This is also a common aspect of philately; some of the most valuable stamps are error varieties. Often, careful examination must be undertaken with a high-powered loupe to identify particularly subtle coin errors, but their presence can bring significantly higher prices than normal issues.

Coin errors can bring large sums, but this again depends on their collector base. Within US and Canadian coins, errors can be worth immense amounts due to the short history of coinage in these countries and their high GDP. It is always worth examining a coin for a potential quirk of production, but it will only increase its value if there is significant demand for that particular type.

III. Patterns, Proofs and Specimens

The need to meet the demands of everyday trade has often led coin production to be an extremely intensive process, with thousands of coins being struck each and every day. This intensity reduces the possibility of strict quality control, leading to the aforementioned errors and varieties; it also leads to a varied production standard, meaning that collectors have naturally come to prefer those coins of superior quality. It follows that among the most popular and most valuable coins today are those produced with particular attention to detail, of exceedingly high quality and intended as presentation pieces: namely Patterns, Proofs and Specimens. These special issue coins were generally never intended to circulate and were produced either as trial pieces or specifically for collectors, their main purpose being to demonstrate the skill of the mint or to propose a new coinage.

Patterns are the oldest of these three presentation types. A pattern coin is typically struck in extremely small numbers and is intended to trial a new coin design (its 'pattern'). The existence of coins necessitates the existence of patterns and the earliest examples of these special issues date back to ancient times. Very few ancient patterns survive, and the small number extant can achieve record-breaking prices when they are offered at auction. In 2012, a US-based auction house sold a pattern or 'prototype' Shekel from the Jewish War of 66-70 AD for more than $1,100,000. In Europe, some of the first known patterns are 'piedfort' Pennies of the 13th century, coins produced with regular dies but struck to twice their regular weight. These were presumably produced to send to regional Mints to instruct them which designs to follow and were struck in double thickness to ensure they were not mixed with regular circulating coins. From around the 16th century the record of pattern coins tends to be more complete. In Britain, hammered patterns from Elizabeth I onwards are synonymous with so-called 'Fine Work' coins, issues produced with an inordinate amount of care. When compared side by side the difference between patterns and regular issues is stark.

Left: Elizabeth I (1558-1603) Pattern Shilling of 1595-1598. Right: Regular issue of the same Shilling type.

With the widespread introduction of milled technology the quality of pattern coins was further enhanced and by the 17th century patterns began to exhibit not only finer standards of engraving and die arrangement but also carefully treated planchets giving a 'mirrored' effect to the coins. Patterns were occasionally produced 'off-metal' - that is, in a metal other than the one in which the intended coin would be struck. Gold patterns of silver or copper coinage are extremely valuable and presumably were intended as elite presentation pieces. By the 18th century it became more common for private individuals and companies to produce their own pattern coins in an attempt to secure royal patronage for their work, leading to an even wider range of types being available to collectors.

Patterns have always been of particular interest to numismatists as they satisfy several of the common desires behind collecting coins. Patterns are always rare and produced in small numbers; their artistic quality is always extremely high (as one would expect for a coin intended to debut a new design in the hope of approval), and they are of significant numismatic and historical importance. Accordingly, some of the highest prices ever paid for coins have been for examples of these trial pieces.

Proof coins are far more common than patterns. The major difference between these two coin types is one of intent; patterns are intended as purely internal trials while proofs are produced specifically for collectors. Special issue coins have been presented to dignitaries and as gifts by monarchs since ancient Greece; in a sense these were some of the earliest proofs. During Henry VII's reign in the late 15th century, piedfort double- and treble-Sovereign coins were struck using the same dies as the regular issues, also presumably as presentation pieces. However, many of these early pieces somewhat overlap with patterns as their true intention can be hard to gauge. What is today considered a 'proof' is a very specific type of coin and usually relates to its finish. Typically a proof is defined as being produced with polished dies giving extremely mirrored fields; often the dies are also treated with chemicals to render the raised elements of the design matte, creating a contrast between the brilliant fields and the 'frosted' devices[6]. Proofs are usually struck several times to ensure a completely sharp strike and a crisp edge. An important

---

6   Proofs have also been produced with fully matte or fully brilliant finishes.

distinction to note is that proofs are struck with the same die designs as circulating coins, and those with any major differences are usually considered patterns.

Proofs tend to be made to limited mintages and are often made as cased sets of multiple coins. In Britain what can be considered the first proof set was struck in 1746, where supposedly 100 four-piece sets of King George II's coinage from Sixpence to Crown were made available for collectors. This initial set did not have a brilliant finish, however. A small set of very limited numbers was also produced in 1787. From 1821 onwards proof sets in the UK began to be produced with a brilliant finish and were issued every time the coinage changed (most often linked with the succession of a new monarch). When first struck, proofs were popular but were not seen as significant as patterns or other rare historical coins. As time has progressed appreciation for their attractive appearance has grown as has their collector base, and today some of the single most valuable coins in each numismatic market are proofs. The 'Una and the Lion' Five Pounds, for example, was the largest coin included in Victoria's 1839 coronation proof set, and is today one of the world's most popular coins.

The lines between patterns and proofs began to blur in the 19th century, however; many coins included in proof sets were types that were never intended to circulate and were struck from unique dies, more in the manner of patterns than proofs. Meanwhile, many patterns were produced in larger numbers and with proof-like finishes, similar to other proof coins and referred to as archival "Proofs of Record".

In 1834, a US proof set was issued with a Dollar coin dated 1804 – this denomination was never struck in 1804, meaning its dies were not of circulation issue akin to a pattern. Its intention was, however, as a presentation piece within a proof set. Regardless of its intention, the unique nature and extremely limited numbers of the 1804 Dollar have led to its being referred to as the "King of American coins", with examples selling for more than $3,000,000 today. As another example, in 1936 a series of pattern coins were struck for the newly crowned King Edward VIII in the UK, including five boxed sets of fully brilliant coins. Edward chose to marry an American divorcee, Wallis Simpson, causing a national scandal and forcing him to abdicate within a year of ascending to the throne. His coinage was scrapped, yet these sets remain. Having been produced in advance of any official widespread coinage, their status would seem to be as patterns, yet their finish and presentation would suggest they are indisputably proofs.

Many coins such as these do not fit neatly into the above-mentioned categories and are referred to as being both proofs *and* patterns for their proof-like finishes and non-circulation dies. Ultimately, the distinction has little impact on value. Most proofs and patterns have been produced to exceptionally high standards, many are extremely rare, and as such they often command significant premiums over contemporary circulating types.

The last special issue coins to discuss are 'specimens', and their definition is a little more vague. Specimens are not intended to circulate but, unlike proofs, are not produced with a mirrored finish and indeed they usually exhibit satin or matte surfaces. Specimens, unlike patterns, are produced through multiple strikes with normal coinage dies, but are also used as purely internal pieces to showcase these finalised designs to banks and government entities. In a sense specimens are a cross between proofs and patterns and can function as either. To confuse matters further the term 'specimen' is used interchangeably and can vary depending on one's native language and numismatic market. In Canada for example, many more coins are referred to as 'specimens' than in other countries and indeed full sets of specimen coins have been issued to collectors in the manner of proofs. In short, as they are sharper, better-made, rarer and more attractive than their circulating equivalents, specimens also enjoy the same value premiums as proofs and patterns.

In general, the higher the quality of production, the more valuable the coin. This is the same for both antique and modern pieces. But be that as it may, improper production can occasionally correlate with increased value as shown through mint errors and varieties. Patterns, proofs and specimens make up a very large proportion of the most valuable coins today for their superior quality and comparative rarity. However, production standard is only one part of what dictates coin value, and in many ways how a coin was made is less important than how it has been cared for since. This brings us to the most important factor behind coin value in numismatics, the one element that can mean the difference between a coin selling for $1,000 and $100,000 – a coin's preservation.

4. Preservation

When I researched that first battered 1799 Halfpenny I bought as a child, I compared it directly with those I saw online selling for £200 and immediately assumed my coin was of equal value. After all, it was the same coin, and surely £200 must consequently be what that type of coin was worth?

It was not until afterwards that I became aware of the significant impact that preservation has on the value of a coin. Distinct from its production quality, preservation refers solely to how much a coin has been handled or damaged since it was first struck, referred to as its 'grade'. My ignorance of the topic was not uncommon, either. Many novices presume that if two coins are of the same type their value will be identical as if there is a standard 'going rate' for all coins. However it is not just having any old example of a given coin type which is considered important, rather it is the quality of the individual coin that denotes its worth. The degree of preservation is the difference between an immaculate representation of ancient or medieval portraiture and a blank expressionless disk of metal. Alongside rarity, a coin's condition is the most important determiner of its value.

This was not always the case, however. Collectors in the 18th and 19th centuries simply aspired to owning any representative of a rare coin with condition being a mere afterthought. Contemporary auction catalogues barely made mention of the state a coin was in; often they merely wrote "in good preservation" or "as made". Comparatively little research had been conducted at this point as to how a coin should look in its untouched state, so all things considered these statements were fairly redundant. Collectors continued onwards paying little heed to the condition of their coins.

Then came Lieutenant-Colonel William Durrant: one of the first truly grade-conscious collectors. Durrant, of a genteel Suffolk family, collected British coins until his death in 1847. His passion and zeal for obtaining the best example of every type he wanted transcended price, logistical hurdles - and even laws. Durrant took advantage of the ill-standardised state of contemporary coin grading by attending public viewings of his late collector-peers' estate auctions, looking through their coins and replacing them with his own inferior examples. He avoided capture because the coins were not photographed, were only occasionally printed as drawings in auction catalogues, and their vague descriptions of quality could not easily be contradicted. That being said, eagle-eyed numismatists finally worked out what he had been doing when he died and his coins were offered at auction. I once had the privilege to flip through an original annotated Durrant catalogue from 1847 in which the annotator had detailed from which collection he presumed each coin was stolen. For his early anticipation of how quality would eventually dictate coin values in the future, Durrant may have actually been a time-travelling numismatist who went back to play the system – we will never truly know.

To avoid such unscrupulous activities and to further the science of numismatics, a standardised coin grading scale was eventually agreed upon which is as follows: *Poor, Good, Very Good, Fine, Very Fine, Extremely Fine* and *Uncirculated* (or *Mint State*). This scale is still used by many European numismatists. Between the different boundaries there are some commonly used border grades such as "Good Fine" and "Almost Extremely Fine". The unscientific nature of these terms meant they still leave considerable room for debate and subjective opinion. However, alongside this grading scale the ability to 'plate' coins for catalogues (photographing wax moulds of them) followed by the development of coin photography gradually allowed for a far more scientific analysis between different examples, increasing collector demand for the finest pieces possible.

Nowadays, coin photography is so sophisticated that even minute differences in quality can be detected and as a result, appreciation of mint state coins has never been stronger. If perfectly preserved, a common coin will receive far more acclaim and attention than an average condition rarity. Perhaps the most significant impact that preservation has on a coin's value is as follows: if you offer an unremarkable coin at auction, only those collectors without their own specimen will bid. Contrastingly if a superb high-grade example of that same coin enters the market, even those collectors who already have their own specimen may seek to buy your coin to upgrade. As such preservation can 'reopen the market' and lead to a huge increase in the final price paid.

There are four main aspects of preservation to assess when examining a coin: circulation wear (I), altered surfaces (II), circulation damage (III) and collector damage (IV). Each of these factors separately affect coin values and it is vital to have an understanding of how each manifests itself. When a coin is first struck it will have mint 'lustre' across its surfaces, a satin effect which is often the first element to disappear with handling. Lustre and its desirability will be covered within the next section.

I. Circulation Wear

Circulation wear - present on almost every antique coin - is what defines a coin's grade. When handled, even the lightest friction from your hands will gently rub away the sharp details of a coin over time, particularly when that coin has been struck in a soft metal such as gold or high purity silver. Wear always impacts the highest, most exposed points of the design first (generally found in the centre of the coin) and so after moderate circulation the centres start to appear somewhat 'flat'. Advanced circulation will cause this flatness to migrate outwards and the rims will also begin to exhibit wear. For beginners it can sometimes be difficult to identify wear without knowing how the complete design of a coin should look, leading many to initially over-grade their coins.

Wear is more than acceptable within numismatics and is fully expected to be present on most coins. Some collectors enjoy knowing that their coin has been widely circulated and has developed its own story – however, the highest prices will always be paid for those coins that show the least wear. Generally the older and heavier the coin the more likely it is to have suffered considerable loss of detail, meaning those examples which have remained sharp will attract substantial premiums. Even if the degree of wear differs only slightly it has a huge impact on prices, and grade is particularly important in the US market.

The three US 'Morgan' Dollars illustrated below were all struck in 1893 at the San Francisco mint and were all sold in the same auction in

February 2020. This is a particularly rare year and mintmark combination. The coins may all appear similar, but each received a different grade; the first was considered Almost Uncirculated 50, the second Almost Uncirculated 55 and the third Mint State 62[7]. These seemingly minor grade differences led to dramatically diverse prices; the first sold for $13,800, the second for $28,800 and the third for $150,000.

From left to right: AU50, AU55, MS62 1893-S US Morgan Dollars

The graph below shows the comparative leap in price for the MS62 Morgan Dollar amongst several other 1893-S examples of varying quality that were sold in early 2020 by the same US-based auction house.

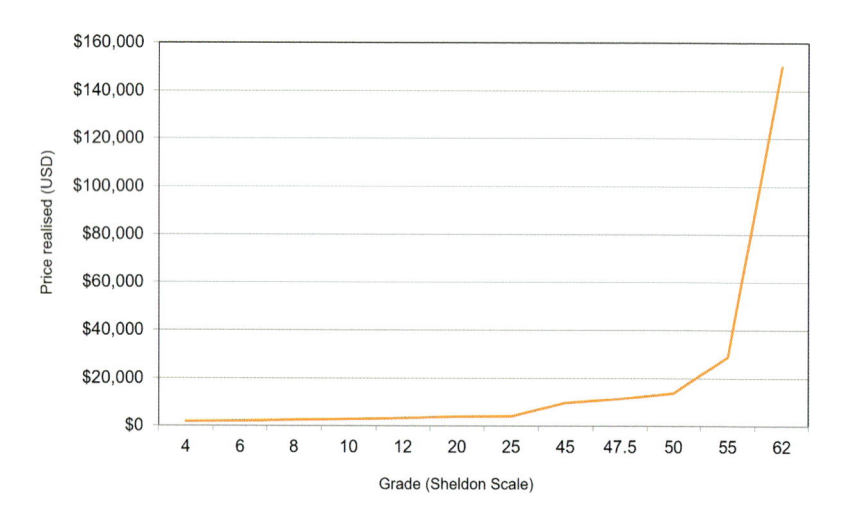

Prices realised for 1893-S Morgan Dollars in early 2020

---

7   These are 'Sheldon Scale' grade boundaries used by US grading companies which will be covered in more detail later.

As grade increases, prices climb proportionally. However, prices can jump exponentially for the very finest examples as there may be only a handful of examples in that high preservation extant (called 'conditional rarities'). When evaluating a coin it is sensible to research the finest known examples to learn what a fully detailed specimen looks like. This way it is possible to assess how much detail remains.

II. Deliberate Surface Alteration

Surface alteration refers to any practice that has changed the original surface 'texture' of a coin by deliberate intention as opposed to through normal use. This process may not have significantly affected the sharpness of the designs, but inspection under magnification will show an unusual or unappealing surface to the metal. Surface alteration can be caused by a handful of actions but by far the most often seen is cleaning.

One of the earliest lessons numismatists learn is not to clean your coins. It only takes one heartbreak where you have unknowingly destroyed the value of a coin by cleaning it to cement this mantra in your head forever. Cleaning refers to any activity intended to enhance the appearance of a coin by removing engrained dirt or toning, most commonly through wiping or brushing its surfaces, and can range from light to extremely harsh. When cleaning is undertaken more intensively it can entirely transform the appearance of the metal, giving it a bright polished finish with no toning whatsoever. When cleaned this heavily, a coin's appeal to collectors has sunk to almost nothing even if the coin is rare and otherwise uncirculated. As the most common surface alteration, it is essential to be able to identify when a coin has been cleaned as the practice significantly reduces coin value.

A less abrasive form of cleaning coins is referred to as 'dipping', when chemicals are used to strip away surface materials or the topmost layer of metal to give the coin a brighter appearance. The mildest form of this practice is submerging the coin in acetone or ammonia to remove surface dirt or discolouration, and as a comparatively non-invasive procedure this is not classed in quite the same way as true dipping. This lesser process is often called 'conservation' and does not involve any friction to disrupt the surface of the metal. As a result, despite being a form of cleaning, conservation can in many cases increase value. True dipping involves treating a coin with an acid-containing solution in order to remove the original patina it has developed with the aim of making it more appealing to the eye. Occasionally this practice causes a more attractive patina to develop on the coin, but in most cases the tone that returns is unnatural and will dissuade potential collectors. For the most part, collectors will prefer a coin that has natural toning.

Coins can also exhibit 'repair' marks. Similar to cleaning, repairs are usually undertaken by those attempting to enhance the appearance of their coins. While older repairs were often the actions of well-meaning collectors, more modern repairs tend to be in the interest of fooling a potential buyer. Repairs manifest themselves as areas of unnatural smoothness in the fields or devices of a coin, usually where a scratch or scuff has been delicately rubbed away or disguised through microscopic scratches.

Finally, a severe form of surface alteration is known as sweating. This refers to the antique practice of artificially wearing down a coin in the interest of removing excess metal, most often occurring with gold coins (as the process was simply not cost effective otherwise). Numerous coins were placed in a bag and shaken, the impact of friction creating a metal dust at the bottom which could then be collected. The coins themselves showed no clipping or filing and so the process was harder to detect by authorities. Sweated coins show an uneven 'blurring' of the devices, the swift shaking motion creating a loss of detail across the entirety of the designs rather than simply flattening at the high points. Whereas normal circulation wear is considered acceptable for a coin even when severe, sweating immediately reduces a coin's appeal to collectors.

A coin with unsightly surface alteration is harder to value than one that merely exhibits wear. Numismatists seek originality above all else, and a coin with surface alteration is not simply one which has been traded often and used for its intended purpose, but is instead treated as damaged goods. Accordingly, values for these coins do not fit neatly onto a graph but rather depend on the rarity of the coin and the extent to which the alteration has affected the eye appeal. Unaltered coins are said to have their 'original surfaces' and will always carry a value premium.

Two British James II Guineas, 1688. The first has been sweated, the second worn through circulation. Notice the 'blurred' effect present throughout the designs of the first example versus the flat upper surfaces of the second piece.

III. Circulation Damage

Circulation damage refers to the scratches or dents on a coin's surfaces and edge that are associated with normal use. Unlike circulation wear which occurs slowly over time, damage is caused by sudden, sharp impacts to a coin's surface. These often appear as crescent-shaped digs known as 'bagmarks', so-called for often being caused by collisions with other coins in a bank bag. Additionally, once they have left the bank coins can easily scratch and dent each other in pockets, vaults, savings pots or anywhere else where they are kept closely together. Damage can also appear as nicks to the edge of a coin, as shallow scratches or surface scuffs.

Circulation damage is very common in larger gold coins as the heft and softness of these pieces means even a light impact will mark their surfaces. Similar to wear, some degree of damage is often expected on coins and does not prevent them from being desirable to collectors. Interestingly, coins can still be considered Mint State even with circulation damage. If a coin's surfaces are still fully original and show no hint of wear then minor nicks are considered to have occurred prior to its being issued for commerce. However as one would expect, the lesser the damage the more valuable the coin.

The two coins illustrated are the same type, both Five Guineas of George II struck in 1748. Five Guineas weigh around 40gm and have a high 22 carat gold purity so these types almost always exhibit at least some minor scratches. Both of these examples were graded as Mint State, one as MS62 and one as MS63. However the MS62 coin had a scattering of digs and scuffs on the obverse whilst the MS63 example had comparatively few. Despite their similar grade, the MS63 example sold for $168,000, whilst the MS62 failed to sell at a price of $72,000.

The extent of damage to a coin's surface will always affect its sale price, as collectors tend to seek out the most untouched example of a coin on the market no matter what its technical grade.

IV. Deliberate or Environmental Damage

The final and most devastating detraction to coin value is post-mint damage inflicted on a coin, either deliberately or due to its environment. Similar to surface alteration, damage can render a coin undesirable to most collectors, and accordingly its value becomes far more subjective (but certainly much reduced). Deliberate damage can take many forms, and is defined by physical changes to the planchet or designs of a coin[8].

Some of the oldest forms of damage inflicted to coins were performed to remove a portion of the precious metal planchet to retain as 'profit'. This could be achieved by either clipping or filing, as well as sweating. Clipping was, as it sounds, the use of tin snips to remove slivers of

---

8   Technically, sweating is a form of damage but as it emulates wear is included as a form of surface alteration.

metal from the edge of a coin which could then be melted down into bullion or to produce new coins. This practice was seen as tantamount to counterfeiting and would occasionally be punishable by death. In fact, clipping was considered such a serious crime that even amongst criminals it was vilified. When the famous pirate Henry Avery (born 1659) attacked the Mughal treasure ship, Ganj-i-Sawai or *Gunsway* in 1695, he ended up taking £600,000 in precious metals and jewels equivalent to around £93.3 million in 2022. He initially shared these spoils with fellow pirate William May. However, when Avery found out that May's crew had traded clipped coins to his own men, he reclaimed almost all of the treasure he had given to May.

Due to the introduction of more regularly shaped coins with protective edge designs in the mid-16th and 17th century, clipping was limited only to hammered coins that pre-date milling. Clipped coins are smaller than their peers (as one would expect) and often exhibit significant wear. Collectors will always prefer a full and unclipped coin, but as this practise was one undertaken in antiquity it will not reduce coin value as much as other forms of damage as it is seen as part of the coin's 'story'. Filing - the removal of metal from the edges of a coin using a rasp - was a similar practice. While undesirable, filing affects value even less than clipping as the effects are subtle (as the original practitioners of filing intended it to be). Filing can be identified by small, parallel scrape marks around the edge or rim of a coin.

Another common form of deliberate damage is inflicted by piercing or 'holing' a coin, the act of punching a hole through the metal itself. Coins were pierced for a variety of reasons; to wear as jewellery, to keep on a ring with other coins to avoid being lost, for the sheer fun of it, etc. There is an oft-stated figure in numismatics that a pierced coin will bring a price just ten per cent of that of the same coin without a hole, but the truth is less scientific. If a coin is extremely rare or of otherwise exceptional quality, it may still fetch a fair percentage of its usual price. Additionally, a pierced coin will sometimes be 'plugged', where the hole is filled in by a collector attempting to restore the coin. This can be undertaken with various levels of skill, and a neatly-plugged coin will be more valuable than one with a crude plug or left with a gaping hole. However, in either case their value will be far less than an undamaged example, and suffice it to say that holed and plugged coins rarely offer a significant appeal to collectors.

Other damage can arise from coins being mounted in jewellery, leaving solder or mount marks around the edges or claw marks at the peripheries. Generally coins that have been housed in jewellery also exhibit heavy polishing in an effort to keep them shiny. The combination of these factors makes ex-jewellery coins some of the least valuable of all, as their altered surfaces and damage completely removes their visual appeal.

Graffiti is another common form of damage on older coins. Many would inscribe notable dates, names, patterns or even just a scrawled 'x' on their coins. Graffiti occurs to various degree of severity and, in most cases, will significantly reduce coin value. However, in a similar vein to clipping, graffiti can sometimes be considered an interesting nod to the coin's past and may therefore not lead to such dramatic drops in value as caused by holing or mounting. Additionally, when a coin is extremely rare or even unique this form of damage (among others) can be seen as almost insignificant. I once catalogued a Norwegian Triple Speciedaler of 1666 - one of just two known examples - that bore graffiti on the reverse, yet its rarity led to it selling to a very satisfied buyer for an immense sum of $432,000.

Norway, Triple Speciedaler, 1666

On the other hand, a particularly insidious form of graffiti called 'tooling' will always heavily impact a coin's value. Tooling is defined as the designs of a coin being re-engraved or the fields completely levelled with a fine stylus, either to deceive a buyer into thinking that the coin has been more lightly circulated or simply for fun by a collector. As this procedure directly hurts the artistic quality and originality of a coin, tooled specimens are worth a mere fraction of the sums that regular issues will bring. Fortunately, even cursory research and comparison will allow numismatists to identify and reject tooled coins.

Similar to tooling, coins can be 'whizzed', or ground with a high-speed mechanical brush in order to create the illusion of mint lustre on their surfaces. While original mint lustre spins across the coin in a 'cartwheel' effect from the centre outwards, whizzed coins create a blanket of satin texture with no discernible direction. Examination of the surfaces will reveal circles of hairline scratches from the brushing process. Despite being a type of surface alteration, the severity of the whizzing process makes it closer to a form of damage and it will certainly hurt a coin's sale price more than most forms of surface alteration.

Environmental damage can also appear in various forms. Many coins with environmental damage have been discovered by treasure hunters or metal detectorists and owe the damage to the conditions in which they were deposited. Shipwreck coins will frequently exhibit saltwater corrosion leaving a pockmarked effect on their surfaces, whilst those buried underground for long periods regularly show chemical reactions depending on the acidity of the soil. Metal detecting-found coins can suffer from plough damage which causes dramatic bends, breaks and tears to the metal. And, even if coins survive perfectly underground they can sometimes, heartbreakingly, be nicked by the spade when being excavated. Environmental damage does not tend to reduce a coin's value to the same degree as deliberate damage, but again it ultimately will come down to how appealing the coin looks or if its environmental damage tells its own tale (saltwater damage, fire damage etc.).

Degree of preservation is a better determination of value than any other coin feature, be it rarity, historical significance or even production standard. The numismatic market has many tiers of quality and the majority of coins fit into a 'moderately circulated' category. This material has the largest collector base, and values for these average condition coins are usually quite standardised; the better the coin condition, the proportionally higher the price it will fetch. However, the finest quality examples will often fetch prices many multiples of lesser specimens because the collectors with the most capital will seek to obtain the best coins they can. Equally, coins with deliberate damage or alteration will usually fetch a fraction of the price of undamaged examples as they are desirable only to those collectors unable to afford an untouched specimen.

A high grade is clearly seen as a universally desirable trait for coins. This is alongside a desire for well-made coins of high quality production. What the combination of these two factors amounts to is a desire for undeniably impressive pieces, coins with the most pleasing appearance and the best presentation – the final of the three P's.

5. Presentation

The story so far: your coin may be rare, have a wide collector base, be well-made and be well-preserved. It will surely sell, and likely sell well. But there is still one hurdle left. Assuming it is not unique, what will make the wealthiest collectors choose to buy your example of that coin as opposed to another?

What it all boils down to, and what the market really wants is: a coin that looks nice – one with impressive presentation.

As previously mentioned, the significant emphasis on coin preservation above all else is a relatively new phenomenon in numismatics. In the 19th century, to judge the quality of your coins you would have to physically take them to other collectors and dealers and compare them side-by-side with whatever examples they had. This approach was so impractical that no formal grading system could be agreed upon. Instead, if you had simply an appealing-looking example, you would be satisfied.

Over time, new technology has allowed the analysis of grade to become increasingly more sophisticated. Nowadays establishing the production and preservation standard of a particular coin is actually quite a scientific procedure, high-resolution photography allowing microscopic comparison with uncirculated examples in order to determine the degree of wear and analyse the quality of manufacture. The standardisation of grading has allowed much of the coin market to become predictable and relatively liquid; trends change over time, but at any given moment the majority of numismatists would be able to tell you the rough value of a given coin from their field in, say, Very Fine condition. Prices rise proportionally to grade, and logically it follows that those coins deemed to have the least wear and produced to the highest standard will carry the largest price tags. But even with this price stability and however well developed the science of numismatics may be, the sum that the finest coins sell for is the furthest thing from scientific.

What truly drives coin value is simply what collectors choose to pay. And collectors are not cold, calculating machines who will only pay accepted market prices. Collectors are recalcitrant and capricious, and will let impulse and desire cloud their reasonable judgement. If a wealthy collector feels a connection between themselves and a particularly choice coin they may well bid as much as it takes to secure it for their collection, creating an unprecedented price spike. This is the cause of the sharp upturn in values for the highest-quality specimens.

As such, numismatics is at its heart a hobby of passion, and a coin must inspire passion in the collector for it to sell well. Collectors will have no reason to choose a particular coin if its quality is decidedly average, and its potential market will only be those collectors who do not own an example. The prestige in owning the very best preserved example of a coin - alongside the myriad of techniques in place to assess coin condition - would understandably lead one to believe that preservation alone will always inspire the greatest passion in the buyer. However, despite the extent to which the hobby has developed in the last century, what collectors still truly seek above all else are coins which look pretty, a factor not merely limited to their technical condition.

Rather than specifically their preservation, it is ultimately a coin's presentation which inspires collectors to buy coins and consequently generates the highest prices. If preservation and ranking were everything then the finest example of a given coin type available to commerce would always generate an extraordinary price, but in practise even the best known examples fail to attract significant sums if they are unattractive to the eye. Excellent preservation will most often equal excellent presentation, but excellent presentation does not always require excellent preservation.

A relevant case study showcasing the importance of coin presentation on value is that of the extremely rare 'Leopard' of King Edward III. In 1344, Edward attempted to introduce the first multi-denominational 'Florin' system of English gold coins consisting of the Double Leopard (Double Florin), Leopard (Florin) and Helm (Half-Florin). These coins did not fit well into the English monetary system, failed to divide properly with international currencies, and were produced for just a few months in 1344 before being recalled and melted due to unpopularity. Only a handful of coins from this issue survive.

In 2006 a well-struck and well-preserved Double Leopard was discovered by a metal detectorist, and became the first to ever enter the open market; it sold for an unprecedented hammer price of £400,000 ($725,000). At the time of writing this coin is thought to be worth over $1 million. Meanwhile, in 2003 a very poorly preserved Leopard/Florin was found in similar circumstances and was put to public auction. This was the only example available to collectors, and yet it sold for a paltry £4,400 ($7,081). It came to auction again in 2016, and this time sold for just £4,300 ($5,579). Despite its age, its rarity, its wide collector base and being technically the finest specimen available, the coin failed to even scrape five per cent of the price of the Double Leopard due to its poor preservation and presentation. Nobody wanted it.

Left: England, Edward III (1327-77), Double Leopard, 1344. Right: Leopard of the same issue

Simply put: if a coin is in excellent condition it will usually be extremely presentable and it is this factor which will inspire collectors to buy it.

However even if a coin is in the highest state of preservation known, if it is imperfect there will always be a cap on the price it can achieve. Presentation is everything to collectors.

Within the hobby, coin presentation is referred to as 'eye appeal'. This is a simplistic term which encompasses several factors, most of which refer to its production and presentation but also cover its lustre (I), patina (II) and its overall 'wow' factor (III).

I. Lustre

When a coin is struck by dies, metal flows from the centre of the planchet outwards to the edges producing parallel micro-striations on its surfaces. These tiny grooves reflect light, the uniform direction often creating a circular 'cartwheel' motion when tilted. Lustre most often appears as a satin, silken sheen on the surface of a coin, or is sometimes reflective like a mirror[9]. Due to their extreme fragility, even minor friction can destroy these striations and damage a coin's lustre.

Lustre, as a delicate and freshly-struck effect, is desired by collectors above many other visual factors. Even if a coin exhibits soft details, the presence of lustre will indicate that it has been weakly struck as opposed to significantly handled. Lustre is technically associated with coin preservation, but it can fade from a coin which is still technically uncirculated. This effect is particularly true for copper and bronze coins; when newly struck they tend to exhibit blazing red lustre, but gentle oxidation over time can cause them to fade to a dull brown. Accordingly lustre tends to be more of a 'presentation' factor than one purely related to preservation.

Unfortunately, one of the reasons that so many novices end up cleaning their coins is due to this ingrained knowledge that these 'shiny' coins are nicer than dull coins. Cleaning, above all else, is guaranteed to remove lustre and produce a flat, lifeless appearance on a coin's surfaces. The desire to restore lustre also leads some to attempt unscrupulous methods, such as whizzing the surfaces in an imitation of a lustrous satin effect. Fortunately whizzing is easily identified through cursory comparison with genuinely lustrous coins.

When choosing between two coins of the same type, collectors are

---

9   Such coins, when produced as normal currency strikes, are often referred to as 'prooflike'.

almost guaranteed to prefer whichever one exhibits a greater coverage of mint lustre even in spite of production quality.

II. Patina

Depending on how reactive the planchet metal is, coins are prone to developing a tone as they react with the air, referred to as their 'patina'. Production relates to how a coin has been made, preservation to how it has been handled, and patina to how a coin has been stored. Many US Morgan Dollars, for example, exhibit fantastically vivid patinas associated with their being stored in sulphur-dyed burlap bank bags. If a coin has been housed in a collection for many years it may develop an iridescent and multi-coloured 'cabinet tone', caused from gentle interaction with the air over decades or centuries. Technically this is the uppermost layer of the metal being damaged by exposure to oxygen, but the process can create a highly desirable effect and one coveted by collectors.

Patina can hugely enhance a coin's eye appeal and plays a significant part in presentation. The most dedicated patina collectors will buy coins exclusively based on their tone, but almost all numismatists will be swayed by an attractive patina when choosing which coins to collect. In a large collection of Shillings struck during the period of the Commonwealth of England (1649-60) I catalogued several years ago, the highest price achieved was not for the best-made or the best-preserved specimen but rather for one which had superb rainbow toning.

Two English Commonwealth Shillings both struck in 1652. The left-hand example showed very little wear and sold for £3,360, whilst the slightly inferior right-hand example realised £6,000 due to its attractive patina.

On the other hand, an unappealing patina can significantly detract from a coin in otherwise exemplary preservation. If a coin has toned too darkly it can appear black and hard to identify, or can occasionally exhibit toning 'blotches' where elements of the planchet sharply change in colour.

Just like any other factor seen as desirable within numismatics, there are practices which attempt to replicate attractive toning on coins. Artificial toning is commonly paired with improperly dipped or cleaned coins and is intended to enhance their eye appeal. Artificially toned coins generally exhibit intense, neon colouration with abrupt changes between colours, whereas naturally toned coins tend to blend seamlessly from colour-to-colour and rarely feature such vivid blushes of hue. Additionally, careful examination of the surfaces will reveal hairline scratches or marks diagnostic of cleaning which will help to distinguish a naturally toned, untouched coin from one polished and artificially re-toned.

III. 'Wow' Factor

Much of the joy of numismatics comes from conversation with those who share your passion, from comparing your coins, concocting theories – and impressing each other with the quality of your collection. Numismatics is, at its heart, a competitive hobby. Partially fuelled by the prominent role of auctions, whether you compete against other collectors or yourself there is a perpetual drive to own the best, the most impressive and the finest coins extant. As you develop your knowledge of your chosen numismatic field, you quickly learn which coins are more common, more rare, more often encountered in higher states of preservation, etc. Before long, some of the novelty vanishes and the majority of those coins seem to you to be quite commonplace and 'average'. But there will still be those few coins that manage to stun you with their eye appeal, and it is these coins which attract the most attention – those which make you, and every other collector, stop and say, 'wow'.

The 'wow' factor can be hard to place and tends to vary depending on the given coin type. It could be an intersection of production quality and patina, lustre and preservation, or any other combination of factors which produces an amazing appearance; after familiarising yourself with a particular coin type, you will simply 'know it when you see it'. So few coins have a perfect balance of qualities producing the 'wow' factor, but if one does its price will always reflect it. This is where numismatics can become somewhat more abstract and prices vary. For example, an auction I attended in London in January 2020 had an appealing selection of British hammered coins. Among these was a James I Shilling from around 1610. These coins are not overly rare, and tend to sell for around £300-500. This example was especially appealing with an excellent portrait, and so its estimate was slightly higher at £600-800. I myself intended to bid £850, was swiftly blown out of the water and after extended bidding the price closed at £6,000 – which after various fees came to a sum total of over £8,000.

England, James I (1603-25) Shilling, c.1610

Technically, this coin exhibited light circulation and had no lustre; it was not of perfect production and had the usual slightly uneven flan. But, despite these factors its appearance was of such high quality that it brought a price greater than any other regular-issue James I Shilling ever had before[10]. The 'wow' factor simply refers to that particular attention-grabbing aspect which can whip bidders up into a frenzy and cause them to pay whatever it takes to secure the coin for themselves.

This universal desire for fantastic presentation and a strong 'wow' factor motivates collectors in choosing which examples of a given coin type to collect, but also determines what type of coins they will collect in the first place. Generally, the rule is that the higher spending power a coin had when circulating, the proportionally higher value it will have today. If a coin is large, gold or silver and with appealing engraving then it has

---

10 One of the most common elements bringing a 'wow' factor for circulated coins is an excellent portrait, an aspect which should always be weighed up when choosing which coins to buy. Many collectors buy specifically those coins with an above-average portrait.

significant 'wow' factor in its very nature and will always have a stronger and wealthier collector base than smaller and less imposing coins.

Once again this element has its root in a desire to impress others. Some coins only have significant value when they fit into part of a wider collection. A diminutive, fractional British Farthing in a high grade or of a rare type will only be interesting to other British collectors of Farthings, or if the owner has hundreds of others alongside it. Its value will always be capped below a certain level, as for the most part if Farthing collectors could afford substantial prices then they would probably be collecting more impressive larger denomination coins. On the other hand, a large gold coin of significant age will stand alone as an object of wonderment even across nationalities and borders, and such a coin will have the largest collector base of all. Whether a proof, pattern or circulating issue, the size and quality of a coin significantly impacts its value, as those collectors with the most capital to spend will seek to buy the best and most impressive they can.

It should be noted that in line with the spirit of competition so integral to numismatics, preservation level now has its own 'wow' factors to collectors. Coin presentation is the truest motivator for buying a coin, but a coin's grade has gradually come to be considered as the universal standard of numismatics. This has led many to compete for top graded coins regardless of their eye appeal, as owning the best preserved example of a coin is guaranteed to impress other collectors. This is why it is always safest to purchase coins in higher grades; they are doubly secure, being technically impressive and also likely boasting strong eye appeal.

All coins follow the same patterns driving their value. Supply and demand determines the size of the collector base while the individual coin's production, preservation and presentation determine how much of that collector base will compete to purchase it. It is one part of the equation to own a rare coin with historical or numismatic significance, another for it to have significant collector demand, and another for its quality to be impressive enough to appeal to most of those collectors.

A – Rarity

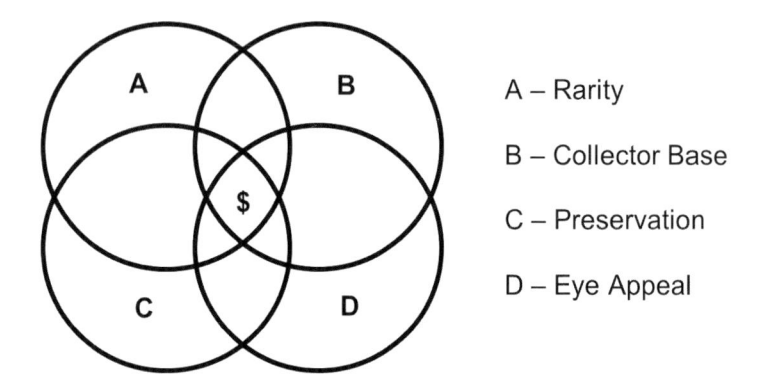

B – Collector Base

C – Preservation

D – Eye Appeal

Venn diagram illustrating the key aspects which intersect to create coin value.

The focus given to coin preservation, production quality and ultimately to presentation has created a competitive atmosphere within numismatics in which collectors deign to obtain the very finest examples they can. As this section has shown, the analysis of quality in coins is an expert skill which takes time and effort to develop. This understandably can dissuade potential buyers simply due to their fears that they will slip up and purchase an inferior coin from inexperience. However, to address this, over the last few decades an even more standardised, numerical system of grading has been introduced, one which has radically transformed how numismatists collect and compete with one another and one which has inspired thousands of new collectors to comfortably participate in the market – third-party certification.

Chapter 1.3.
Third-Party Grading

1. Background to TPG

Third-party coin grading and encapsulation (TPG), also called certification or 'slabbing', is perhaps the most polarising area of global numismatics. This procedure is as it sounds: the submission of your coins to a third-party operator who assesses them for quality and returns them ultrasonically sealed in plastic capsules bearing a numerical grade. Seen as a primarily American procedure with European auction houses generally being less fond, depending on whom you ask TPG is a) absolutely imperative for the integrity of the business or b) merely a means of transforming historical artefacts into soulless commodities. Many collectors and dealers retain their painful memories of the 1989 coin market collapse and the part that TPG played, and so choose to reject the practice entirely. My career has included positions at an anti-TPG European auctioneer and a very pro-TPG US auction house which has helped me to understand both sides of the argument. However, no matter your viewpoint, the practice has undeniably revolutionised the trade and allowed scores of new numismatists to confidently participate in the market.

As we covered earlier, traditional coin grading has historically allowed subjectivity as a result of the scale's vagueness; additionally, mishandling of coins (ie cleaning, tooling, mounting) has often gone unnoticed or undescribed by sellers, leading to widespread distrust. This vague assessment of quality also meant that prices were difficult to standardise. Consequently, third party certification was developed in the late 1980s by two companies: Professional Coin Grading Service (PCGS) and Numismatic Guaranty Company (NGC) with the aim to standardise grading across the market, identify forgeries, and facilitate honest trade. Other grading companies do exist, but PCGS and NGC are the main operators and the most widely used. These two companies both adhere to the same numerical system of grading known as the "Sheldon Scale", put forward in the late 1940s by

William Herbert Sheldon, an American numismatist. The Sheldon scale consists of similar grade boundaries to the older system in place (*Poor, Fair, About Good, Good, Very Good, Fine, Very Fine, Extremely Fine, Almost Uncirculated* and *Mint State*) coupled with a numerical 'score' from 1-70. The scale is as follows; most tiers skip some numbers, so those listed are only those that you would actually see on a coin's holder.

The Sheldon Scale

Grade / Prefix	Number Range
Poor (P/PO)	1
Fair (FR)	2
About Good (AG)	3
Good (G)	4, 6
Very Good (VG)	8, 10
Fine (F)	12, 15
Very Fine (VF)	20, 25, 30, 35
Extremely Fine (XF)	40, 45
Almost Uncirculated (AU)	50, 53, 55, 58
Mint State (MS)	60 – 70 inclusive

Two opposite-end examples of English James II Crowns dated 1687 in NGC holders graded 'Good 4' and 'Mint State 65'.

There are a few variations within this system. If a coin is considered a pattern, proof or specimen its prefix will read PR/PF (these two are interchangeable) or SP respectively. Despite not having a grade prefix, in these instances the accepted numerical boundaries means that the number itself indicates the grade level. Additionally, should the designs of a proof coin be frosted and matte in contrast to its fields it will be designated a 'Cameo' coin. If it is particularly frosted and the contrast is stark, it will be designed Ultra Cameo (NGC) or Deep Cameo (PCGS), i.e. 'PR65 Ultra Cameo'. A cameo contrast has a significant impact on a proof coin's value.

If a coin has exceptional eye appeal, it will receive a star symbol (★) after its grade number (a designation unique to NGC), an extremely desirable accolade. If it is at the upper end of quality for its grade it will receive a plus '+'; and if it is proof-like (ie with very reflective fields and frosted designs) but not actually a proof, it will either have a 'PL' prefix or suffix to the numerical grade (ie 'PL65 / MS65 PL') depending on the coin type[11]. Those coins with particularly pronounced proof-like qualities will be called 'Deep Proof-like' (DPL). All of these accolades can attract substantial premiums compared to other coins of the same grade.

Most importantly: if a coin is genuine but has been significantly mishandled (cleaned, placed in jewellery etc), then it will receive what is referred to as a 'net' or 'details' grade. This appears as its relevant grade prefix followed by 'Details' and an explanation, for example, "AU Details (Cleaned)". Such coins will often be considerably less desirable than those with a numerical or 'straight' grade, and their value will be contingent more on their eye appeal and the severity of whatever mishandling they exhibit.

It is noteworthy that the Sheldon Scale is not employed for ancient coins, as these archaic types are far too varied and irregular for it to be universally applicable. Instead, a modified 'adjectival' scale is used in which coins are deemed to be Fine, Very Fine, Poor etc and instead of a numerical grade they instead feature two scores out of 5 for both their 'Strike' and their 'Surfaces'.

---

11 PL is only used as a prefix for coins described as being produced as definitively 'proof-like' by the issuing mint themselves as opposed to simply appearing reflective. The most commonly encountered examples are Canadian Dollars of the 1950s and 60s.

Both major grading companies maintain an extensive online database of coins and their grades known as their 'population reports'. These give quantities of all examples certified and the grades awarded for any given coin type, allowing collectors to ascertain precisely where their own coin sits in this global ranking. Additionally, PCGS and NGC let collectors produce 'registry sets', where collectors register their certified coins and build up online collections tied to their accounts. Registry sets are intrinsically competitive, with points awarded for the comparative quality, extent and preservation of your collection which occasionally bring prizes.

Since the 1980s, TPG has migrated from being purely associated with US coins to permeating every corner of numismatics. It is now common to encounter encapsulated coins in European auctions and uncommon to encounter un-encapsulated coins in US auctions. The value of the practice is known inside and outside of the numismatic market; recently, Collector's Universe (who owns PCGS) was acquired by an outside investor for an immense $700 million. As this section will go on to cover, TPG has had probably the greatest impact on numismatics than any other innovation since the Age of Enlightenment.

2. The Certification Process

This is a run through of how third-party certification operates. First, you have a coin. Perhaps you have bought it at auction, inherited it or found it, but the most important thing is that you actually own it. If it is rare, of high quality or you are unsure whether or not it is genuine, you may well decide to have it third-party certified. This process consists of three main steps: submission (I), assessment (II), and encapsulation (III).

I. Submission
After creating an account with your chosen grading company, you can choose to either submit your coin in person or ship it with permission and the correct paperwork to their head office. There are also several submission centres and authorised dealers through whom you can submit your coins to a grading service. You will need to have a rough idea of your coin's value in order for it to be placed in the correct 'grading tier'

as the price for the service is contingent on value (due to risk, insurance, skill required etc). Typically, for coins worth less than $3,000 the price is under $50 and in almost every case this fee is ultimately inconsequential. The grading companies are helpful and will answer any questions you have regarding your submission.

Once you have completed the relevant forms, your coin will be securely shipped to your chosen company's head office for assessment.

II. Assessment

After arrival - and completing a grading queue - your coin will be examined closely by a specialist grader. Firstly, they will identify what the coin itself is: its country of origin, age, whether it is MS or proof, if it has any errors, what metal it is, etc. This will usually include consulting several reference works and more often than not the specialist will include one or two of these reference numbers on the grading insert. It is at this stage that any counterfeit coins will be identified and returned to the sender as "Not Genuine".

If your coin is deemed to be authentic, it is next inspected for mishandling. The grader will look for significant scratches, Mount marks, edge filing, repairs, tooling, cleaning, excessive hairlines, artificial toning, environmental corrosion, whizzing, any damage whatsoever that would prevent the coin from receiving a numerical 'straight' grade. Should any such damage be identified the coin will receive a 'details' grade, and if its surfaces are deemed to be heavily altered it will not be encapsulated at all.

Assuming your coin is free from these detriments then the grader will move on to assessing the level of circulation wear it exhibits. This is judged by how sharp the designs remain and how flat the highpoints may be. If the coin exhibits any wear whatsoever it will be exempt from entering the category of Mint State. Minor scratches and bagmarks are assessed separately, as Mint State coins can still feature these contact marks if they show no other signs of circulation. Once every facet of your coin has been suitably inspected, the specialist will decide a fitting numerical grade.

III. Encapsulation

With its identity, authenticity and quality determined, your coin will be sealed in an airtight plastic holder featuring a paper insert bearing its grade and specifications. Often there will be a review process in which additional graders examine the encapsulated coin to evaluate the accuracy of the provisional grade. The paper insert also includes a barcode which, if scanned, will pull up the relevant result on the company's online population report allowing instant knowledge of its global ranking.

Your newly-encapsulated coin will then be returned to you. After this point, your coin is guaranteed by the grading company, and so should it turn out to not be genuine or not as described then the grading company will pay fair market value to the affected party. If the holder is breached, then this guarantee is void.

An important element to note is that both NGC and PCGS offer their own services dedicated to removing environmental detriments from coins; NGC offers 'conservation' whilst PCGS 'restoration'. Should your coin appear to have unappealing surface stains, verdigris or other reversible detriments, the grading company of your choice may offer you their services to attempt to remove these undesirable substances and enhance your coin. This typically costs a fee equal to a small percentage of your coin's value due to the risk involved, but can have dramatic effect on the eye appeal.

Since its inception, TPC has become the industry standard and graded coins are seen more and more even within traditional European auction catalogues. To date, PCGS has graded 42,000,000 coins of total value $36,000,000,000, whilst NGC has graded another 46,000,000 still. This practise of 'slabbing' has even expanded outside of numismatics, today being employed in the assessment and evaluation of banknotes, comics, trading cards and many other collectibles. TPC does, however, encounter fierce opposition from some more traditional industry sectors resulting in many coins still being commonly sold 'raw' (a term for uncertified coins) by many auction houses and dealers.

3. Criticisms of Encapsulation

I recently saw a conversation regarding TPG take place in an online UK coin collecting community; traditionally, British collectors have not taken well to coin encapsulation. A member posted a photo of an Edward VI

Shilling in a PCGS holder and asked "to set him free or to not set him free?" The thread received dozens of comments from British collectors and dealers alike saying "set him free!", "let him out mate" and most uncomfortably: "he must be feeling cold, he needs the touch of a warm hand".

The thread quickly broke down into a discussion about the evils of slabbing with only a minority standing up in favour of encapsulation. One commenter stated his position as "don't understand this slabbed thing anyway... adds cost and perceived value, but [you are] paying for plastic". In the end, the coin was cracked out of its holder to much jubilation. And this incident was not isolated. TPG encounters considerable scorn and hatred from a wide swathe of the market, a feeling positively encouraged by more traditional collectors and dealers. Numismatics, with its roots in an appreciation of the past and neoclassicism, carries antiquarian and curatorial ideals in many collectors' minds; as such the prospect of trapping coins in plastic where you cannot hold them seems decidedly counterintuitive and not in keeping with the soul of the hobby.

There are admittedly some valid concerns with the practice of third-party grading. Despite there always being an absolute, determinable degree of circulation wear a coin exhibits, grading will always be subjective. If a type is engraved shallowly then it can appear more worn than it actually is and be marked down accordingly, frustrating those familiar with the issue. The same coin can receive a different grade each time it is submitted, clouding the trustworthiness of the graders. Additionally, trying to encapsulate delicate hammered coins can introduce a real risk of them breaking, holders may omit to mention coin weights (an important attribute of these earlier issues) and some holders obscure the coin edge entirely. Sometimes a production quirk such as a flan flaw or metal starvation is deemed as damage when the coin is in fact 'mint state', negatively affecting its potential value. And, finally, there are just some coins for whom the Sheldon scale simply does not neatly apply[12].

The impact of encapsulation on market price also poses an issue for traditional collectors. In some instances it can provide negative value and

---

12 There is an ongoing discussion that the grading of hammered coins should be treated the same as ancient coins, with a score out of 5 for surfaces and strike.

coins which had been bought and sold for literally centuries without issue may suddenly be flagged as 'cleaned' by a grading company and their value instantly decimated. Moreover, some coins with an undeniable 'wow' factor may be unfairly reduced to a mere technical grade when encapsulated, their eye appeal superseded by whatever number they receive.

Encapsulation is not merely criticised for lowering market prices, however, but also for inflating them by creating positive value. The particular phrase from that online conversation I witnessed which stayed in my mind was 'paying for plastic', alluding to a common perception by collectors that many encapsulated coins are significantly overpriced. Generally this refers to high-grade common coins, usually seen as being worth little by normal standards yet achieving unprecedented prices if their numerical grade is high enough. This perception can potentially be attributed to the 1989 collapse; despite that circumstance being specifically linked to institutional investors buying from collector markets, many still carry an unshakeable conviction that coin encapsulation equals unsustainable prices.

Despite its shortcomings, the decision of whether or not to certify your coins is not one which relates to the benefits of the broader practice itself, but rather is limited to the nature of the individual coin. Grading itself is not in question; its advantages are clear and it is folly to allow one poor grade or outdated stigma to condemn the entire practise of TPG. Instead, common sense must be practiced as to which coins suit grading and which do not. Firstly, the grading fee must be cost effective. Collectors with on-average lower value coins are understandably less willing to pay an additional $30 per coin to be housed in plastic when that amount may be equal to the coin's cost, whilst that amount is trivial to, say, a $2,000 coin. Secondly, if your coin is delicate, it may not be worth the risk of having it certified in case it breaks or is returned as 'too fragile to holder'. Finally, and most importantly, by familiarising yourself with the standards of the major grading companies you can choose to submit only those coins which stand a decent chance of grading well. As mentioned, minor coins in high grades can have their value significantly increased through prudent use of the grading companies.

For the most part, wider opposition to professional grading simply comes down to individual preference. Traditional collectors enjoy housing their coins in mahogany cabinets, physically holding the coins themselves, stating that you are 'feeling the history', and that encapsulating a coin is 'imprisoning' it. Coin cabinets are not (as some would lead you to believe) necessarily the best way to store coins, and instead represent an entirely personal decision made by those who choose to adhere to traditional numismatic values. As previously mentioned, the patina that coins develop in cabinets is technically damage, and the longer that coins are exposed to the air the more they will oxidise. Accordingly being ultrasonically-sealed will offer far better protection from the environment as well as reducing risks of being dropped or scratched. Simply put, those who oppose third-party authentication tend to do so from emotion rather than logic; it is a collector decision, not an investment decision.

Whether or not to certify your coins is your choice, and a healthy market will likely always exists for 'raw' coins. However, the advantages TPG has brought to the global market vastly outweigh the handful of disappointing grades collectors have received over the years. Third-party grading has transformed the numismatic market place in much the same way that banknotes did the global economy, by removing the speculative barter component of trade, significantly increasing liquidity and ultimately converting an archaic, academic pursuit into effective commodity trading.

4. Coin Commoditisation

The single-most significant element TPG has brought to collectors? Confidence. At the beginning of this book I stated that a combination of belief and trust formed confidence, and without confidence no investor would ever part with their capital. When traders of ancient times did not trust their coins, they refused to accept them or would only take them with a discount. To new and inexperienced numismatists it is difficult to have any confidence at all, as the biggest barrier to liquidity is a lack of knowledge. What TPG has done for the industry is inject this confidence all at once into numismatics worldwide. By assuring collectors that their professionally graded coins are genuine and that their quality is indisputable, they have removed the need for collectors to have their own advanced knowledge. It is this confidence that has allowed prices to standardise and for coins to turn from purely collectables into commodities and assets.

You can think of a coin's third-party grade as being comparable to bond credit ratings issued by one of the top three credit rating agencies: Moody's, Standard and Poor's or Fitch. Just as these three institutions issue letter ratings to assess the credit risk of a bond (AAA, AA, A, B etc.), TPG scores are issued to reflect the quality of individual coins. Experienced collectors will often have their own concept of how appealing the coin is and its scarcity/significance within the market, but what TPG has achieved is global confidence in their product amongst numismatists and non-numismatists alike.

As such, the door is wide open for investors to enter the market without needing to undertake an assessment of the coins themselves, as the expert work has already been done by the grading company. This influx of new capital significantly bolsters coin prices. Admittedly it was this same inexpertly-wielded capital that spurred the calamitous events of the 1989 coin market collapse, but the ability to research prices and auction trends online (not to mention learning from past mistakes) has helped to lower the risk of such unsustainable price growth occurring in the modern market.

Most significantly: the major grading companies offer a financial guarantee for their encapsulated coins and in a sense the numerical grade is a bond with the grading company. If that grade is found to be inaccurate or the coin to be inauthentic, then the affected party will be compensated fair market value for a genuine coin of the specified grade. Collectors need not simply take the grading companies at their word; they can expect fair compensation if the technical grade is incorrect. It is this aspect more than any other which helps commoditise coins. The guaranty behind grading has created a reliable perception of market value for coins of any given grade and has meaningfully contributed to the global standardisation of prices.

Many opponents of TPG become fixated on the specific numerical grades that coins receive, but the role of encapsulation goes further than this mere number. Grading equals authenticity. Many collectors do not mind overpaying for a coin with some damage or cleaning if its appearance is to their liking, but nobody wants to purchase a fake or forgery. An encapsulated coin has a subjective grade but can be guaranteed to be genuine, and for many collectors that is enough.

TPG scoring gives collectors the confidence to bid without needing to examine a coin in detail. It also, however, allows collectors to bid without ever needing to see the coin at all. As numismatic markets extend throughout the world across national boundaries, demand for coins can come from basically anywhere; once, bids for a coin in our auction turned out to be coming from a naval ship posted off the coast of Antarctica. The internet has created an entirely new market in the last few years, and anyone who has attended an auction in-person recently will attest to how often the auctioneer must stop to 'allow the internet to catch up'. Accordingly, the independent assessment of a third-party with no vested interest in the value of the coin gives collectors the confidence to bid from wherever they are, without ever having seen the coin in-hand. This dramatically increases the potential market for any given coin type which will almost always correspond with an increase in price and, through reducing transaction time, result in a more liquid market overall.

Numerical grading is also the perfect means of allowing collectors to compete with one another – an additional element helping TPG to boost prices. By issuing precise grades, there is no longer subjectivity amongst collectors as to whose coin is better as it is the work of a moment to pull up the online rankings to see for oneself. This has created a separate major factor dictating which coins generate the largest prices alongside presentation, that of obtaining the 'technical finest' coins[13]. PCGS and NGC positively encourage this with the introduction of their competitive registry sets. In August 2018, the auction house for which I worked offered a common Athens Tetradrachm with imperfect centring but which happened to be the single-finest of the type certified by NGC. Starting with an estimate of $4,000-6,000, it continued to climb in price

---

13 Bizarrely, the opposite is also true, and some seek to obtain the *worst* graded registry sets possible. Coins graded as "Poor 1" can carry premiums over higher graded examples due to the rarity of a coin having such advanced wear yet still being recognisable.

and resulted in a final sum of $36,000 – no doubt destined to become part of an elite NGC registry set.

Athens Tetradrachm, 440-404 BC, graded NGC Choice MS ★ 5/5 - 5/5

Results such as these lead some to refer to TPG as a practice which increases liquidity solely for coins 'sight unseen' and based on their grade alone. I would argue that it actually increases liquidity 'knowledge unknown'. Those who oppose TPG outright tend to do so because they feel they are better informed than the grading companies. Grading is a greater help for those with less knowledge of coins than it is for those with more, and can help to bring new collectors into the hobby as a result; in some ways, grading is the collector's friend and the expert's enemy. There is a valid argument that the positive and negative values created by TPG do not represent liquidity as these values may be said to be artificial. However, numerical grades generate these prices repeatedly and reliably. After a market has accepted a global standard, the negative and positive values it has created may henceforth simply represent new actual values.

TPG has not just affected prices, however; encapsulation has also gone some way towards improving the actual appeal of individual coins. During my teenage years I worked at a number of museums. Not all of them were world-class museums, but they gave me the opportunity to learn a few basic principles about arranging displays. The visual effect and visitor engagement you receive is roughly 40 per cent what an item itself is and 60 per cent how you present it. You can exhibit the most fabulous piece of Saxon jewellery in the world, but if it is left in the corner of a large display case packed with other antiquities it will largely be ignored. However if you take that same piece of jewellery, give it its own informational plaque and suspend it in the dead-centre of a glass case with a white backdrop, you will have people queuing up to ooh and aah.

The same is true of coins. The moment you put a coin in a transparent plastic holder and give it a write-up, people start to give it a second glance. In a sense, you are emphasising the individual value of the coin to collectors. Victorian auction catalogues would often group lower-value coins together as a single lot, as many other auction houses still do today. These groups of coins are, more often than not, bought by dealers with the capital available to afford several coins they were not primarily looking for and can then resell. But by splitting these lots up and certifying them, you increase the chance of collectors forming attachments to individual coins – and it is basic economics that the more coins you offer individually, the more collectors and capital there is to go around. TPG has in many ways helped to market coins specifically to collectors.

Despite these major improvements to the numismatic circulatory system, the wide use of TPG by most major auction houses has also, unfairly or not, drastically altered the perception of 'raw' coins in major auctions. Regardless of their protestations, many traditionally anti-TPG dealers and auctioneers will now have their finest coins certified so as not to miss out on the positive values this may bring. Comparing catalogues of European auction houses from ten years ago to the present, one sees an on-average 1,000 per cent increase in the numbers of coins now offered in holders. This then raises scrutiny as to those coins they have chosen not to have certified. After all – as they are somewhat playing the market by encapsulating their best, would it not follow they would avoid encapsulating their worst? Could that raw coin be fake, or not as described? TPG has created unprecedented confidence in the market for encapsulated coins, but this has come with a corresponding drop in confidence for those coins left raw. Many dealers take advantage of this effect by travelling to examine raw coins, estimating their approximate grade and bidding accordingly. The returns can be higher if you purchase and encapsulate uncertified coins, but the risk is higher too. If buying uncertified coins, it is always recommended to seek an opportunity to examine them in person first.

Numismatics has a long memory, and TPG still carries associations with the 1989 collapse for many. The radical upheaval that TPG has caused in the numismatic market within just 40 years has been condemned by some as mere hype associated with an ugly and new-fangled practice and one which damages the market's integrity. Nowadays, the immediate impact it has had on prices for coins which had remained relatively stable for decades beforehand has led some to call TPG a fad for those "more interested in coin value than the joy of collecting". Whether or not you choose to grade your coins, and whether you are collecting with a greater focus on enjoyment or profit, the hobby is undeniably expensive and TPG cannot be ignored as an immense presence within the market and a major determiner of coin value.

TPG should be embraced as a tool that can be used to fill the gaps in your knowledge, to instil confidence in a coin type and to ensure you are purchasing with the best chance of a positive resell. An attractive coin's plastic 'coffin' will never stop anti-slabbing collectors from bidding on it, while an uncertified coin may not receive the attention it should from those vast markets concerned with numerical grade.

Beginning in the US, TPG has now completely diffused throughout the global trade. The value and swift growth of the practice has been recognised both inside and outside of the numismatic market, leading to shrewd investment from external sources; in late 2020, Collector's Universe (which incorporates PCGS) was acquired by a private investment group for an immense $700 million, while in the summer of 2021, NGC was acquired by the leading investment firm Blackstone for another $500 million. The confidence that TPG has spread worldwide has blurred the borders of numismatics and begun encouraging many to collect material they had previously avoided, and some new collectors to participate in the market where before they were afraid. Collecting habits radically differ from country to country and TPG is now favourable in every market, but simply essential in others. An understanding of which regions demand TPG - and which do not - represents an essential part of turning a profit from numismatics, and is a cornerstone of a wider subject: the dynamics of the global numismatic market.

Chapter 1.4.
Global Markets

It is an exciting era for numismatics. Seen for centuries as simply an academic hobby, the introduction of grade standardisation has transformed coins almost overnight from redundant antiques into fully tradable and transferrable assets, their standardised prices enabling substantial liquidity. Encapsulated coins flit from country to country, their capital-backed numerical grades acting as passports allowing entry to every corner of the global market and facilitating international trade.

But whether treated as a collectable or an investment item, coins are at their heart a luxury commodity. The time, effort and money needed to build a collection of coins are impossible for some while comparatively easy for others. Just as the larger commercial centres of the Islamic Empire drew precious metal away from European capitals a thousand years ago, the numismatic market today is far stronger in certain countries and regions than in others. Coins depend on the demand of the collector market to determine their prices; there are not many coins worth over, say, $100,000 and those that do exist are mostly limited to a small handful of countries.

The factors which contribute to the strength of a national numismatic market come down to two simple elements: the wealth of the country of production and the international interest in that country's coins. The wealthier a country is, the greater the proportion of its citizens will have the time and money to invest in numismatics. As many of these collectors will focus exclusively on acquiring those coins produced by their country of birth, prices will be generally higher for coins made by countries with a high GDP. This effect is also prominent in countries with very large populations such as Russia and China.

Some countries have relatively low GDP and a correspondingly weak domestic market but a strong international interest in their coins. This is the case in many Latin American countries. Logically then, it follows that the strongest markets are those which not only have healthy domestic markets but also encounter outside investment in their coins from multiple foreign collector bases. The nature of these markets in which capital comes from several separate sources means that liquidity is relatively easy to maintain; if there is a reduction in one particular country's buying power or a prominent collector dies, coin prices are still likely to stay stable or only dip a small amount.

Global markets do not merely show which coins from which countries are collected but also how collectors from different regions operate. Depending on where you look, the habits of coin collectors can vary widely. Attitudes towards numerical grading, provenance, quality and damage differ from country to country and it is vital to understand these different regional collector mind-sets so as to buy accordingly and avoid mistakenly overpaying.

Collector attitudes can be broadly categorised by region, but there is admittedly considerable overlap which makes it impossible to describe them country-by-country. As such, the four very broad collector trends and their locational bias are distinguished as follows: 1. European markets (EMs), 2. Satellite markets (SMs), 3. US markets (UMs) and 4. East Asian markets (EAMs). These trends only apply to those regions that actively participate in numismatics; there are many countries that have weak or non-existent numismatic markets and have thus been excluded.

Within each market there are some constant themes that will always guide collectors: preservation, eye-appeal, high-denomination, and famous rarities. Regardless of regional collecting habits these aspects will always be prominent drivers of value.

1. European Markets

'European' markets (EMs) descend from the practices of the first scientific numismatists handed down from the 18th century Numismatic Revolution. In EMs, coins are collected largely for their historical intrigue, eye appeal is considered to trump technical grade, and the discipline is seen as far more passionate and academic a pursuit than commercial. I have referred to them as 'European' as they are most common in Europe, but they embody a mind-set found in many different numismatic markets including almost the entirety of the ancient coin market.

EMs are prevalent in countries with long and extensive numismatic histories; the longer a country has been producing its own coins, the higher the chance that it will lean towards the EM mind-set. Tradition is everything in these markets. Collectors prefer to keep their collections in wood-panelled drawing rooms within mahogany cabinets, inspecting their coins with a brass loupe while swirling a glass of brandy in their hand! Provenance is often referred to as 'pedigree', and there is significant interest in the ownership history a coin holds and its part in any notable collections. Rather than attempting to obtain coins in top grades, collectors seek examples of the most famous rarities with the strongest eye appeal. Much focus is given to the academia of numismatics with collectors commonly releasing articles regarding their theories on ancient mint practises or coin die varieties. EM collectors will always favour physically holding their coins over anything else, and thus third-party grading is widely rejected.

As the EM attitude largely stems from a desire to conform to those 18th century upper class ideals which first revolutionised numismatics, EMs are 'parent' markets and generally belong to some of the oldest coin centres of the world. The longer a country's numismatic history, the earlier there would have been collectors and the greater the likelihood that a long and illustrious tradition of coin collecting has been established. Coins of these countries stretch further back, to a time where each one is old enough to be seen as a veritable archaeological artefact in itself rather than simply a collectable item. Not only do these archaic coins carry a different significance, but many also do not fare well under the standards of the Sheldon scale and so TPG is rarely an appealing prospect for EM collectors. Thousands upon thousands of coin varieties exist and there are ample opportunities for research and academic discovery. Due to the exceptionally wide range of coins to choose from, it is more common for EM collectors to heavily specialise in one area (such as by denomination or monarch) rather than competing for all of the absolutely best coins in the series. The strong academic leaning of EMs means that historical discovery and artistic appreciation of coins is first and foremost and commercial aspect trails far behind.

These factors combine to render EMs the *least commoditised of all*.

That is not to say that coins traded in these markets cannot fetch impressive prices. Rather, prices are far less standardised and the market is thus comparatively illiquid. EMs are most often associated with wealthy countries whose denizens have copious free time for numismatic research, but the wide range of choices available to the collector naturally disperses buyer capital into a range of areas and coin types creating smaller satellite markets. Some of these satellite markets can be extremely thin, with their entire collector base made up of only a handful of individuals. New coins are discovered frequently by metal detectorists, constantly expanding collector options and changing the balance of supply to demand. Additionally, the desire to be able to physically hold coins means that TPG struggles to gain traction, hurting price stability further and reducing the prospect of internet bidders buying sight-unseen. In some cases this lack of commoditisation can actually create positive coin value, as any significant rarities or coins with a strong 'wow' factor can fetch colossal prices far above the market standard. By the same token, however, EM collectors attempting to resell often risk substantial losses.

As one would expect, most European markets conform to the EM mind-set with some of the more prominent followers being England, Ireland and Scotland, Italy, Germany, Russia, Poland, Spain and much of Scandinavia. With their extensive coinage history, many Middle Eastern countries also exhibit an academic leaning towards numismatics. Due to its being so embroiled in the foundations of coin collecting itself, there are collectors with EM attitudes in even the most commoditised numismatic markets.

Most prominently, the majority of the ancient coin market follows EM collecting standards. Ancient coins are specifically those of the ancient Greek, Roman and Persian empires alongside Byzantine coins and those of ancient China[14]. This numismatic market is the oldest and one of the widest in the world with collectors scattered all over the globe. Its very nature is embroiled with classical history and archaeology and accordingly the vast bulk of ancient coin collectors prefer to abide by traditional practices and keep their coins outside of holders.

---

14 The definition of 'ancient' in coins can be somewhat vague as British Iron Age coins are not considered ancients by many.

Some EM countries more than others are beginning to show a partial transition to a more commoditised numismatic market. Prominent international investment in UK coins has led to widespread encapsulation of some types and corresponding rises in price, a factor which even the most traditional collectors cannot ignore. This has pushed some to try their hand at having their coins third party certified, at least when they come to sell. Encapsulated coins are also becoming more sought after in the Polish and Russian markets.

It is important to note that collectors who are 'following the money' are jumping from the EM mind-set into the US commodity mind-set rather than the other way around. As aforementioned, the European market is incompatible with more commoditised markets and if certified and uncertified coins are offered together, collectors will ponder why some coins are slabbed and others are not – and will usually opt for the slabbed coins. EM collectors will still bid on encapsulated coins in order to break them out, but sellers will risk alienating potential commodity bidders by offering coins raw. As such, pure EMs are shrinking every day.

2. Satellite Markets

The propensity of collectors to choose those coins with which they feel some kinship or historical affiliation leads most to collect numismatic emissions from their own country of origin. This means that a country's GDP can be a solid indicator as to the strength of its coin market, and that for many poorer or smaller countries coins will never rise above a certain value - as the depth of collector capital is simply not there. However, the exception to this rule is when those poorer countries have had some colonial or imperial history shared with a richer country. This colonial element introduces new, wealthier collectors to the market and creates what are referred to as 'Satellite' markets (SMs).

SMs can be defined as belonging to those countries that have a colonial past, most often with comparatively low GDP per capita or in the developing world. It is its original colonising country that is most active in a given SM market, and these foreign collectors typically choose to buy specifically those coins associated with their colony. As such, SMs are 'child markets', extensions of particular EMs, and will share several characteristics with their parent market. Much British, Spanish and Dutch colonial material is collected in the same way as EMs with focus given to eye appeal and to rarer varieties. SMs see considerably less research or academia associated with their coins than in EMs as their numismatic series is generally shorter and more recent.

Typically, the larger the colony the stronger the market; a prominent parent market can instil interest amongst a SM country's own citizens in the history of their coinage. Some of the world's largest SMs are present in former colonies of Spain. Spain's colonial presence stretched throughout Latin America and their 'Reale' coinage represented one of the world's first international currencies (indeed the US Dollar is itself based on the Spanish Eight Reales coin). Spanish coinages of similar appearance were issued from Mexico, Bolivia, Peru, Guatemala and Colombia, each bearing regional mintmarks. Prices for this colonial material tend to be very stable as the wide spread of these colonies helps to diversify the collector base across regions. It is not merely Spanish collectors buying colonial coins; each of these countries has collectors who feel their own kinship with the Spanish colonial coinage. As such, the wide collector base for Spanish colonial material has helped create a secondary market for post-colonial Latin American coinages – making these newer coins worth comparatively more than for countries with similarly low GDPs but without their own colonial past.

Smaller and more recent colonies usually fail to create the same rise in value for post-colonial coinage. Germany's colonial history, for example, is far less extensive than that of Spain. The small colony of German East Africa covered what is today Burundi, Rwanda and some of Tanzania. Coins of German East Africa can fetch thousands each and are popular with German collectors, but later domestic issues of these three African countries are worth very little to collectors.

Parent numismatic markets are among the world's most active, and so their wealth and developed collector base will usually dictate the trends of their child markets. Each SM will have its own dedicated collectors buying its own domestic material, but for those coins which fail to engage international collectors the competition at auction will be much reduced and prices will remain low. As such, a characteristic trait of SMs is a particular handful of famous and valuable colonial rarities which see considerable international interest, but a sharp drop in price for less well-known types. The specific focus on colonial material means that there is a far wider gap between prices for the top ten per cent of coins and the next 90 per cent; only a few coins are popular, while the rest are worth comparatively little. This is in contrast to EMs where every coin tends to have some degree of collector interest and prices drop down in a far more regular and controlled manner. When buying in a SM it is important to conduct research to ensure you are buying a coin with a strong collector base as opposed to a less avidly collected type, and to take into account the wealth of the parent market itself.

A prime example of a SM and its parent market are the various vassals of the Islamic Fatimid Caliphate in Northern Africa. Domestic coins of these North African countries are worth little to most collectors but anything struck during the Arab dynasty will have a significant following in the Middle East. Other examples of SMs and their EM are Latin America and colonial Spain, as well as India and colonial Britain and the Netherlands.

In many ways the ancient coin market also has a similar appeal to collectors as SMs do to their parent markets. Collectors seek coins they feel a connection with and the breadth and interconnectedness of ancient empires means many feel kinship with this ancient ancestral history. The vast array of countries covered by the ancient world - alongside a wide following of classical history - is one of the major driving forces behind the strong global market for ancient coins.

Historically, SMs have mirrored the attitudes of their parent market. However, a major component of SMs is their shorter and more recent numismatic history in direct contrast to EMs. Accordingly there are far fewer coins to collect, and a greater emphasis is placed on their condition and quality of production leading to a more common use of TPG. In many ways these smaller colonial markets are in a period of transition from traditional to more commoditised attitudes. Additionally, if a country with a colonial past is also relatively wealthy then its SM becomes something far more developed – a market type which is today amongst the world's most prominent.

3. US Markets

'US' Markets (UMs) wield some of the greatest power in numismatics today. UMs are defined by their primary emphasis on the technical quality of coins alongside rare varieties and series completion, with grade considered above all else. Heavily commoditised, UMs exhibit exceptional price standardisation for coins and focus more on logic and good business sense than other markets. As so-called, the largest UM is certainly the USA but the influence of its attitudes is quickly permeating every other market.

UMs are almost always associated with wealthy countries that have short numismatic histories. UM collectors may buy foreign and ancient coins but the majority focus heavily on their domestic emissions. This popularity, underpinned by wealth, typically drives prices for rarer pieces prohibitively high and as such it is unusual for international collectors to collect domestic UM coins. A coin's preservation is considered the most important factor and strongly correlates with its value; accordingly, TPG is simply essential in these markets and the vast majority of coins have been encapsulated. This corresponds with strong commoditisation and very consistent prices paid for coins. An academic approach is still maintained in UMs but, due to their comparatively short numismatic series, most rare varieties and discoveries have already been extensively documented and so their prices have also become rather standardised. With their focus on commodity value and reliance on TPG, in many ways UMs are the polar opposites of EMs.

By far the biggest contributor to the differences between EMs and UMs is the age and length of their numismatic series. You can think of a country's coinage history being like a map of an unexplored land. In EMs, the land is vast and collectors are still exploring the extent and filling in the edges. Some are unwilling to stop as their map is incomplete and territories are yet to be explored, while those that do settle down have plenty of room to spread out in. In UMs, this land is small. Collectors have completed their map long ago and run out of room, so they end up piled in on top of one another.

What this means is that there is not necessarily a greater capital base in

UMs, but rather the *price per coin* can be much higher than in EMs. Many consider UMs to be the strongest markets, but the truth is that collectors simply have limited scope to collect and so are forced to compete heavily for coins of the same type. This results in a much higher average coin value. In most markets a coin worth $1,000,000 is extremely unusual yet many American coins fetch multiples of this sum every year. The smaller range of options available assists with commoditisation as multiple collectors for each coin type help keep prices consistent.

Additionally, the shortage of available coin types encourages collectors to seek the finest possible examples of each coin in order to introduce new objectives to collecting. Much of the enjoyment of assembling a collection is that it is never truly complete. EM collectors can continue collecting for their entire lives and never have to buy the same coin type twice. They will give comparatively little effort to improving on the coins they already have, as there are so many entirely unrepresented coins still to obtain. On the other hand, UM collectors with enough capital can quite swiftly complete their collections; they will then seek to continuously upgrade each coin they own until the logical end result is their owning the finest of every type (an impossible feat for most). This difference means that the correlation between grade and coin value is far more pronounced in UMs than in EMs. For the same reason, UMs also have a far stronger emphasis on errors and varieties than any other market, simply as they have had the time to explore and categorise them all.

The spirit of numismatic competition also drives the significance of coin grade within UMs. To obtain an example of every coin type in an EM would be simply impossible, and so traditional EM collectors impress their peers with appealing examples of the rarest types. Within UMs, the shorter series means that completing your set of coins is actually a possibility and so collectors instead impress their peers with the highest graded examples. This competition is further encouraged by NGC and PCGS through their registry sets, whilst TPG online population reports are typically more useful than in other markets as there is a greater chance of the bulk of examples having been certified.

Alongside the significant presence of the US itself, other UMs have developed from SMs. A colonial history means a country will often have a shorter history of coinage, and if these former colonies have since developed a high GDP then price per coin will rise significantly. Within the Commonwealth of Nations, many former British colonies have developed their own strong domestic collector bases, and the limited range of coins for collectors has instilled the same focus on grade and rarer varieties. Notably, the international interest associated with SMs is still present in these Commonwealth countries – both British and Commonwealth collectors will seek those coins with links to both countries. The combination of domestic and foreign investment has created some of the world's most valuable coins, demonstrated in 2012 when an example of the extremely rare Australian 1920-Sydney Sovereign sold in London for over $1,000,000 hammer price.

Australia, George V 1920-S Sovereign. Sold in September 2012 for £650,000 ($1,052,000).

As discussed, EMs are the world's most commoditised markets. This has benefits and disadvantages. Prices are very stable overall and do gradually increase, meaning that coins purchased as buy-and-hold investments can hold value well and potentially appreciate over time. However if one seeks to turn a quick profit from the resell of US coins, the uniform use of TPG and wide awareness of the 'market value' means that any margins stay extremely thin. The strength and saturation of this market also means that new discoveries herald immediate and overwhelming collector interest. If a new coin type is discovered for, say, a French Louis d'Or of the 18th century, it may generate a slight premium of around ten or twenty per cent but will be unlikely to achieve much more. If a new US coin type is found, collectors will pay tremendous amounts to be the first to add it to their collection.

The US is the largest UM as one would expect. Alongside are members of the Commonwealth of Nations such as Canada, Australia, South Africa and New Zealand. The Canadian numismatic market is especially similar to the US and is renowned for its incredibly precise analysis of even the most minute errors and die varieties[15]. Comparatively few ancient coin collectors subscribe to a UM attitude, but increasing numbers of higher grade ancient pieces are being encapsulated.

Through their focus on coins as commodities, UM markets have attracted sneers from more traditional collectors for being overly concerned with value and not enough on the coins themselves. However, UM collectors are not ruthless numismatic businessmen. The US market is fundamentally different to those in Europe, and US collectors would be foolish to reject TPG or buy coins for arbitrary prices. Market prices are so established that the prospect of buying coins for above their 'intrinsic' value is seen as far less sensible. By buying encapsulated coins, collectors have relative assurances that their values will be consistent.

Certainly not limited to the US, in recent years UM attitudes have entered every market worldwide. Those who condemn the practises of TPG and its obsession with grade still sit up and pay attention when they see remarkable prices achieved for coins in plastic holders. As more and more encapsulated coins are appearing in Europe and across the world, two countries in particular have taken to grading practises and contributed to the immense sums that third-party graded coins can bring – the twin numismatic behemoths of China and Japan.

4. East Asian Markets

The majority of global numismatic markets can be placed somewhere on a scale from a European attitude to a US attitude. One represents the past of numismatics, and the other represents the future. However, another type of market – the 'East Asian' (EAMs) – plays a unique role in transitioning EMs to UMs through an immense injection of capital

---

15   In a previous position I was tasked with cataloguing the extensive George Cook Collection of Canadian Coinage – the 'world's most comprehensive assemblage of Canadian coins'. Hours were spent examining the precise varieties of each type.

into international markets. Mostly driven by China and Japan, above all else EAMs focus on the appearance and quality of their coins and are perhaps the most investment-minded of any global market today.

EAMs share a desire for large-sized gold coins of the highest possible grade and concentrate more on the appearance of the individual coin itself rather than how it fits into a harmonious collection. Engraving quality is held in high regard with a preference for the bold and beautiful; it is often said by Western collectors that EAMs prefer those coins bearing female rulers. These aspects mean that EAMs tend to prefer well-made relatively modern coins to more irregular older coins. Despite some EAMs having a rich and extensive coinage history - Chinese coins for example stretching back to the 4th century BC - the highest value coins of the domestic EAM markets are those produced in the 19th and 20th centuries. EAMs have a love for beauty and perfection in coinage but also treat coins as assets to be traded with a wide use of TPG.

EAMs share characteristics with every other market. They emulate EMs in that they often have long numismatic histories and an academic collector focus; they also represent parent markets to SMs, heavily collecting those coins which have some link to their countries and past empires. Their strongest overlap is with UMs, with a comparable focus on technical quality and a desire for highly certified coins. However, EAMs are unlike any other market for their willingness to spend immense sums on foreign coins. Their domestic markets are stable and yet they also participate actively in international numismatic trade.

The impact that Japan specifically has had on foreign markets in recent years has been huge, particularly for British coins. Japanese culture emphasises the importance of *kakeibo*, the saving of money, and couples with a widespread custom of placing these savings into international investments. Japanese buyers commonly follow market trends but in such numbers that they ultimately generate their own market trends. During the "bubble period" of the Japanese economy from the mid-1980s until the early 1990s, the impact of Japanese buyers heavily investing in art dramatically influenced art prices worldwide. The same is now true of coins. Japanese collectors tend to buy on advice from their trusted dealer or investment programme, and most of these have been marketing the

British 'Una and the Lion' 1839 Five Pounds in recent years. As such, it is largely this Japanese interest contributing to the incredible price growth of the 1839 Five Pounds, and nowadays almost every example of this coin offered at auction will be bought by a Japanese buyer.

In China, since the economic reforms of 1978 allowed foreign investment and individuals to start businesses, the economy has become the world's fastest growing with an average growth rate of six per cent per year over the last 30 years. This period of increased prosperity has brought with it many eager and wealthy numismatists. A large proportion of these collectors participate exclusively in China's domestic market, leading to immense prices being paid for rarer Chinese coins in high grades. These are not limited to vintage coins and indeed the Chinese 'Panda' series of bullion coins produced from 1982 onwards are amongst the nation's most popular. Alongside a growth in domestic numismatics the rise in wealth has also produced a drive to invest in foreign coins comparable to that of Japan, and some rather unique collecting practises. I once heard of a Chinese buyer purchasing the only known example of a particular Spanish gold coin for over $90,000 in the US; when asked after the auction what had made him choose that coin, he announced that he had a collection made up entirely of unique coins.

EAMs have a more commercial and investment approach to buying coins, and their motivations for buying are similar to other markets: high grade, eye appeal, rarity etc. Like UMs, this investment approach leads EAMs to prefer encapsulated TPG coins over raw coins; but their market is not like that of UMs. Rather than being commoditised with standardised prices, EAMs will occasionally pay far above what is expected for coins they want - but only occasionally, and not even this is predictable or standardised. In many ways, EAMs are the most enigmatic markets in the world and the hardest to predict. Sometimes the highest-grade example of an extremely rare Chinese coin expected to exceed $2 million will only scrape $1 million, and sometimes an innocuous variety will explode in popularity and fetch $100,000 on an estimate of $10,000-15,000. This capriciousness often leads auction houses and dealers to overestimate what EAMs will pay, much like a child sporadically receiving payments from an elderly relative.

What the market does know is that the pattern of international investment exhibited by EAMs favours particularly appealing, large-sized milled gold and silver encapsulated with a high technical grade. As such, many traditional EMs are grudgingly moving towards encapsulation for their higher grade and more valuable coins in the interest of appealing to EAMs and UMs alike. This means that EAMs are accelerating the global transition from traditional numismatic values to a more commodity-based market.

The dominant EAMs are China and Japan, with Singapore and South Korea following as more minor players in the international market. Smaller Eastern and Southeast Asian countries mostly adhere to their domestic markets and their values are accordingly based on their GDPs.

★   ★   ★

Trends vary significantly across the world in how and what numismatists collect. Some choose to keep their coins in fine wooden cabinets, some in sterile plastic holders; some prefer interesting errors and others perfectly preserved rarities. These tendencies can be roughly grouped by region, as the age, wealth, traditions and cultures of a country will dictate the collecting habits of its denizens.

But despite their clear distinctions, the lines are now blurring between each of the four major regional collector attitudes. Markets turn like sunflowers to face their greatest profits, and what ultimately fuels the dynamics of the numismatic market is the capital underpinning it. The desires of collectors in the wealthiest centres of the world – the US, Europe, the Middle East and Asia – decide how the market operates. Coin grading and commoditisation in the US and Asia has led to unprecedented price growth and this has attracted the attention of even the most traditionalist European collectors. TPG, that cornerstone of UMs originally introduced merely to create a universal standard of grading, has taken on a new role as a means of providing confidence for coins sold worldwide. By allowing international transactions to take place without viewing coins in person, TPG has spread numerical grading and an emphasis on coin condition throughout the market.

In a bustling international trade, it is those few coins which manage to straddle the boundaries between markets that generate the highest prices overall. Numismatists who observe widely accepted market practices such as TPG and concentrate on buying those coins that will appeal to multiple regions stand the best chance of turning a profit when they come to resell.

Chapter 1.5.
Market Participants

1. Collectors

Collectors were the hobby's first participants and are the most wide-ranging, diverse and pervasive presence in the entire numismatic market. From the kings and noblemen of antiquity who could afford to put coins aside as curiosities, to the modern-day collector of pennies, the slow growth of interest in coins began long ago and started a chain reaction which has resulted in the worldwide trade we know today.

And collectors are the numismatic market, first and foremost. Without their demand, there would be no value in the supply. Collectors transform inanimate disks of metal into marketable assets through their interest in history, art and society itself. The lowest level of collector might have a handful of modern curios pulled from their change which they take out and look at time to time. The highest level will have a bank vault filled with millions of dollars' worth of coins. But whether casual or dedicated, every collector knowingly or unknowingly fuels the worldwide numismatic market and represents the foundation stone of numismatics. Collectors are the ones who write the coin catalogues and also the ones who buy from them.

Firstly, the bulk of numismatic research is undertaken not by archaeologists or museums but by coin collectors themselves. Knowledge and inspiration comes easiest to those with unlimited access to their artefacts of study, just as those proto-archaeologists of the Age of Enlightenment first began as antiquarians accruing curiosities. The passion of collectors drives them to not only purchase coins but also to categorise and catalogue them, to inspect them minutely and identify varieties, quirks and any potential historical significance they might hold. Academic societies of collectors are numerous, formed with the aim of contributing to the study of coins worldwide. Without these scores of volunteer historians adding daily to the knowledge base of numismatics, we would know far less about the extent of coins or their history.

But it is not the research which collectors undertake that places them at the foundation of the numismatic food chain. It is collector *capital* which provides the very basis of the global numismatic market. Coins can act primarily as an asset class for much of their life – but like any hard or soft commodity, ultimately there will still need to be a 'consumer' at the end of the process to whom the coin will represent more than something to be merely traded. It is these collectors who underpin the market by providing this unconditional capital base, and the market follows their whims.

Due to the vital part played by such 'foundation' collectors, the entire numismatic market will react based on their buying practices. Over the course of two decades, Japanese collectors purchasing 'Una and the Lion' Five Pound coins transformed a type traditionally offered raw and tucked away in the middle of an auction catalogue to an encapsulated commodity worth hundreds of thousands of dollars, its photo emblazoned proudly on the catalogue's front cover. Many collectors are oblivious to how their coin purchases cause the market wheels to turn, but even the most trivial splurge can cause a butterfly effect felt the world around which has an impact on coin prices everywhere.

Like coins, no two collectors are truly alike. Coins may appear identical, yet minute differences in metal quality and strike - if only at a microscopic level - cumulate in a varied finished product each time even. The same is true of collectors. Most will hold some interests in common, but each will have different affiliations, preferences and habits leading them down different paths, an effect magnified between regional and national numismatic markets. Collectors may buy coins based on their age, composition, denomination, country of origin, errors, numerical grade, or any other number of factors which can overlap significantly.

Some collectors are obsessive and hoard every coin they can find with no intention to ever resell. Some are less attached and will consistently upgrade and shift their collecting interests. Collectors may be academic and buy coins for their historical significance; others may be collecting solely as stores of wealth. Just as it is those coins that manage to appeal to multiple market types simultaneously which generate the strongest prices, coins which satisfy the largest number of collector desires are ultimately the most valuable.

The majority of these collectors are hobbyists, buying as they please with profits being an afterthought or not a thought at all. Nonetheless, almost every professional operative within numismatics began as a collector of some sort. By collecting one is able to familiarise oneself with the market, and collectors are akin to numismatic stem cells, each with the ability to go on and specialise as any other participant in the trade.

Collectors are the grassroots of numismatics, assigning value to coins, researching new types and mapping out the hobby for generations to come. However, when a collector takes on a more market-savvy mindset and begins to buy and sell coins for profit, they represent the first step in the numismatic 'industry' – that is, the hobby's professional infrastructure, in which the passions of collectors are transformed into a buoyant commodity market.

2. Dealers

Whenever a market arises, so do those who capitalise upon it. Just as the first electrum coins allowed Lydia to become a nation of *kapeloi*, merchants, soon after coins began eliciting significant premiums above their face value from collectors the first numismatic 'dealers' came into being. Originally selling coins alongside other works of ancient art and antiques, gradually more and more sellers began to specialise in coins alone and concentrated on expanding their market knowledge of this particular asset class. Today, these specialist operatives are an essential and invaluable step up from collectors. Dealers are individuals or groups who have become well-versed enough in numismatics to offer advice to collectors and simultaneously generate their own income.

The term 'dealer' may sound overly vague or have certain narcotic connotations, but within the industry it is understood to mean specifically those who generate a profit from buying and selling coins. Dealers come in all shapes and sizes. Some operate individually, and some as groups comprised of multiple market professionals. The services they offer to collectors are wide-reaching; collection, storage, sourcing particular coins, offering market tips or news and providing overall numismatic consultation. However, the root of their business model is simply to sell coins for more than they have bought them.

Dealers achieve their profits through a variety of methods but can be split into those conducted by individuals, groups (or 'dealerships') and those who privately buy and sell as a form of speculation. Almost all dealers and dealerships follow a similar model. Coins are bought at major auction or in person and offered as stock for collectors to peruse, marketed online on the dealer's website and occasionally consigned privately with an auction house. Dealers will maintain an active client base, informing them of any particular coins they have in stock that may interest them or offering to re-purchase coins they have previously sold. They will often hold on to specific coins for long periods of time waiting for them to sell at their price or in anticipation of a market change. In a sense, dealers are the stockbrokers of numismatics.

Some dealers or speculators follow a more private model and are comparatively hands-off. Rather than forging relationships with clients, these individuals will buy what they consider to be undervalued coins and immediately place them into an auction, often with a reserve. Many private dealers specifically focus on arbitrage between regional markets, purchasing coins from one country and selling them in another. The majority of successful arbitrage comes from differences in the US and European market models; popular European types offered encapsulated in US auctions with sub-par grades can be purchased, broken out of their holders and sold raw in Europe, whilst high-grade European coins sold raw at auction can be bought, encapsulated and sold in the US. In my time at various auction houses I have seen the same coins jump from company to company, often selling for far more on each occasion depending on the placement. If conventional dealers are the stockbrokers of numismatics, then private dealers are the day traders.

No matter what their business model, one of the most significant issues dealers face is that of cash flow. Many coins are expensive and may take time to sell, and so much of their available capital is tied up. As such, several times a year dealers congregate at regional and international trade shows or conventions, lists of which can be easily found online. These shows allow collectors to browse the stock of many individual dealers at once and present a welcome opportunity for dealers to free up capital. Additionally, these shows facilitate inter-dealer trade. One of the most crippling impacts of the Covid-19 pandemic on dealers was the cessation of numismatic trade shows, which forced the entirety of the market online.

Most collectors forge healthy relationships with a number of dealers and gain a sense of whom to trust from comparing prices and experiences. Through their links to the industry, dealers are the first point of contact for collectors to turn to when seeking specific coins and often when looking to sell. It is important to remember that dealers may sell to one another or offer their coins at auction but they are ultimately entirely dependent on their clients and the actions of collectors.

3. Numismatic Auction Houses

During the 18th century, auction houses began to be widely introduced for the sale of art and antiques. Coins at this early juncture were seen as antiquities and were offered alongside more traditional auction pieces, and continued to be so for almost two centuries. As the world's two largest auctioneers, Christie's and Sotheby's, sold off or abandoned their numismatic interests in the late 1990s and early 2000s many think of auction houses as today being primarily concerned with art, furniture, cars etc. However, numerous other auction houses still subsist primarily or even exclusively on the sale of coins, banknotes and other currency items. As they allow buyers to compete with each other for price in real time, these establishments are the single most price-defining entities within numismatics.

Auction houses are yet another step up on the numismatic food chain from dealers, acting as the apex predators of the market. Typically auction houses are the logical choice in which to offer the most valuable coins of the trade, and by catering to collectors and dealers alike they can generate record prices. Many new numismatists are nervous at the prospect of participating in major auctions as they seem too advanced and complex for them, but the process is actually very simple.

Clients will approach an auction house with coins they would like to consign. A representative of the auction house will examine these and quickly make an assessment as to whether they would be of sufficient value for one of their sales. Value minimums vary depending on the auctioneer; in my career I have worked at houses with value minimums ranging from around £100 ($125) up to $5,000. If the coins are accepted then the auction house will make a commission offer based on their value – the more valuable the coins, the better rate they will usually be willing to give. However, this heavily depends on the average value per coin, as more coins equal more work cataloguing. An auction house will be far more likely to offer a favourable rate for one coin worth $100,000 rather than 100 coins worth $1,000 each.

Once accepted, your coins will be processed, catalogued, photographed and placed within an upcoming sale. Depending on your chosen auction house, they may also be sent for TPG and encapsulation. Potential bidders will have opportunities to view them as they please prior to the auction, after which the lots will open for sale. Participants will bid in small varying increments that tend to be proportionate to the current auction price, and your coins will sell for the maximum amount that bidders are willing to pay, called the 'hammer price'. You will receive the hammer price minus auctioneer's fees sometime after the sale. However, each auction house also charges a 'buyer's premium' which is at present an average of 20 per cent; this is a surcharge paid by the buyer. Accordingly, say your coin sells for $100 and the auction house is charging you a 10 per cent commission. You will receive $90, the buyer will pay $120 plus tax and the auction house pockets $30.

Numismatic auctions are one of the major aspects that allow coins to operate as a commodity – by letting international supply and demand determine their value. Auctions rely on coin prices to be bid up until the most motivated buyer bids one increment over the second highest bidder (called the underbidder), and if there are no further bids then the coin then sells for that sum. Accordingly prices will always represent market demand. This element works in tangent with a unique aspect of coins: their lack of uniqueness. Whereas pieces of art are generally produced as one-offs and their prices are wildly subjective, coins have known mintages and most types are represented by several examples meaning the price that one coin sells for has an impact on the value of all other coins of that type that exist.

This effect means that auctions contribute to the price growth of coins over time. A single passionate or competitive bidder might pay an increment or two more than they at first intended for a coin. This then cements that price in the auction record for all to see. Accordingly there is an increased chance that next time a coin of that type is offered, buyers will calculate what to pay based on that recent strong result.

Numismatic auction houses provide market insight for all other participants in the numismatic trade as their public offerings of coins help to inform the market what coins are 'going for'. Auction results inform the various annual coin guides what updated prices they should list, which in turn dictate the prices that dealers charge for their inventory. In line with the 'people will pay what they want' mentality some US-based auction houses are even doing away with estimates entirely, particularly for already-heavily commoditised US coins. For their ability to define market prices based on demand, auction houses are seen as the 'stock market' of numismatics.

Whether large or small, most auction houses will operate in much the same way. However, their internet presence may vary, and this online aspect is vital for prices to be truly representative of the market. If an auction house does not have a sophisticated enough online platform for bidders to view and participate in the auction then collectors may be either dissuaded or remain unaware of the sale. I heard of a recent case where a buyer picked up three coins at a tiny regional auction house without internet in the UK for less than $50, placed them in a more prominent auction, and after heated bidding they achieved a total of more than $300,000. For a coin to achieve its highest price it must be visible to as many potential collectors as possible and these collectors must also be confident enough to bid. In this way, TPG has been instrumental in commoditising coins as it attracts the widest possible swathe of the market to bid online from all over the world.

Dealers and auction houses represent the main facilitators of the antique coin trade, both guided by the base of collector capital. The majority of numismatic transactions will take place through one of these entities. However, two other participants also have major influences in the market for the prestige and the authority they command: museums and mints.

4. Museums

Public institutions have maintained collections of coins for centuries, often donated and maintained by wealthy families - such as Joachim II Hector, Elector of Brandenburg (1505-71) who began the Berlin coin cabinet – but these early collections were sporadically assembled and generally poorly studied. As the numismatic market grew in the 18th century, so did the numbers of coin collections held by museums and the depth of their study. The British Museum, the world's first public national museum, was established in 1753 and immediately began accruing and cataloguing rare antique coins. By the early 19th century some of the earliest coin auctions in the world consisted entirely of the British Museum's coin duplicates. Today, most of the world's rarest coins are housed in various museums. Even without playing a significant part in the operation of the market, these institutions have helped guide numismatics for centuries through their academic resources, experience and by lending legitimacy to the hobby.

Museums and their collections can influence major decisions within numismatics on both macro and micro scales. Through their research, new coin types can be identified and their significance studied - but the long memories and knowledge-base of museums can also assist with the analysis of individual coins and their authenticity. For example, one of only three known examples of the rare Brutus 'Ides of March' gold Aureus was thought for decades to be a forgery and treated as such, with considerable suspicion surrounding the fact it only first appeared in 1953. While conducting their research on the coin, an auction house contacted the British Museum for advice and found in the museum's collections an original cast of the same coin with a label dated 1932. This earlier date as well as the record of the coin within the museum's archive played an instrumental role in the coin being accepted as genuine. It sold most recently in 2008 for 230,000 CHF ($226,000) and is now itself displayed at the British Museum.

Rome, Marcus Junius Brutus "Assassin of Caesar and Imperator" Aureus, 44-42 BC

Museums have also been known to assist the TPG services. If a potentially valuable coin raises any suspicion as to its authenticity, NGC or PCGS will happily involve a major institution to conduct analysis. If the coin is deemed authentic by the museum then it will be encapsulated and accepted by the market. In this sense, museums and the authority they wield have a major impact within numismatics by assisting with high-level research.

The role of museums in the academia and science of numismatics is vast, but where the wider market itself is concerned the part they play is far smaller. Despite their holding some of the first major numismatic auctions, museums nowadays are extremely unlikely to sell any of their coins as the practice of 'de-accessioning' (removal of items from a museum's collection) is, according to a curator at the British Museum, "an absolute nightmare". As such, museums in a sense represent the final destination a coin can reach, as a coin in a museum is unlikely to ever again enter the collector market. This can be a source of considerable frustration to the industry when a collector bequeaths his impressive coins to a museum after his or her death. More often than not the museum will already have examples of those coins, and yet the conditions under which they were donated means they cannot be released.

But although they stay their hand where selling numismatic material is concerned, very occasionally museums will participate in the buying of rarer coins. Some museums have a unique relationship with metal detectorists; under UK treasure laws, if a hoard (more than one coin deposited in a find spot) of coins over 300 years in age is discovered, the British Museum must be allowed to examine them to assess their archaeological significance. If the coins are deemed to be of historical importance then the museum will retain them for their collection – but will pay fair market value to the detectorist who discovered them. This is not necessarily the case in every museum, as many European countries have far stricter treasure laws which allow the seizure of any antique coins without offering financial compensation. Unfortunately, this has led to a prominent black market for smuggled antiquities in these countries.

There is currently a loophole in the UK's treasure act which means that if a single coin is discovered, it is not considered treasure and thus does not have to be assessed by the British Museum first. This means that, alongside their purchasing of detector-found hoards, museums must very rarely make forays at major auctions. In 2001, a gold Saxon coin was discovered by a riverside in Bedfordshire, a Penny or 'Mancus' struck during the reign of King Coenwulf (796-821). This is one of only a handful of gold coins known from Saxon Britain and is thus of immense historical importance. Due to it being a single find, the British Museum was powerless to seize it, and the coin was put to major auction in October 2004. An American buyer bid an immense $350,000 for the coin, meaning the museum was forced to raise this comparable sum from donations in order to secure the coin for its collection.

This was a very unusual circumstance and one which so infuriated the British Museum that there are currently changes being reviewed in the UK treasure act to prevent such an occurrence ever happening again. Nonetheless, a government-funded institution paid $350,000 for a coin, and even this very limited museum participation in the market helps to legitimise the trade and 'intrinsic' value of coins. Museums are by no means an active player in the numismatic trade, but their experience and authority provide invaluable resources to collectors and dealers alike whilst also helping to instil an element of confidence in the trade as a whole.

5. Mints

For 2,500 years, local and national mints have produced the coin supply to meet the demands of their region or country. Countless mints have been established throughout history and across the world, each one producing completely different products which have their own distinct collector bases today. Just as their coins originally satisfied economic needs, mints nowadays help to provide modern material for some of the largest collector groups in numismatics as well as assisting those who collect antique issuances. Alongside dealers and auction houses, mints represent one of the primary sources for collectors to buy coins, and their presence not only satisfies present collector demand but also serves to inspire new collectors to enter the hobby every day.

Circulating coinage is used to a lesser degree nowadays than in previous eras, but it nonetheless still represents one of the primary means of introducing new collectors to numismatics. This is usually through the finding of either antique or unusual coins. It is rarer to find antique coins in circulation, but in some countries such as the US and Switzerland coinage has not undergone a major upheaval in more than a century. As such, coins of significant age or even silver content can be occasionally pulled from one's change. For the most part, however, it is new designs or potential errors which cause spenders to put a coin aside for later analysis. The widely held belief that unusual coins equal value means that by far the most common queries we professionals in the trade receive are regarding modern coins. It is only one small step from researching an unusual coin you have found to ending up buying another, and so by consistently introducing new designs on their coins, mints help to constantly refresh the collector base.

Alongside their production of circulating coins, almost every active mint today will strike its own distinct range of proof and commemorative coins for collectors and offer investment in its range of bullion coins. Every year new coin varieties are produced and are met with considerable excitement from collectors who vie to be the first to obtain their own example. The advantages of these new issues is that they cater to some of the prevalent desires of numismatic markets: they are made with excellent engraving quality, often to known quantities, and will be immaculate as they are brand new and perfectly suit TPG. This has led to occasional instant and dramatic leaps in value. In late 2019, the British Royal Mint produced a reissue of the 'Una and the Lion' Five Pounds as a 2oz gold coin priced at £4,395. Just 225 were struck and they sold out almost instantly. By January 2020, top-graded examples of this type were already attracting prices of almost £30,000 at auction. By September, their price had doubled to £60,000.

Great Britain, Elizabeth II "Una and the Lion" 200 Pounds 2019

    The high quality and popular subject type of this coin combined with its large size and gold content generated unprecedented interest from collectors. This particular coin was an outlier, and most mint products will appreciate at a much slower rate. Most modern coins should be bought wisely with market insight, but with the knowledge their value may not significantly increase.

    Mints, like museums, curate their own collections of coins and will answer collector queries regarding their products. Mints are especially capable when it comes to the analysis of modern issues and errors as they are in control of the production. A potential error coin will immediately have a greater appeal to collectors if it is accompanied by a letter confirming its unusual status from the mint that originally struck it. Some mints have expanded this role and provide dedicated collector services, carrying a stock of historic coins and offering formal certificates of authentication to accompany them. As such, mints provide an authoritative presence in the industry similar to museums, yet with a more commercial and collector focus.

Extensive research is absolutely vital when considering purchasing a mint product to ensure that you are buying directly from a country's official mint itself. There are numerous private organisations with names similar to those of mints that strike their own unofficial coins marketed solely at investors; these coins are often very unreliable stores of value as their collector base is extremely limited. Often, as their coins are geared at those buying to resell, the vast majority have no consumer base whatsoever, and when the first investor attempts to sell their coin the value entirely collapses. National mints are far safer choices when looking for coins which will retain or increase their value.

Since the first proof set was produced for collectors in 1746, the role of mints has transitioned from solely a functional necessity of a country's economy to an avenue for historic and artistic exploration. Unlike the finite supply of antique coinage traded by dealers and auction houses, mints release new and innovative coins every year and provide consistent enjoyment for collectors worldwide.

6. The Internet

The participants of the numismatic market have remained unchanged for centuries. Mints have produced the supply of coins which have eventually been offered through dealers and auction houses to ultimately end up in either museums or private collections. Those in collections were eventually recycled and re-entered the market, and those in museums generally remained there as part of the numismatic archive. The numismatic process had continued more or less uninterrupted with no signs of imminent alteration. That was, until the mid-1980s to mid-1990s, when the development of online connectivity gave birth to the internet and, in combination with TPG, caused the relationships between numismatic entities to change forever. By facilitating transactions between parties and introducing absolute transparency, the internet transformed how the numismatic industry operated from the bottom to the top. And alongside this upheaval, the internet has had such a profound impact on how coins are bought and sold that in many ways it acts as an additional market participant by itself.

Major numismatic auctioneers were among the first to witness the effects of the internet on the trade. Formerly, auction houses would command a client base of only those collectors physically capable of getting to the auction house to examine coins in person – this would often be limited to dealers acting on behalf of collectors. With the introduction of online bidding, collectors from around the world were suddenly able to view and bid; coupled with TPG, the audience for every auction instantaneously underwent massive expansion. Those collectors who were unwilling to reveal their identity no longer had to bid over the phone, but could instead participate in the auction by simply placing a bid online. Nowadays, anyone who has attended an auction will be very familiar with the auctioneer's sigh as they wait for the internet to finish its frenzied bidding before anyone in the room has even had a chance to raise their paddle. Internet bidding introduced the maximum possible buyer base for coins sold at auction.

With this immediate ease of bidding came a corresponding ease in reviewing auction results. Auction houses began releasing their prices realised online and the first numismatic search engine, CoinArchives, was introduced. Collectors who were formerly reliant on books and mail catalogues were now able to scroll through recent coin prices online. Prices began to be more actively tracked, perceptions of intrinsic coin values began to rise and arbitrage between markets dropped off sharply.

The combination of increased auction participation, ability to research recent prices and the growing influence of TPG led to unprecedented price standardisation within numismatics. For much of numismatic history, dealers were able to justify charging higher prices for their coins because the market was more subjective and collectors would pay these sums. Online resources meant that collectors who had previously been buying coins at inflated prices were suddenly made aware of lower prices being charged for coins elsewhere. This meant that in order to compete with one another, dealers were forced to switch to a system of selling high volumes of coins with low profit margins; equally, those dealers who had previously been charging too little for their stock became aware of this and adjusted their prices accordingly. As such, coins of the same type began to sell for similar prices across the world, and the introduction of TPG meant coins of the same grade would sell for more precise amounts still. The commoditisation of coins had begun.

And with this liquidity - this new concept of 'established' prices and market trends within numismatics - came a newfound confidence in collectors to not only purchase coins from dealers and auction houses but directly from one another. Whereas previously the lack of market transparency had led the inexperienced to fear transacting with those who were not industry professionals, TPG and standardised coin values meant collectors could be certain of both a coin's authenticity and also its approximate market value. Consequently, the internet allowed an entirely new online marketplace to spring up on its own, one that allowed collectors to directly market their own coins for sale on online auction sites and through social media platforms. Every collector suddenly had the ability to become a dealer, and buyers and sellers were able to find one another instantly. By creating unprecedented liquidity the internet has permanently altered the existing infrastructure of the global coin market, and yet through its offering buyers and sellers a place to transact directly it also represents an entirely separate entity within numismatics itself.

The Covid-19 pandemic rocked the economies of every country by bringing face-to-face interaction to a screeching halt. The majority of coin shows in 2020 and early 2021 were cancelled, and auction houses stopped hosting physical sales. In the past, this would have simply put the global numismatic market on ice; no transactions would be able to take place and nothing would happen. However, the internet has not only allowed the market to continue through this crisis but to actually grow in strength. Bored social isolators have been able to absent-mindedly browse the online markets and snap up those coins they hadn't had the time to find before, leading to record breaking prices being achieved. How society will adapt and change as a result of Covid-19 in the long term is still yet to be seen. But this disease has shown us all that the true lifeblood of numismatics is no longer found in auction rooms or in dealers' trays, but is instead crackling through the cables and radio signals that keep us all online.

★ ★ ★

Numismatics thirty years ago was a far less exact science. Coin grades and values were subjective; collectors would have to travel to view coins and so only those few able or willing to do so would have a true insight into the appearance of the coin. The individual collector or professional was required to have an in-depth knowledge and understanding of grade and condition and so only the most eager and quick to learn could persevere without risking considerable losses. Numismatics was an academic discipline still entrenched in 18th century practises and haphazardly propped up by collector capital; its one attempt to incorporate an investment approach crashed and burned in the collapse of 1989.

What the internet has done is to transform that market entirely. Now, collectors can buy from wherever they are with whatever knowledge they have, online auction platforms coupling with third-party grading to produce a sprawling network of bidders stretching to every corner of the globe. New markets are allowed to rise and prosper through this interconnectivity, coins which had spent their entire history within the confines of one island shooting back and forth across the globe, collections breaking and reforming into newer and superior assemblages. Prices have never before been so stable nor coins so easy to invest in.

Throughout this transformation have been the naysayers who condemn any practice that treats numismatics as anything more than a passion and a hobby. Price rises and profits are seen as a secondary consideration and ones that should be considered separately from the joy and discovery of collecting coins. While it is sensible to approach numismatics primarily from a place of enjoyment and curiosity, it is impossible to ignore the fact that many do indeed turn a profit from buying and selling coins.

Equipped with an understanding of the past and present of the numismatic market, the factors that drive coin value and the variety of markets around the globe, one can begin to evaluate the performance of coins as not only a collectable piece of history but also as a store of value and a class of asset.

OFFERING THE BEST IN NUMISMATICS

SPINK
WHERE HISTORY IS VALU[ED]

Henry III Gold Penny
Realised £648,000

The most valuable single coin find ever made in British soil

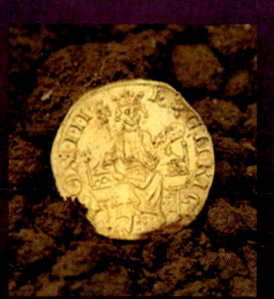

#SPINK_AUCTI[ONS]

Follow us on social

SPINK LONDON

Tel: +44 (0)20 7563 4000 | Email: concierge@spink.com
69 Southampton Row | WC1B 4ET | London

WWW.SPINK.C[OM]

Section 2
Coins as an Asset Class

SPINK

Where History is Valued

GLOBAL COLLECTABLES AUCTION HOUSE WITH OVER 350 YEARS OF EXPERIENCE

CONSISTENTLY ACHIEVING WORLD RECORD PRICES

SPINK OFFERS VALUATION FOR INSURANCE AND PROBATE FOR INDIVIDUAL ITEMS OR WHOLE COLLECTION SALES ON A COMMISSION BASIS, EITHER OF INDIVIDUAL PIECES OR WHOLE COLLECTIONS

For more information, please contact Spink:
Tel: +44 (0)20 7563 4000 | Fax: +44 (0)20 7563 4066 | Email: concierge@spink.com
SPINK LONDON | 69 Southampton Row | Bloomsbury | London | WC1B 4ET

LONDON | NEW YORK | HONG KONG | SINGAPORE | SWITZERLAND

STAMPS | COINS | BANKNOTES | MEDALS | BONDS & SHARES | AUTOGRAPHS | BOOKS
WINE & SPIRITS | HANDBAGS | COLLECTIONS | ADVISORY SERVICES | SPECIAL COMMISSIONS

In 2013, it was estimated that the coin market was worth over $3 billion per year in the US alone. In all likelihood, that figure merely scrapes the surface. As mentioned in the previous section, the third-party grading service PCGS has certified 42 million coins to date with a combined value of around $36 billion, and NGC has graded another 46 million still. Even when allowing for a 20 per cent overlap, that still brings the total value to more than $50 billion - and that is only for encapsulated coins. When combined with the huge numbers of coins that are still sold raw it is likely that the total value of coins worldwide is somewhere between $75 and $100 billion. This is also a constantly recycling system; coins are bought, retained, re-sold and so on. The wheels keep turning and, as very few coins leave the market or drop significantly in value, this number is constantly increasing.

In June 2021, the world's most valuable coin came up for auction for the first time in almost twenty years. This impressive title is held by the famous USA 1933 Twenty Dollars or 'double eagle', a coin produced in numbers nearing half a million - yet the majority of which were melted down in accordance with a US law forbidding private ownership of gold coins in the wake of the 1929 Wall Street Crash. Only a handful of examples of the 1933 double eagle survived through theft. In the mid-1990s, one specimen resurfaced in the collection of King Farouk of Egypt, and after a lengthy legal debate, the coin was made legal to own by the US Treasury and was sold in 2002 by Sotheby's for a then-record price of $7.59m. The coin reappeared at Sotheby's once again in 2021, this time selling for a new world record price of $18.872m. This made it the 27th coin to have sold for over $1m up to June 2021, to a total of $83m.

USA 1933 Twenty Dollars, the world's most valuable coin.

With figures such as these it is hard to retain an image of numismatics as merely a bookish and academic pursuit. The combination of the internet and TPG has created a commoditised atmosphere in which even the uninformed can confidently buy coins in the hopes of generating a profit. But while treating coins as investments has returned as a far more prevalent mindset in recent years, the shockwaves from the 1989 collapse still ring in the ears of numismatists and investors alike. That first major foray of investors into numismatics failed so spectacularly that many are hesitant to try again, and numismatic investments still remain mostly unexplored and somewhat half-baked. Occasionally, coins do make their way into financial publications; an article published in the Financial Times in 2019 purported to be a discussion of coins as investments, but instead merely listed a few prominent collectors in history alongside a handful of auction results, without offering any advice to the investor. Guidance remains patchy and actual advice non-existent.

Many still consider an investment mindset within numismatics as decoupling coins from what underpins their value – that is, the desire of collectors to collect them. Akin to 1989, they consider there to be a price bubble which is overdue to burst when these investors come to sell. Even some who consistently profit from the trade hesitate to advise their clients how to buy coins as investments, as there is now an ingrained belief that coins must represent a hobby first and foremost with any profits merely a fortuitous happenstance.

However, the truth is that when any consumer market is bustling, outside investors will always seek to participate. Some of the healthiest markets in the world have both a consumer base and an investor base; real estate, bullion, art and other alternate assets. What is more, the vast majority of the global capital markets consist solely of those exchanging securities at market prices without any intention of actually 'consuming' anything. So long as a market is liquid and has fixed supply, the part played by the consumer does not have to be significant. One does not need to commit to permanently placing capital into an asset, and it is the active transferring of assets that creates liquidity; accordingly the impact of investors has vastly contributed to the stabilisation of coin prices worldwide. The rejection of coins as an asset class is thus inimical to the numismatic market as a whole.

Should the market for a coin type only consist of investors then it will admittedly represent a less stable asset; this is why there is wisdom in buying primarily for enjoyment. If you buy the coins you like then you also stand a better chance of buying wisely as the majority of collector interests intersect and you will organically grow your knowledge. But whichever way you might side on the debate, every collector has a vested interest in considering how their coins will operate as stores of value. As the market does allow for substantial capital gains it is prudent to observe correct procedure and treat one's coins as a balance somewhere between a hobby and an investment.

By now you will hopefully be comfortable with the workings of the numismatic market and the aspects which govern the value of individual coins. The second section will evaluate the overall performance of coins as assets, the infrastructure that allows price comparisons before buying, how coins function as stores of value and the dynamics of the global market as a whole. It will also compare the trends within the numismatic market against those of more widely traded assets such as real estate and bullion, as well as the stock market itself.

Chapter 2.1.
Knowledge is Power

The first stage of every investment is conducting thorough research, assessing whether or not it is the correct time to enter the market, how present prices compare to historical prices and speculating as to how values might grow in the near future. Investment confidence is impossible to achieve without a solid perception of market value, and only through an easy means of tracking prices can a market be truly liquid. Accordingly, every major financial and securities market allows for detailed analysis of price history, their trends and their growth.

Liquidity is a given aspect of securities markets; multiple units of each security exist and each has a known buy/sell price that is governed by market demand. What makes a market more subjective and illiquid is when specific assets are limited in number to a handful of examples or even to just one. The real estate market is an example of this, as each property is unique. Observable trends exist within real estate that are impacted by demand and international investment, but individual houses have a subjective appeal and their value is more difficult to define. The art market is even worse; price growth can be massive for a popular work, but every piece of art is unique and subjective. You are limited to one data point per asset and the information past prices provide are by nature unreliable. Each of these assets carries considerable idiosyncratic risk.

What distinguishes coins from these other asset classes is that investors, collectors and industry professionals can reliably track the market; various tools and resources exist to allow real-time prices and results. Multiple examples of each coin type exist, meaning that you do not have to wait for the same coin to re-enter the market to establish its market price but can simply observe prices for comparable pieces at auction. TPG assists further in establishing a commonly known 'going rate' for a given coin in a given numerical grade, whilst the wealth of market information prevents investor participation from overinflating prices. This is the first essential factor that allows coins to function as an asset class – universally accessible market knowledge.

1. Auction Records

The commodity with which coins share the most characteristics is bullion. Most gold and silver is traded not for its few industrial uses but for its function as a store of value. Investors enjoy tangible assets, and bullion can be an excellent investment in times of financial uncertainty. Accordingly, prices for bullion are based on constantly fluctuating market demand. Successful bullion traders must pay constant attention to the market in order to ensure they sell when market conditions are favourable and buy similarly. If the structure allowing them to keep track were to fail then the bullion markets would descend into chaos; nobody would know if they were charging over or under market price and bullion value would cease to have any meaning or stability.

For most of the history of the numismatic market, similar disarray prevented coins from acting as commodities. Individuals who wanted to track price changes in coins would have to painstakingly attend every auction they could or instead wait patiently for printed sheets of prices realised to be issued. This would also only apply to local auctioneers; the sheer numbers of auction houses worldwide meant that tracking the global market was simply impossible. Coin price guides were assembled but these were released far too occasionally to meaningfully advise collectors and were perpetually running to catch up with market trends. Grading was inconsistent and subjective and bidders could only be certain of quality if they had examined coins in person and had the skill to properly assess them. Therefore, standardised coin values could not exist and prices remained uncertain.

Once again it was the internet that radically altered this market climate. From the 1990s onwards, auction houses began to list prices realised online and CoinArchives, the coin auction search engine, was created. Within ten years almost every auctioneer was publishing the results of their coin auctions on the internet; accessibility of results would vary from auctioneer to auctioneer but CoinArchives would assemble them all in one location. TPG became more widely used and grading became precise. Collectors and dealers no longer had to rely on the inexact science of 'book values' and their own subjective grading but were instead able to update their auction estimates and prices based on current market trends. Nowadays, it is extremely easy to research price history for a coin going back at least twenty years. Many catalogues earlier than this are not digitised, but this is largely inconsequential as their prices have little relevance to today's market.

The upshot of this transparent system is a reliably accurate perception of market price that gives collectors and investors the confidence to trade. Coin values are based entirely on demand, and collectors need to know that that demand is present and stable in order to have confidence to bid. Auction records provide up-to-date coin values which may seem to outsiders as immense sums, but collectors are perfectly willing to pay these as long as they are seen as the proper market prices. Perhaps you are buying the finest known example of a coin and are therefore comfortable paying double the market rate – but you would not want to pay ten times the next highest result. So long as what is paid can be measured proportionally in some way against a recent result, collectors will be able to justify their spending to themselves and the market (and to their other halves).

Additionally, this easily accessible market information means that even outside investors can gain an accurate understanding of coin prices that would otherwise seem extortionate. If coin values were cryptic and known only to real experts (like some more niche collectables markets), then the market would be immensely illiquid as only true professionals would be willing to pay what the assets were truly 'worth'. On the other hand, the investor market can also overestimate and drive prices beyond the reach of collectors and reality. However, auction records mean that even a novice might purchase a coin for $1,750 if they are able to see that it sold recently for $2,000. In short, without this market transparency there would never be a guarantee of price stability and market continuity; the coin you bought for a supposedly reasonable price might fetch a more reasonable price still when you come to resell if there is no widespread perception of its intrinsic value. Universally accepted pricing prevents coins from 'slipping between the cracks'.

Auction records provide both a guide to a coin's market value and also form its provenance. Even if desirable and high grade, when a coin has no auction record the market will simply not know what to pay for it. A collection I handled a few years ago had some of the rarest British Halfcrowns of the 1650s; two in particular stood out, both patterns struck in 1651. One of these was the tenth example known; the other was thought to be unique. The former was quite weakly and crudely engraved and exhibited light wear, whilst the latter was pristine and of much higher quality. Despite this, the more common former specimen sold for £54,000 ($73,000) and the latter a comparatively modest £31,200 ($42,000).

England, Commonwealth (1649-1660), Unattributed pattern Halfcrown 1651. An image of the more common Halfcrown can be found in Chapter 1.1.3 "The Numismatic Revolution"

The market has become reliant on auction records to prove a coin's collector base, authenticity and ultimately to determine its value. The first of these two Halfcrowns was a known rarity and although an example had never achieved a comparable price previously, there was enough data available to show bidders that it was a desirable type. The other specimen was attractive and enticing but could not generate the same certainty of a return on investment. This would have been enough to stay many bidders' hands. However, should this Halfcrown come to auction again, it will surely achieve a significantly higher price, as it now exists in the auction record[16].

---

16   This effect would not be so pronounced within a US type market; UM series are so well-documented and heavily commoditised that a new coin type would always attract strong bidding.

Auction records have helped to stabilise the numismatic market worldwide. The reduction of arbitrage has hurt the profits of those who previously enjoyed the subjectivity of coin values, but helped those who sell their coins publicly. Past records, by providing a history of heavy collector demand, can validate the sums coins fetch at auction and foster confidence in the minds of experienced and inexperienced collectors alike. Alongside maintaining consistent pricing, auction records also set value precedents which can lead to an increase in prices and provide some measure of protection to sellers.

2. Value Precedents

Some years ago in Dallas, while taking an Uber on my way to work, I ended up in a conversation with my driver. It transpired that he had previously been a very successful executive at Microsoft and since retiring he simply traded stocks in his spare time and drove with Uber as a hobby. We discussed his methods and how he had made his fortune, and he told me that his secret was one simple, fairly self-explanatory method. He would track the history of a stock and find out if it was now trading for less than its historical peak. If it was, and there was no glaring indication of imminent market disruption, he would assume that that peak represented the stock's 'potential' and as the market had valued it at that level once, it could do so again.

What this illustrates is not necessarily a reliable financial trend but instead a truth of any market: that past performance heavily influences the behaviour of investors today. People base what they pay on the value others attribute to it; we often trust others more than ourselves and if everyone else is doing it, then surely we should be doing it too. In coins, auction records provide the current going rate but every result is by nature a value precedent. Unless multiple examples of the same coin are offered in an auction together, then there will always be a lag in auction appearances between any two examples of the same coin type. Value precedents have two main implications for numismatic markets. They can lead to price growth, and also protect buyers when attempting to resell.

Collectors are usually happy to pay a percentage over what they perceive to be the intrinsic value of a coin in order to secure it for their collection. This usually stems from a similar approach in bullion where a given percentage is paid over the precious metal value for a coin or piece of jewellery in recognition of its quality. Through this approach buyers feel that it is only that percentage above intrinsic value that they are actually paying; the rest of the transaction is simply a movement of capital into a different form. However, as true to-the-minute values do not exist for coins, collectors will instead use the most recent auction results to establish the 'intrinsic' value of a coin. If that result was an increment or two higher than average, then this may be treated as the new value level for that coin type. This process can repeat multiple times and will result in a coin undergoing rapid price increases within a relatively short period.

Value precedents can also protect those who pay a significant amount more than what a coin would usually achieve at auction. Even if you have paid three or four times the previous record for a coin simply because you liked it, that result will stay in the record. Every market professional and collector will forever be able to see what was paid for that example. Accordingly, even though the sum paid was unprecedented and you may not break even, unless there has been a major crash to the buyer base there is only a limited amount that coin's price will drop down from that previous amount. You will have paid only one increment above that of the next most motivated bidder and have thus proved that coin's potential value to the market as a whole. Nevertheless, for the most part it is better to refrain from paying such excessive prices if you hope to sell your coins at a profit. You may have artificially stretched the market thin for that coin by bidding aggressively and will have no guarantee of achieving a resale price even close to what you paid.

Precedents offer opportunities to the numismatic investor. By keeping close track of a coin's auction records you can hope to catch a coin undergoing price growth in its early stages; you may also find a coin which had previously seen aggressive bidding and attempt to purchase it for a percentage below its historical level. You can then attempt to resell it for a higher percentage of that previous result.

The competitive nature of auctions means that they are almost always directly indicative of present market strength and demand. The prices coins achieve at these public offerings ultimately determine the price they achieve next time, and the time after that. Values from auctions set a precedent that investors can follow, and by hedging various coin types in this manner you increase the likelihood of incurring ongoing gains. Auction records have rendered the numismatic market so transparent that it is now difficult to buy coins for below their market price, but without the availability of value precedents one would also struggle to resell at acceptable levels. On balance, the availability of market knowledge reduces individual profit margins but dramatically increases overall confidence in the industry.

3. Population Reports

Alongside the prices that coins have sold for and their value precedents, the population reports of major third-party grading companies allow for an additional layer of analysis to be applied: that of conditional values. These databases describe the exact numbers of a given coin type certified which aid in assessing their rarity as well as ranking coins by their grades. As so much of the market is concerned with technical quality, these population reports can be invaluable in assessing which coins to buy and what sums to pay for them.

The simplest application of population reports is checking how an encapsulated coin you are considering purchasing compares to other certified specimens. If you enter the barcode associated with your coin on the relevant TPG website, it will pull up the record and list how many examples are in lower or higher grades. If it is an average graded example with some examples certified lower and some higher, it will be considered more innocuous and its price should be conservative. If it is higher up the rankings, it will generate more interest. This will assist you in determining the sum for which to either sell or buy a coin.

Additionally, should your coin have a known mintage figure you can then quantify the total percentage of examples that have been graded. This can give you an idea of the popularity of TPG within that market whilst also evaluating the risk of newer, higher grade coins suddenly being certified and eroding the value of your example. If a coin is from a mintage of 400 and 350 of those have already been certified, you can be reasonably assured that there is a low risk that the grade rankings will dramatically change. And, like auction records, these population reports are entirely open and available to all collectors. As such, should your coin be towards the higher end of known grades, the market will know.

Population reports are especially useful when considering buying or selling a particularly high-grade coin. By consulting the databases, you can easily establish if that coin is the single highest graded specimen; and if so, it will almost always carry a significant value premium. The abundance of those who collect by grade or assemble competitive registry sets means that the collector can justify spending considerably more for the finest graded specimen whilst the dealer can justify charging more.

If you are able to develop a sophisticated enough understanding of how TPG grading operates, population reports can also advise on the buying of raw coins. This should only be attempted by the very experienced as the potential downside is significant. By examining a coin sold un-encapsulated (raw) you can estimate the approximate grade it might receive, check the population reports to see how that grade would rank in the database and judge your bid accordingly. Although a gamble, this is where your expertise might pay off; it is through this method that many dealers generate their greatest profits

Finally, population reports provide an additional means of assessing a coin's rarity - whether encapsulated or not. Often I will research more unusual coins offered raw in European auctions to glean an idea of how the rarity of its date may compare with others of the series. If few or no examples of a type have been graded whatsoever and the associated market is heavily grade conscious – such as the US, Canadian or another UM market – this can be an excellent indication that it is rare and worth buying.

Population reports, alongside auction records, allow the investor to research a coin type for its rarity and comparative quality. Their most valuable resource, however, is that they allow for an estimation of how a coin's grade might govern its value - even if none of that technical quality have ever sold before. By cross-referencing results for encapsulated coins at auction against their placement in the population report, you can develop an idea of how strong the market is for that type and estimate how prices will drop or rise for differently graded examples.

4. Indexes

By conducting adequate research it is possible for anyone to gain a measure of understanding of the price history of an individual coin at auction. One can also extrapolate from this the health of the wider collector base for that type. However, some have taken this analysis further and have assembled indexes of rare and valuable coins to act as overall market indicators. While stock indexes follow selected stocks within a subset of the market using a weighted arithmetic mean, rare coin indexes follow the market prices of a 'basket' of coin types year on year. These indexes can give a valuable overview of numismatic market performance, while inviting comparison with the wider financial market and other classes of alternative assets.

One of the primary functions of coin indexes is to allow the new investor to evaluate the strength of the market overall in comparison to its past peaks and troughs. This can aid in deciding whether or not to participate in the market. The PCGS 3000 (also known as the CU 3000 Rare Coin Index) Index tracks the values of valuable US coins from 1970 to the present. Cursory inspection of the PCGS 3000 graph shows how prices climbed exponentially in the 1980s, ending with a crash at a high of $181,088.48 on 5th May 1989. After the 1989 market collapse, the PCGS 3000 took six years to recover before the internet rebuilt the shattered market. It once again began to pick up pace in 1995. Analysing the current data can inform the investor how the market is currently faring and assist in analysing buying opportunities.

Indexes can also be used for direct comparison with other alternative assets. Coutts, a private bank in London, keeps a running 'passion index' of rare collectables that has seen a 90.4% overall increase since 2005. Coins are at present the second fastest-growing asset after vintage cars and are ahead of jewellery, watches and fine wines; since the Coutts index began in 2005 it has recorded a 228.8% increase in values for rare coins. In this manner indexes can be used for prudent comparison of coins against similar classes of asset.

In some cases, indexes can even be used for comparison with the wider financial market itself. A British-specific rare coin index maintained by Stanley Gibbons, the GB 200 Rare Coin Index, was the subject of several national articles in March 2016 as it had appeared to have outperformed the FTSE 100 in 2015. The GB 200 had produced a return of 6.2 percent in 2015, beating the FTSE 100 which lost 4.9 percent that year. Numerous quotes and statements emphasising the 'perennial value of coins to investors' floated around and there was a widespread patting of each other's backs.

Indexes have their place in the usefulness of analysing the numismatic market and even when comparing with other alternative assets, but the investor must exercise caution when using them in comparison with wider financial markets or as a reliable representation of market strength. Coin indexes are only as good as the accuracy of their components, and whereas the FTSE 100 and other indexes generally operate on the buy/sell prices of their individual stocks, coin indexes use 'book values', the listed values for coins listed in price guides. These values are inspired by recent auction results rather than being truly representative of the market, and so the impression they give of market performance is more approximate than precise.

Indexes allow a transparent insight into the historical performance of the coin market and offer some opportunities for comparison with other markets, but are more illustrative than they are actually useful when assessing which coins to buy. They are effective when first educating a potential investor in the trends and legitimacy of the numismatic market, but are merely a jumping off point for more in-depth and directed research. For the individual it is far more useful to track the performance of coins on a one-by-one basis as and when they appear for sale.

★ ★ ★

It is always a numbers game. For every numismatic transaction you will need to gamble and use your best judgement based on available data. For example, you might be considering buying a coin from a small mintage graded MS61 and priced at $9,000. You see an example graded MS63 at the top of the population reports for NGC and PCGS, and an MS62 piece sold for $13,000 three months previously. You can assume that as that MS62 was not the finest graded it will not have the accompanying disproportionate value premium; and, for a coin to reach those prices it must also have a fairly healthy collector demand. If you buy that MS61 example you may be able to sell it reasonably fast for $10,000 using the MS62 example as substantiation, or instead hold onto it for two years and try for an even stronger market then. You may also lose out and be forced to sell it two months later for $7,500. But by analysing the wealth of data available for grade, auction records and value precedents, you stand a far greater chance of making educated decisions than in asset markets with fewer data points and easily accessible information.

The accessibility of such information for coins is one of the key factors underpinning their reliability as an investment. The ease of establishing the past price a coin has sold for, how its grade compares to others and the overall strength of the market all aid in encouraging even the relatively novice to participate. These factors, coupled with the standardisation of grading across the industry, allow for multiple value data points to be accessible for most coin types.

Chapter 2.2.
Putting Cash into Cash

1. Liquidity

A vital consideration of any investment is its liquidity. In short, an asset can be considered relatively liquid if it can be bought or sold quickly at a price that reflects its intrinsic value; that is, neither the buyer nor the seller has to wait to achieve the correct market price for that asset. If the spread between buy and sell prices grows, then the market for that asset becomes more illiquid. Cash is the most liquid asset class as it holds a universally accepted value; bullion is the most liquid tangible asset, tradable instantly at market price but slightly harder to use in everyday transactions. The real estate market is comparatively illiquid as its assets are immobile and far more subjective in their value. Those selling a property may have to wait a long while to find a buyer at the price level they seek.

Most collectables markets are reasonably illiquid. These alternative assets often do not have a true 'intrinsic' value accepted by the wider market, and their buy/sell prices will differ from specialist to specialist and collector to collector. If only one example of a particular asset type exists (say, a Van Gogh painting), then the owner will only know its current market value when they come to sell their example and there is no anticipating whether it will be lower or higher than their expectation. The price is so arbitrary that it will usually either drop or rise significantly from its previous level. This means that the market perception is always of either a sudden prohibitive rise or a dramatic fall in 'value'. In illiquid markets, everything is either 'cheap' or 'expensive' and as such these words have no meaning. Auction houses thus provide the bulk of the liquidity within collectables markets by matching buyers and sellers together for a quick sale, but offer no guarantee of price stability.

As discussed, coins stand head and shoulders above most other classes of alternative asset for liquidity. The ease of researching past coin auction records and value precedents means that the market knows what intrinsic value a coin has to collectors and assists in determining their buy and sell price. Although this factor is also prevalent in many other collectable categories, coins are unusual in that they exist in multiple units, meaning that collectors do not need to wait for specific examples to re-enter the market but can simply observe prices paid for similar coins when they appear at auction. Various price guides informed by recent auction results also assist with liquidity; many collectors abide by the prices suggested in these books and values remain consistent.

Not only do coins have significant market recognition for their intrinsic price, but also have a widely held perception of value by members of the general public. Liquidity also applies to how easily you can use an asset as a form of payment in a transaction for its intrinsic price. If you were to show the layman a piece of art, a bottle of fine wine or an antique book each worth $10,000, the chances are that in most cases they would not be able to appreciate their true value. If however you showed the same individual a large gold or silver antique coin, they would be more likely to be willing to accept it as a form of payment.

Both internal and external to the numismatic market, TPG considerably assists with coin liquidity. By establishing a quantifiable standard of quality decipherable by outside investors - coupled with the ability to research past prices to keep values realistic – coins can be exchanged for far more precise amounts with minimal spread between their buy and sell prices. This is a particularly observable trend within US coins which almost always fall into razor-thin value ranges based on their numerical grade. The confidence that TPG has instilled sight-unseen means that the widest possible swathe of the market will participate for encapsulated coins at auction, keeping prices strong and at similar levels.

Coins have a unique advantage over almost every other form of alternative asset that contributes to their liquidity – their portability. Shares, stocks and other securities can be held online and do not require physical movement but this carries its own risks; as such, most investors prefer to keep some measure of their wealth in tangible assets. The Coutts passion index reports that vintage cars are the sole alternative asset class presently beating coins with a +245.8% increase since 2005 against +228.8% for coins. But to physically store your collection of vintage cars will require space, security, considerable maintenance and upkeep and even after all of these your assets will still be vulnerable to theft or damage. Coins have some of the most 'condensed' values of any asset besides perhaps diamonds, but - unlike diamonds – coins are not naturally occurring and so the risk of the market becoming flooded by new discoveries is lessened. A handful of coins can feasibly be worth multiple millions. They can be stored in a bank vault with ease or in a relatively cheap home safe or other protected environment, and are resilient so unlike art they are less prone to environmental damage and require less attention to their storage. If times became tough and you were forced to flee with whatever you could grab, you could not take your home, your art or your wines, but you could easily transport your most valuable coins and be relatively certain that they would be tradable for their intrinsic values.

However, like most other alternative asset classes, liquidity is in short supply for the very highest and lowest echelons of the market. For more common or average types – and particularly those below $1,000 in value – liquidity is very high as this sector has the largest collector base. Additionally, being more commonly seen at auctions there are a wealth of data points available to consult to determine the correct buy/sell price. But as you approach the crème-de-la-crème, the coins of $100,000+ in value represented by only a few surviving examples, liquidity becomes more difficult. The market is thin at this level and collectors more capricious. Prices for these coins are subject to greater change according to the whims of buyers; the potential profit can be much greater but the likelihood of a loss correspondingly high. This effect exists for the lowest levels of the market too. When particularly inferior coins are offered they will only have a few interested collectors, and these too can fetch disproportionately high or low prices.

On the whole, liquidity for coins is comparatively high. There is a generally widespread perception of how much coins are worth and the spread between buy sell prices is on average, low. Even outside of the market coins are known to hold significant value and their portability makes them an enticing store of wealth. This liquidity has changed the face of numismatics in recent decades; the substantial profit margins formerly attained by dealers have shrunk as more and more collectors have become familiar with current market prices. As such, the most common means of generating a short-term income from numismatics is now through a model of high volume and low margin.

2. Margin and Volume

By breaking down the barriers between buyer and seller and allowing scrutiny of auction records, the internet has served to vastly reduce spread between the buy/sell prices of most coins. As such, rather than buying coins for below their value or attempting to overcharge, the modern coin dealer must generally focus on a "low margin, high volume" approach as their bread and butter - similar to bullion trading. This highlights some of the advantages of the numismatic market whilst also drawing attention to the challenges that would-be participants face.

This business model is quite hands-on and tends to be practiced by only dedicated dealers for whom numismatics is a primary livelihood. Low value coins (<$1,000) are either bought in quantity or higher value coins (>$10,000) are bought individually at auction for what is perceived to be a few per cent below intrinsic value. The dealer will then seek to sell these for either market price or a few per cent above and achieve somewhere in the region of 5-10 per cent return on their investment. This is not easy money; for every $100,000 transaction the dealer might make somewhere around $5-10,000. These numbers are purely illustrative and will change depending on the market or the coins themselves but the proportions will remain similar. The advantage of the volume>margin model is that it stands a better chance of a swift turnover; dealers could charge a higher price for their coins but would be forced to wait longer to sell. This is possible for some coins but impossible as a consistent business model.

The volume>margin method primarily works on the perception of an intrinsic value which the coin is bought for a small percentage below and sold for a small percentage above. This is the same manner as gold transactions; higher spreads are not possible in such a standardised market and bullion traders must conduct huge numbers of transactions simply to remain afloat. Much of the numismatic industry operates via this volume>margin approach, but it is certainly not standard across the board. Exceptions to this rule are encountered constantly, and arbitrage is still very possible in numismatics. Despite the interconnectivity of the internet no auction house ever has a full audience of potential buyers in attendance; auctions will always command a greater domestic audience than international, and 'foreign' coins will often sell for below the values they command in their domestic markets. Often, dealers will use the volume>margin system to keep their business ticking over while their windfalls arrive in the form of arbitrage opportunities or encapsulating high-grade coins offered raw.

The presence of the volume>margin approach in coin dealing highlights several advantages of the numismatic market: complete transparency, relative stability and significant liquidity. But despite the market liquidity for numismatics, on an individual basis liquidity can be somewhat more difficult and the margin/volume method can fail to deliver. A given coin type might sell for a sum between a tight value range of $400-450 each time it comes to auction, but if you consistently buy at $450 and sell at $400, you will quickly lose capital and likely become disillusioned with numismatics as a whole. Often there is a need to slow down transaction speed and to price a coin including your profit margin and wait for a buyer. The more you are forced to do this the more of your capital is tied up in coins – leading to potential issues arising concerning your cash flow.

3. Cash Flow

Where liquidity is in short supply, you will struggle to sell your coin for the amount you paid. Technically speaking the market needs to be somewhat illiquid if you are hoping for a quick and profitable turnaround when buying and selling coins, but occasionally you must wait for either the market to pick up or the right buyer to come along before you can sell a coin. This effect is exacerbated by the volume>margin system in which huge amounts of your capital may be tied up in coins for which you can only hope to make a small profit. On these occasions you may encounter cash flow problems.

Cash flow is arguably the biggest challenge faced by coin dealers. If you are merely a collector or passive investor putting some of your capital into coins then cash flow will not be a significant issue as you will have other more easily liquidated assets to fall back on. If your livelihood is built on the buying and selling of coins for profit then it is another story entirely. A dealer might buy a coin during a dip in the market for, say, $10,000. For the sake of argument, let us say that this was $2,000 less than that same coin sold for the previous year. The dealer cannot now simply turn around and sell that coin for $12,000 immediately as the market is still in a downturn. Accordingly, that $10,000 is tied up in a coin until such time as the dealer can find a buyer. If they have bought several coins in the same downturn then even more of their useful capital will be locked away in coins.

Unlike real estate or shares, coins do not offer any income or dividends and so you cannot live off your investment as you wait for it to mature. Fortunately there are some options available if you are in an emergency and need to liquidate swiftly.

The fastest means of freeing capital from a coin is by bringing it to a coin show and allowing multiple dealers to inspect it. You can take advantage of this gathering to generate a small unofficial 'auction', comparing different prices and potentially leveraging offers against one another. Once you have garnered enough interest you can accept the highest offer you are given. If no coin show is on the horizon or another pandemic hits, then you can achieve a similar effect online by emailing various dealerships and auctioneers. Unless you have bought very cheaply this method is almost guaranteed to result in a loss; you are prioritising speed of sale over percentage return and will be marketing directly to those who must generate a profit margin. If you have bought wisely then the loss you are forced to take will likely be minor or you may break even; accordingly, your coins will have stored value relatively well. However, you should usually expect to take at least a 10 or 20 per cent loss when selling in this manner. Overall this is an advantage of the numismatic market, that there is an abundance of market-savvy specialists who can assist with quick sales.

If you have either more time in which to sell your coin or do not need to unlock its full value immediately, you can turn to auction houses. By selling at auction you stand a chance of offering your coin directly to collectors and may generate your full investment back - or even a profit. Auctioneers will require time to catalogue and market your coin and you will be forced to abide by whatever their auction schedule is; in some cases this will be several months away. As such, an instant liquidation is not guaranteed. Fortunately, some auction houses will instead offer advances on consignments. For example, if you have a coin for which you hope to receive $100,000, the auction house may conservatively estimate its value to be $60,000-80,000. You can accordingly expect to receive anywhere from $30,000-50,000 as an advance payment. If you need the majority of your coin's value instantly then this method will not be satisfactory, but if you only require 30 per cent upfront to reinvest, auction houses offer an excellent resource.

Finally, some banks and dealerships will accept coins as collateral for loans – a testament to the universally accepted value coins hold. Due to their established values and portability, coins are a widely accepted form of collateral which can be transferred with relative ease. Assuming that you do not want to part with your existing coins but have located a profitable and fast buy/sell opportunity, you can exchange your coins for a loan, conduct your transaction and then receive your coins back. Having a store of rare coins on hand thus affords far more opportunities for transactions than one would at first realise.

Cash flow is imperative to track if you are actively buying and selling coins; you never know when a coin will appear at an enticing price and you will need a bank of capital on-hand for such occasions. There are a variety of options available to swiftly liquidate coins in emergencies, but for the majority of investors these will not be necessary.

4. Diversification

One of the key principles in investing is ensuring that you sufficiently diversify. It is never sensible to put all your eggs in one basket; for example if you put the entirety of your capital into the shares of one company then you would be completely at the mercy of that particular firm's performance. If the company prospered then you would benefit but if it the market turned for the worst you could lose everything. Accordingly it is prudent to diversify, to spread your capital out over a range of securities and asset classes to maximise the strength of your position. These investments should be as far-flung as possible, not merely separated by industry but also by region and nationality. This way you will be able to weather most storms in the financial market and your capital will be protected.

The same principle of diversification is true within individual asset classes. You can diversify your bullion to include palladium and platinum alongside gold, you can diversify your real estate across several countries and locations, and you can diversify the range of coins you buy. Just like in the wider financial market, numismatic markets are prone to swift change and it is vital to be aware of how they will respond to world events. If you limit your collecting to a handful of coins from the same country then your risk will increase; any change in the collector base of that particular market and your coins may begin to dip in value, hurting your chances of a swift resale. However if your coins either span a range of countries or instead appeal to several distinct markets, you will considerably increase your chances of retaining or growing your capital.

There are two primary means of diversifying your numismatic position. The first is to buy a diverse group of coins from a range of distinct markets (I), thereby ensuring individual losses are offset by individual gains. The second method instead focuses on buying those coins with a strong cross-market appeal and takes advantage of the links between wealthy SMs and EMs (II).

I. Single Markets Diversification

Single Market Diversification is the simplest form of numismatic diversification – but is also the most time-consuming. This method involves the buying of popular coin types each from its own distinct market. The tracking of auction prices for specific coins can give you an impression of that market's health but this is never completely reliable. As such, it is wise to spread out your position and to buy an educated assortment of different coins. Although each coin will primarily appeal to its domestic collector base, when grouped together this 'basket' will represent a variety of markets and the total risk is significantly reduced.

It is important to buy according to each separate market's collecting customs; US coins should be bought in high numerical grades, rare UK coins with strong eye appeal should be chosen etc. Market trends should be observed, and only those wealthier countries with solid histories of price increases should be chosen for this basket. Due to the amount of research necessary, single-market diversification is more hands-on but ultimately means that your position is as strong as possible.

Case Study – Coin Price Changes, 2015-2020

Imagine you had decided to invest in coins in 2015. You chose to diversify and bought a basket of six coin types diverse across market and countries. You choose to omit SMs and stick with the more secure choices of EMs, UMs and EAMs, and to buy only TPG coins. After buying two coins from each market type, you hold on to them for five years and resell them in 2020. Here is how your investment looks:

Country	Market Type	Coin Type	2015 Price ($)	2020 Price ($)	% Change
UK	EM	Victoria Gothic Crown 1847 PR64	$8,000	$13,000	+62.5%
Germany	EM	Prussia 2 Thaler 1840-A MS63	$900	$1,550	+72%
US	UM	1897-S $20 MS65	$14,000	$16,000	+14%
Canada	UM	1921 5 Cents VF25	$5,253	$3,400	-35%
China	EAM	Sun Yat-Sen Dollar Year 21 (1932) MS63	$3,600	$9,250	+157%
Japan	EAM	20 Yen Year 9 (1920) MS66	$3,750	$3,800	+1%
TOTALS			$35,503	$47,000	+32%

The coins listed here were picked more or less at random and represent either common or representative types from each country and market. The value range of these coins in 2015 was from $900-14,000; there is a general rule in numismatics that to allow for a greater percentage growth you should not buy coins with a market price below $500. After five years, this basket was up by $12,000 or +32%. The largest single increase was that of the Chinese Dollar at +157% and the only decrease was the Canadian 5 Cents at -35%. Some value increases were so negligible as to be pointless by themselves, and others were so large as to stand alone as desirable investments[17]. However, it is only by diversifying across markets that you will truly stabilise your position and stand an excellent chance of your collection increasing in value.

II. Multiple Markets Diversification

The multiple market method of diversification turns the equation on its head. Instead of buying a range of coins from several distinct markets, this technique involves buying only those types of coins that themselves appeal to multiple markets. By conducting thorough research on which coins have the widest and most diverse collector base, you can choose only those coins that have the most diverse demand and can accordingly represent more stable investments. The wider a collector base for a coin the more collectors must compete for it at auction and the swifter its price will increase. Unlike the single market method this involves researching fewer countries and coin types, but as it involves a smaller number of coins the risk is admittedly higher. When evaluating which coins to choose, it is wise to evaluate the strength of a coin's domestic market, its links to other countries, its visual appeal and its relationship with TPG. High-GDP SMs are good markets to start with, as they by nature carry links to other markets whilst retaining their own wealthy domestic collector base.

---

17 It is worth noting that since this table was put together, prices for PR64 Gothic Crowns have increased a further 177% to $36,000 in January 2022.

Case Study – Sovereigns

Great Britain, George III (1760-1820), Sovereign, 1817

The milled Sovereign is a British coin first struck in 1817 during the reign of George III; it is perhaps one of the best known gold coins in the world with its iconic depiction of St George vanquishing the dragon. Outside of US coins, Sovereigns boast perhaps the widest collector base of any coin denomination for the following reasons:

a) Their issuing country (Great Britain) has a high GDP per capita; the British coin market is strong and there are numerous collectors of Sovereigns.

b) As modern gold coins they carry no VAT when purchased.

c) Sovereigns are considered legal tender within the UK, meaning they incur no capital gains tax when they are resold.

d) Sovereigns were struck in London, Australia (Melbourne, Sydney and Perth), South Africa, Canada and India; their appeal is thus diversified across several markets.

e) Sovereigns were distributed widely during WWII leading to collector bases in even some countries that never produced them (eg Greece).

As discussed earlier, an Australian Sovereign became one of the few non-US coins to exceed $1,000,000 in 2012; indeed, at time of writing five of the 100 most expensive world coins to have sold in auctions since

2000 have been milled Sovereigns, with ten more represented by Five-Sovereign coins. The numerous tax benefits associated with buying and selling Sovereigns coupled with their exceedingly wide market appeal means that they arguably represent one of the soundest coin denominations to invest in. By applying similar analysis to other markets and tracking past auction prices it is possible to identify those coins with the most diverse collector bases.

Diversification can to some extent go against the individual collector's mentality. We feel an affinity for those coins produced in our country or which have some historical significance to us personally. Accordingly, rather than diversifying, many collectors will prefer to take their chances operating within a single market and will buy only those coins they actually enjoy. Despite diversification offering a far more stable position to the numismatic investor, it is a primarily longer-term approach. There are other short-term strategies one can employ to maximise potential profits for coin purchases - even for those within the same market.

5. Investment Strategies

The core principle of numismatic investments - or indeed any investments - is to buy low and sell high. In any transparent financial market this can be difficult to achieve as the buy/sell prices will be well-established. Investors can either choose to buy an asset or security at market price and hope that values will increase, or otherwise act creatively to take advantage of market fluctuations and inefficiencies. Within the numismatic market there are three main tactics one can employ to generate a return on investment: Buy and Hold (I), Speculation (II) and Value Investing (III).

I. Buy and Hold
Buy and Hold is a passive investment approach where a security or asset is bought at market price and held for a long period - regardless of any market fluctuation - in the hope that its value will increase. No effort is made by the investor to pay less than the intrinsic value of the asset as the onus is on the market itself to change over time. Single market diversification, the buying of multiple coins from different markets, is a buy and hold approach as the intention is to let natural price changes for

each coin balance each other in a hopefully upwards trend.

This long-term approach is the most commonly practiced among collectors and has undeniable advantages. The trend of the numismatic market is almost exclusively positive, and over longer periods a return is often a certainty. It is the least hands-on method and, if you are also buying coins out of enjoyment, means you get to own them for a longer period of time. Easily accessible auction results aid in establishing previous price trends and can instil confidence that your coins will appreciate in value. Several of my clients who bought their collections in the late 90s and early 2000s have each made hundreds of thousands of dollars in profit simply by buying at market price, hanging onto their coins and selling when they were ready.

Buy and hold is a sensible approach when buying truly exceptional coins that cannot fail to escape collector attention. Even if you buy these coins at an expensive price, that value precedent will stay in the record; meanwhile, collectors will be hungry for them when they return for sale. In a sense, you will be both limiting and controlling the supply of that particular rarity. In some cases, dealers who originally sell unusually choice coins actually end up contacting their buyers years later and offering as much as double the original price for the coin to be returned to them.

The only disadvantage of buying and holding is that you are not so responsive to market bubbles or trends. Many coin prices do tend to rise year-on-year, but they can also drop suddenly. A client of mine bought an 1826 proof Five Pound coin in 2001 for £8,000 ($12,000). He then held onto it for a total of 17 years. During this period, prices climbed steadily; if he had sold ten years after he had bought it, he would have made a respectable $18,000 profit. However, he eventually sold in January 2018 just as the market peaked, resulting in a sale price of $190,000!

Great Britain, George IV (1820-30) proof Five Pounds 1826 PR63 Ultra Cameo NGC

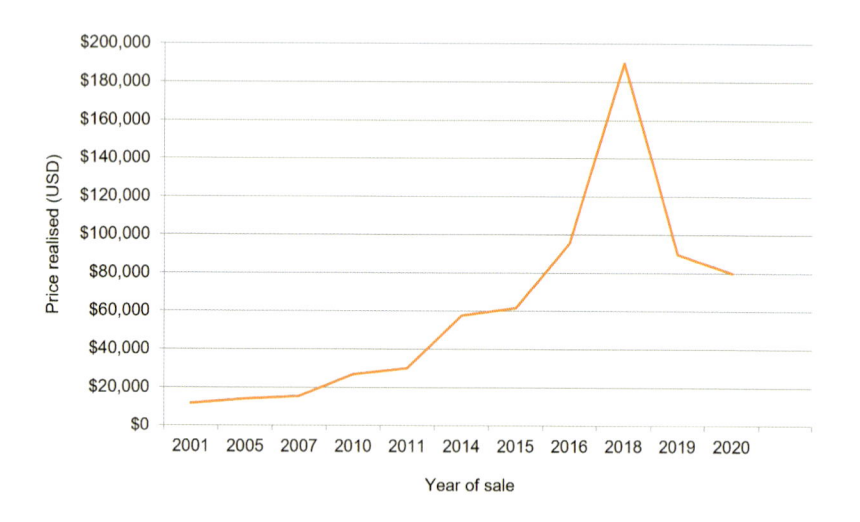

Prices Realised for PR63-graded 1826 Five Pounds

Immediately after he sold his example, prices began to drop. Until recently a PR63 1826 Five Pounds was worth around $80,000, as the market became saturated and collector interest dropped off. Only in later 2020 and 2021 have prices begun to pick back up in the wake of the Covid-19 bubble. Accordingly, the formula is not always "more time since purchase = greater return". Had the owner of that Five Pounds waited two more years to sell he would have lost out on more than $100,000 profit. No matter what this collector did he would have made a substantial gain, but by keeping track of the market he was able to maximise his return. This introduces a different form of investment: speculation.

II. Market Speculation

The opposite of buy and hold is market speculation – a generally short-term and highly active investment approach. Speculators take advantage of price fluctuations to achieve a relatively quick return on their investment; these fluctuations can be small but with consistent re-investing a substantial profit can be made. The risk is far greater for speculators but the potential gains are correspondingly high.

Numismatic speculators operate at a slower pace than securities speculators. Auctions take place between reasonably long intervals and there is ample time to compare current prices with those achieved in recent auction record. If a coin in a healthy market seems to be stalling at a lower price than its last result, speculators will purchase and re-consign the coin in short succession in the anticipation the pendulum will swing back the other way. Bidders can be unpredictable but this approach often bears fruit; unless there is a significant market decline, coin prices will rarely drop twice in a row.

An illustrative example demonstrating the relative risk/return proportion of speculation in numismatics is provided by the US 1915-S 'Panama $50 Round' graded MS64. This coin in this specific numerical grade is common enough to provide a wealth of data points between 2000 and the present day.

Prices Realised for MS64-graded US 1915-S Panama $50 Rounds

THE ROYAL MINT®
THE ORIGINAL MAKER

Consign Your Coins to a Royal Mint Auction

If you are looking to sell your coin or coin collection, The Royal Mint's Collector Services team can help you find them a new home. By consigning your coins to The Royal Mint's regular auctions, you can reach a wide audience of potential buyers and make sure you get a fair price, with competitive selling fees, often as low as 0%.

To find out more, visit royalmint.com/consignments

royalmint.com

CELEBRATE | COLLECT | INVEST | SECURE | DISCO

Coin
Country of Issue
Monarch
Denomination

The price for this coin has dipped and risen as regularly as a heart monitor over the last two decades. However, the US market is highly commoditised; notice how prices will rarely increase more than 20 per cent at one time and will very rarely show consistent short-term growth or drops. Price change is gradual but in a decidedly upward trend.

If you were buying and holding, and had purchased an example of the Panama $50 in 2000, had you sold it any time after 2003 you would have made a profit. If you had decided to sell after ten years, you could have made anywhere from $50k-80k. This is a sound investment strategy, with low risk and low effort. If instead you decided to be more active in the market and had speculated repeatedly, you could have made upwards of $175k just from buying and selling the same coin type - without ever needing to learn about the wider numismatic market.

Speculation can attract considerable profits but the high number of individual transactions means risk is far greater. It is best employed in the mid-market for strong and preferably highly commoditised markets where prices are reasonably consistent. When one speculates, one is taking advantage of the fluctuations in current market price for a coin; linked to this is the concept of paying below this market price, otherwise known as value investing.

III. *Value Investing*

Value investing is distinct from both buy and hold and speculation in that it involves the buying of an asset or security at below its intrinsic value. Coin prices are arbitrary and are based solely on supply and demand; nonetheless, there are usually accepted market values that collectors and dealers follow. With conventional securities, value investing isolates those stocks or shares that the market is perceived to be underestimating, whilst in numismatics it generally involves taking advantage of market inefficiencies and arbitrage.

Despite the transparency of the numismatic market, prices will never be truly watertight. Within every auction there will be bargains - diagnostic of an inefficient market - that can be taken advantage of, typically by reselling across borders or markets (essentially a form of arbitrage). Attentive collectors and dealers will sit through entire auctions watching and waiting for these attractive deals. In 2019, I purchased a coin from a

US auction – a George III Shilling from 1763. This example was graded AU58 and I could see in auction record that it had sold for $1,200 in 2015 at the same auction house. I bid and won it for $800, 33% less than it had previously sold for at its last auction. Two weeks later I showed it to a collector and, by referencing the 2015 value precedent, was able to sell it once again for $1,200.

Great Britain, George III (1760-1820) 'Northumberland' Shilling, 1763, AU58 NGC

As market values are typically determined by auctions, it can be difficult to both buy and sell at auctions with the hopes of reliably generating a profit from value investing. Some dealers will address this through buying in one market and offering in another, some prefer to place extortionate and unrealistic reserves, but most either buy from an individual then sell at auction, or buy from an auction and sell to an individual. These collectors may have missed the auction, and as the value precedent is in the auction record they will usually be happy to pay a percentage over the auction hammer price.

The strategies you choose to employ come down to how passive or active you would like to be in the numismatic market. You may be looking to become a collector, or simply to put some money into coins. However, no matter their objectives the most successful numismatic investors apply a combination of tactics in their buying practices instead of sticking to one strategy. If you can manage to avoid cash flow issues, then you can buy coins and hold on to them for as long as is needed until the market begins picking up. Equally, you can speculate a few times on a specific coin type and then hold it for a longer period in order to weather turbulence in the market. To consistently achieve returns on your investments you must stay flexible and vigilant, as the market has a number of inefficiencies which can make it vulnerable and prone to change.

Chapter 2.3.
Market Dynamics

By this stage you may have carefully selected a diverse range of coin types from active markets, each of which has a solid history at auction. Having conducted your research and planned your investment route, you can now set sail with your coins in tow across the murky waters of the numismatic market. But you are not home and dry yet. The numismatic market is tumultuous, as is any financial market, and before you participate you must be fully aware of the different factors in play. Coins are an often stable and consistently appreciating asset but numerous elements can impact their value after they have been purchased; an influx of new examples entering the market will affect the supply, and a change in the collector base will affect the demand. Vogues will send coin prices shooting through the ceiling, and crashes will bring them back down with a thud.

This chapter concerns the subtleties and undercurrents of the trade itself, and attempts to give an accurate impression of the risk that the numismatic investor is exposed to between buying and selling coins.

1. Pyramid of Buyers

Assuming that NGC and PCGS's numbers are correct, there is more than $50,000,000,000 in coins certified by these two companies combined, and the global total including uncertified coins will be even higher still. The numismatic market has a considerable capital base – but this capital is not evenly distributed and does not necessarily flow in predictable patterns. The vast majority of capital flooding the coin market is contributed by fewer than 20 per cent of collectors, and this imbalance can create an immensely fragile market for the most valuable coins.

Every numismatic auction has a 'pyramid of bidders'. The largest number of bidders in an auction will only have limited capital or will be trying to buy cheaply, and will drop out as prices increase: these form the base of the pyramid. A new, more narrow step is formed as more and more bidders drop out, and by the end of an auction bidding will come down to just two individuals - the point of the pyramid. This effect is true not just for coins at auction, but for the numismatic market as a whole. Most collectors are hobbyists who will only spend trivial amounts on coins, and the collector base thins out rapidly as prices increase. This unequal distribution of buyer capital, this 'pyramid of buyers' is perhaps the most significant contributing factor to the inefficiency of the numismatic market.

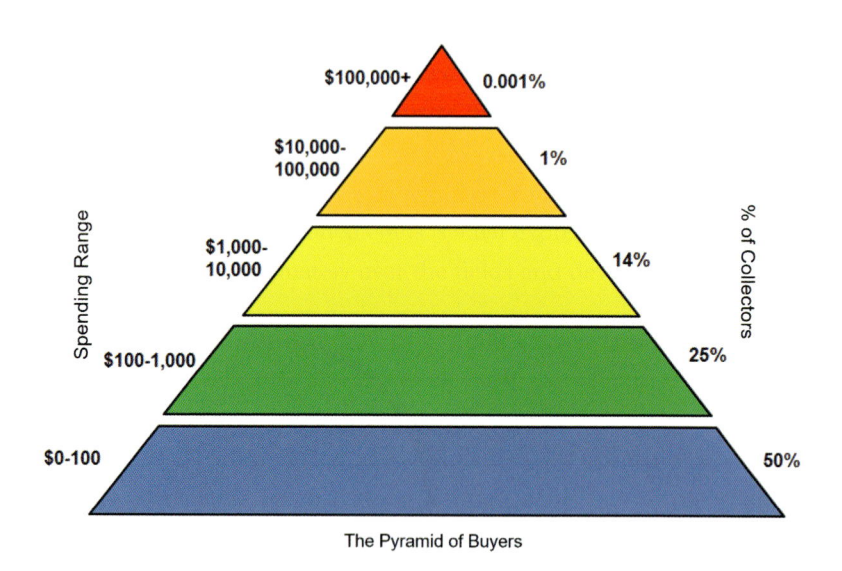

The Pyramid of Buyers

- $100,000+ — 0.001%
- $10,000-100,000 — 1%
- $1,000-10,000 — 14%
- $100-1,000 — 25%
- $0-100 — 50%

(Spending Range / % of Collectors)

As a coin's price increases you will climb another step of the pyramid, and the higher you climb the more collectors will fall behind and the fewer your peers become. It is important to note that what this pyramid truly illustrates is not collector interest at each level, but rather the ability of collectors to maintain price stability at that level. On the bottom tier, a low-grade Roman bronze coin worth about $5 will have hundreds of thousands of potential buyers and its price will be identical each time. A Roman silver Denarius with a clear portrait worth perhaps $100-300 will still have thousands of interested collectors and may vary by 20 or 30 dollars in price but will be otherwise stable. However, a far rarer Roman gold Aureus of Brutus worth $500,000 will only have a handful of collectors either able to or willing to spend that sum, meaning that just one collector deciding not to participate may be catastrophic for the price. It will always sell, but the price paid at auction will be far more prone to change – either upwards or downwards.

The very lowest levels have by far the greatest price security but the lowest actual prices. At this tier the 'curiosity appeal' of coins outweighs collector appeal. Collectors will always be willing to spend the largest sums on coins due to their understanding of coin values and their comparative dedication to the hobby. However, the greatest numbers of those buying coins are not doing so as collectors, they are buying in isolated incidences purely for the minor curiosity value that coin offers. A classical history student might decide on a whim to purchase a worn Tetradrachm of Alexander the Great for $50 because they enjoy its appeal as an artefact. They will have unknowingly participated in the global numismatic market, but their participation may well stop there at one coin – they are not a collector, and they need no other coins[18]. This 'curiosity' spending will always be far weaker than that of collectors as these are often uninformed impulse purchases; with no knowledge of resale potential or intrinsic values, these casual buyers will be unwilling to part with large sums.

Prices at these lower levels tend to be quite stable in that they rarely fall, but this tier does offer opportunities to make multiples of your original investment. Due to the values involved being relatively low, there are no percentage 'value caps' on transactions – in this tier of the market, an enticing example of a coin that typically sells for £100 can achieve a price of £500-600 if two collectors take a fancy to it. 600 per cent of 'intrinsic' value would usually be outrageous, but as the actual figure paid is just £500 above the market standard it is not seen as hugely significant. On the other hand, at a higher level a superb example of a coin which generally achieves £10,000 would rarely garner £50,000-60,000 as the price difference would be considered too steep by most. In this manner lower level coins sold at a considerable mark-up in quantity can net impressive returns.

---

18 Impulse purchases like this are vital for the market as they are a major cause of new collectors entering the hobby.

Many dealers and collectors do choose to buy at the lowest market levels to make their living – but it is undeniably the highest levels of the pyramid where one can hope to generate the largest profits. This is where the titans clash, where the wealthiest collectors come together and fight for the absolute best of the best. There is an expression in numismatics that you should always buy the absolute best coins you can – this is because if anyone *else* then decides they want the best, they will have to come to you and you can name your price. Values become more arbitrary at this height as collectors begin to pay essentially whatever they want to ensure the coin goes home with them and not someone else. A coin which sells for $150,000 and is then reoffered shortly afterwards can sometimes generate as much as a 50 per cent higher price; quite the payday for the dealer who bought it originally. Additionally, should the coin be held onto for a longer period of time the profits can be greater still.

However, there is a reason why coins of these values are at the top of the pyramid. Coin values are entirely collector-driven, and the top tier of purchasers might be represented by only half a dozen collectors. This is where liquidity entirely breaks down in the numismatic market: the impact of an individual buyer can hugely impact the buy or sell price.

Imagine a coin sells at auction for $1,000,000. Newspapers would report that the coin was worth $1m, and most would presume this to be true; after all, it had just achieved that price at auction. But consider: the most motivated collector in the world bought it, and it was only through their participation that the price reached that level in the first place. Logically, as no one else was willing to pay that much - and the one collector who was now owns an example and will be unlikely to buy another - it is fair to say that the coin is thus guaranteed to now be worth less than $1m.

In practice, should another coin of the same type come to market, one of two things will happen. Either the handful of high-tier collectors remaining will compete even more aggressively using the $1,000,000 as a value precedent and the price will exceed this initial sum; or equally likely, the same few bidders will put forward their original bids and the coin will sell for, say, $800,000. It is near impossible to anticipate which of these two scenarios will play out.

Unfortunately, due to fragility of the highest tiers of the market, the loss of just one collector (ie the original buyer who has chosen to sell) can have devastating effects on prices. In late 2020, arguably one of the most famous US coins was offered at auction as part of the Bruce Morelan collection – the 1794 'flowing hair' Dollar, graded SP66 by PCGS and purportedly the first Dollar struck at the US mint. This same coin was last sold at Stack's Bowers in January 2013 when it attracted an all-time record hammer price of $10,016,875, the highest price ever paid for any coin, even beating the famous 1933 Double Eagle. As such, for years this Dollar has been dubbed 'the world's most valuable coin'. Due to the astronomical increase in prices in 2020, this coin made its reappearance at Legend Numismatics' auction with an estimate of $8m-9m. Various numismatic and non-numismatic news outlets picked up the story, expectations rose and pulses raced – only for the coin to fail to sell at its estimate. Morelan had pushed up bidding at the original auction to such an extent that when re-offered, without his influence the coin failed to reach its price level of almost eight years earlier.

USA, 'Flowing Hair' Dollar 1794, SP66 PCGS.

You can minimise your risk by limiting your buying to the middle-tiers of the pyramid. Here values are reasonably high, and yet prices are still relatively standardised. Due to the spread between buy/sell prices being limited, undoubtedly the profits at this level will depend chiefly on volume>margin trading; for greater returns you can try to pay under the usual price and value invest.

It is not the level of the pyramid you choose to operate at that determines your success as a numismatic investor, it is the strategies you follow and the discipline you keep. Profits are relatively easy to generate in the lowest tiers although your volume will need to be high; the middle tiers offer similar opportunities with minimal chance of drastic price changes. However, the most lucrative returns will always be generated by the absolute crème-de-la-crème of coins, but therein also lies the greatest risk to the investor. Numismatists express that you should buy the best coin you can to ensure a profitable re-sale, but this mantra becomes risky at the absolute height of the market – because when the dust settles and you victoriously hold up your prize, you might look around to see that you are all alone at the top of the pyramid and that the only way is down.

2. Market Inefficiencies

"It is however hardly necessary to caution our readers, that the prices frequently given at the public sale of well-known collections… are by no means a fair criterion of the average marketable value of the coins under ordinary circumstances; and for that reason…, we refrain from giving any list of the sums produced by the more remarkable pieces. Such a list would only mislead the uninstructed; to the initiated it would give facilities for extortion. Every dealer in London knows full well that prices are frequently given at public sales, the half of which he would find it utterly impossible to obtain for the identical piece in the regular way of business."

-The Numismatic Chronicle and Journal of the Numismatic Society, volumes 9-10, Taylor & Walton, 1847

According to economic theory, an inefficient market is one in which an asset's market prices do not consistently reflect its true intrinsic value – as such, an inefficient market is highly illiquid. The numismatic collector base is thin at the top, and this will admittedly lead to price vulnerability. But, if a valuable coin sells for far less than it did at its last auction appearance, this does not mean the coin has sold for less than its value, but rather that its market value itself has actually dropped. Alongside price volatility, it is also important to understand the various inefficiencies within the numismatic market that dictate how much a coin will sell for. Market inefficiencies are generated not only from the absence or presence of bidders participating in an auction, but also from the whims and capriciousness of those bidders that do participate. This section addresses bidder behaviour and addresses those occasions where a coin sells below its current accepted market value.

The efficient market hypothesis states that in an efficient market, asset prices always reflect their intrinsic value. This would mean that an asset or security would always have a price reflecting its past performance and current market information. This hypothesis has three forms: weak, semi-strong and strong. The weak form describes an efficient market as one which reflects all publicly available historical information about an asset or security including its past performance and returns. Semi-strong describes an efficient market as reflecting both historical and current publicly available information, and the strong form states that an efficient market will reflect all current and historical publicly available information alongside non-public information.

Using the semi-strong form of the hypothesis, the numismatic market can be considered efficient. The historical performance of coins is publicly available, and in a sense so is their current performance - although unlike stocks, 'current' info is rarely current and represents only the most recent auction results. According to the efficient market hypothesis, in an efficient market if one investor is successful then every investor is successful. This is a clearly flawed model, and means outperforming markets would be impossible. Without inefficiencies there would be no scope for a numismatic investor to profit in any manner beyond a buy and hold approach. This is clearly untrue, and so despite the wealth of information available about historical and present coin values, in practice the numismatic market is highly inefficient and is prone to considerable human error and irrationality. Numismatic markets have their major inefficiencies in their market reach, the behavioural economics of bidders and both the presence and fear of 'irrational exuberance'.

The most common cause of inefficiency within the numismatic market is the tendency for auctions to have 'incomplete' audiences. Unlike the loss of a prominent collector or when a market is in a decline, this inefficiency refers to those occasions when some collectors and dealers are not in attendance who would have otherwise bid on a coin. Their absence can be said to be causing a coin to sell for a sum below its potential maximum market value. Some older collectors refuse to use the internet and buy solely from those catalogues shipped to their door, but even with internet resources, there are simply too many auctions for every collector to monitor at once. Incomplete audiences are most common when coins are sold outside of their domestic market; as such, one of the most practiced methods for dealers to generate profit is to arbitrage by buying in one market and selling in another. Despite its failure to introduce total efficiency to the market, the internet has undoubtedly decreased inefficiency considerably and does make for a more transparent global marketplace.

Even if a coin has its full audience of potential buyers in attendance, this will not equal total efficiency. Within any market, behavioural economics – that is, the balance of emotional to rational decision-making – will dictate how its participants react, and this is certainly true within numismatics. Due to the emotional aspect of coin collecting and the fact that various personal and financial motivations come into play, buyers are more prone to react irrationally in auction situations than in other financial markets. Once, while sitting in an auction room in Chicago, I watched a lot open for bidding: a British gold proof Five Pound coin of George V struck in 1911 and graded PR65. This coin had several bidders and, being in vogue, hammered at an impressive $26,000. Two lots later, a similar offering opened for bidding: a four-piece gold proof set of George V struck in 1911, including another PR65 Five Pounds alongside three other gold coins in similarly high grade. This lot hammered at $24,000: $2,000 less, even with extra coins in the group. Clearly a bidder had formed an individual attachment to that first Five Pounds, and was not interested in participating for the next lot. Sometimes, bidders will stay their hand on the spur of a moment and then regret their lack of participation shortly afterwards; other times, bidders will become frustrated at their lack of success and bid desperately just to ensure they win something. By bidding you change the outcome of a sale through either encouraging others to compete or instead decide to back off prematurely. Auctions suffer at the whim of human error.

	Auction 3075	Lot 32252 › World Coins › Great Britain Great Britain: George V gold Proof 5 Pounds 1911 PR65 PCGS,... Bid Source: Internet	SERVICE: PCGS	GRADE: PR65	Auction Archives Sold For: $31,200.00
		AUCTION ENDED Aug 15, 2019		Make Offer to Owner $40,560 or more

	Auction 3075	Lot 32254 › World Coins › Great Britain Great Britain: George V 4-Piece Certified gold Proof Set 1911 PCGS,... (Total: 4 coins) Bid Source: HA.com/Live STUNNING HIGH-GRADE GOLD PROOF SET	SERVICE: PCGS	GRADE: N/A	Auction Archives Sold For: $28,800.00
		AUCTION ENDED Aug 15, 2019		Make Offer to Owner $40,000 or more

Market inefficiencies can keep prices down or push prices up – but an additional layer of disruption is provided not just by these artificial peaks or troughs, but also by the market's fear of falling foul of these effects. The quotation at the start of this section is from an 1847 British Numismatic Journal covering the sale of Colonel Durrant's coin collection. The market was far less transparent or standardised at this time, and intriguingly, to prevent artificially inflating the market these Victorian numismatists decided to not include prices realised as they considered them "utterly impossible" to attain in normal circumstances. In some ways, this echoed the 1996 speech that then-Federal Reserve Board Chairman Alan Greenspan gave to the American Enterprise Institute during the dot-com bubble of the 1990s. Greenspan famously asked "*How do we know when irrational exuberance has unduly escalated asset values?*", interpreted as a warning that the stock market was becoming overvalued.

Collectors and investors will spend large sums on coins but as aforementioned, there needs to be some perception that they are investing, that they are only paying a percentage over intrinsic values. At its heart the numismatic market is unscientific and inexact and its prices completely arbitrary, but a collector will know when they have paid significantly above the odds for a coin. Sometimes the quick climb of a coin's price is representative of a market upswing, and other times it is a bubble soon doomed to burst. What can cause the largest inefficiencies in numismatic markets are fears that it is the latter and not the former, a fear which causes would-be bidders to stay their hands.

Just as on motorways one slow moving car can trick the entire system into triggering a traffic jam which need never have happened, the same is true of numismatic auctions. The memories of the 1989 crash and the knowledge that markets can swiftly and artificially inflate prices persists, and this may cause bidders irrational trepidation and prevent them from bidding. The slow trickle of data points (eg numismatic auctions) means one erroneous result can cause months of fearful anticipation of a dip in the market, even without any actual drop in collector demand.

Case Study – 'Una and the Lion' Five Pounds prices, 2018-2021

Great Britain, 'Una and the Lion' Five Pounds, 1839, graded PF61+ Ultra Cameo by NGC, sold for $204,000 in August 2018.

Having increased in popularity every year for around 15 years, the market for 'Una and the Lion' Five Pound coins (often referred to as merely 'Unas') seemed to have peaked in April 2018 with the sale of a PR62 Ultra Cameo example for nearly $300,000 hammer in a Japanese auction. This was an exceptional result, and one which had never been achieved for an example in such a grade. Collectors did not know whether to rush to consign their own examples or watch and wait to see how the market would continue onwards.

Four months later, I accepted a consignment of another Una graded as PF61+ UCam. This example sold for $204,000 in August 2018, and one month after that a PF62 UCam in a UK auction hammered for just $150,000. In five months, the hammer price had halved: one sub-par result skewed bidder confidence and led to a fear that the inflated bubble had burst.

One year later, a Proof Details (Repaired) Una sold for $132,000 in an August 2019 sale in the US, and then in January 2020, a PR61 UCam Una sold for $300,000 and a PR64 UCam realised an incredible $690,000. Four months later in the midst of the Covid-19 crisis, a PR65 example realised $930,000, and in October 2020 the then-highest graded example – PF66 UCam - achieved $1,148,000 at a sale in Monaco. Finally, in August 2021, the single highest certified piece graded PF66 'star' UCam by NGC sold in the US for a record-breaking $1.44m.

The collector base for Unas had never actually changed or weakened, but many had paused to draw breath and refrained from bidding to see how prices would change. Whoever bought those PR61+ and PR62 examples in 2018 could feasibly have made $100k+ apiece within the space of a year – and potentially free from capital gains tax.

Since the beginning of the Covid-19 pandemic and the market boom that has followed, the process of commoditisation within numismatics has rapidly accelerated. Now, many rarities are being offered and reoffered at auction with third-party grades; this is leading to much smaller variations in sale prices as the market gains insight into the going rate for given coin types in given grades. This has allowed the inefficiency of the numismatic market to show itself in a new way – irrational exuberance where uncertified or 'fresh' coins are concerned. Fresh coins entering the market – those from old collections that have been unavailable for many years - are now being seen in a similar light to initial public offerings of previously private companies, where competition is fierce and the market decides their value. This is diagnostic of an inefficient market, as there is no data to support these new strong prices. However, collectors will still bid for these coins with the perception that, no matter what they pay, they are still getting a good deal as no market precedent has been set.

Inefficiencies are an inevitable part of any financial or asset market, but can be as much of a blessing as they are a curse. No auction will ever have its full attendance, each bidder will have their own allegiances and irrationalities, waves of fear and doubt and excitement will sweep the market on a regular basis, but it is possible to learn to surf these waves to generate substantial profits. Through familiarising oneself with these inefficiencies one can also learn to exploit them, and without their presence the market would be impossible for the average investor to actively participate in.

3. Vogues and Crashes

What goes up, must come down. That is the law of gravity. But imagine if instead of this certainty, the law was as it is for financial markets: "what goes up, *might* come down". Everyone would be perpetually staring straight upwards at all of the floating objects fearful that any of them might suddenly plummet, and very few would have the confidence to walk beneath them.

The numismatic market, like any market, sees particular coins or markets undergo rapid price increases or 'vogues', which can help make all those within those markets reasonably wealthy reasonably quickly. Unfortunately, vogues often correspond with crashes, sudden drops in individual or wider market prices. Both vogues and crashes can be small scale and large scale, but their speed, severity and fallout are contingent more on market irrationality than actual changes to coin values or their collector bases. Vogues come from market excitement, and crashes from market fears. Market response can sometimes be impossible to predict, but the numismatic investor should try to remain vigilant and to learn to recognise the difference between organic price growth and unsustainable acceleration.

Small scale vogues refer to a period of heightened interest in a particular coin type or types within a given market. This is the case for many British Five Guinea and Five Pound coins which have begun to attract strong international attention, raising their prices somewhat disproportionately to their rarity within the series. These particular trends are distinguished from wider vogues by only applying to specific coin types whilst the rest of that market remains stable and with slower price growth. The causes can vary, but price growth will typically be either from increased competition within an existing collector base or an outside expansion of the collector base (ie international investors and collectors).

These small scale vogues are not necessarily short term vogues, however. Indeed in some cases, repeatedly high results at auction set such a strong value precedent that the value of that type has been raised forever – the 'going rate' has been permanently altered. Generally, this only occurs over longer periods of time (eg 10-15 years). The gradual increase in price for British 'fivers' started roughly 15 years ago, and has increased year on year since. Accordingly, it is far less likely that this vogue will suddenly collapse as collector interest has been allowed to grow and develop over a reasonably long period and, in turn, international buyers have shown no decline in interest.

Large scale vogues are far more unusual, and far more dangerous. These refer to periods of significantly heightened market activity, where prices for an entire section of the market rapidly increase; for example, all coins for a given country might begin to rise in price over a short space of time. For the most part, this is just not how people collect. Numismatic collector bases do not simply double, and quickly growing prices across the board will mean one of two things: either two collectors are competing at auction for all available material (leading to an ultra-thin market), or all collectors/investors are paying over the odds for some reason – generally due to the introduction of a new standard. It was the introduction of TPG that caused the acceleration in buying activity in the US market in the lead up to the 1989 crash; suddenly, collectors and investors were able to appreciate previously innocuous coins for their numerical grade and prices rose accordingly.

A recent exception to this rule manifested itself during the first Covid-19 lockdown, in which prices did begin to see rapid growth across almost all numismatic market sectors, staying proportionally greater for famous rarities or top-graded pieces. Collectors suddenly had limited outlets for their capital, the stock market had tanked, and the numismatic market saw exceptional difficulties due to cancelled conventions and delayed postal services. As such, coin prices immediately jumped due to increased demand for tangible assets coupled with constrained supply. At the time of writing, these increased prices remain stable, but only time will tell whether these represent new value levels or are doomed to drop.

Within any market, when prices start to climb exponentially investors become nervous that there will be a peak or a bubble due to burst. In the numismatic market this effect shows itself at auctions. When coins are offered publicly, all eyes are on their prices realised as these help to ascertain the current health of the market. If a dealer or online seller has listed a coin for a particular price and it is not purchased, the perception is not that it has failed to sell, but simply that it has not sold yet. However, when a coin sells cheaply or does not sell at all at auction, it sends a message to buyers that the market is not healthy.

The numismatic market has a slow heartbeat, and the time gaps between auctions gives ample opportunity for speculation and concern and can cause numerous artificial slowdowns. Numismatics is an inefficient market based on the whims of collectors and so in actual fact, auction results rarely give a true, accurate perspective on the market's health. As such, just a small drop in value for a coin in vogue can cause collectors to close their purse strings completely until they have had time to observe the market.

This market trepidation can easily cause market hiccoughs for small scale vogues – despite collector demand not actually dropping. When a coin has been increasing in value for years on end, the market is constantly waiting for prices to plateau or start to drop. As the 'Una bubble' of 2018 shows, even a coin with well-established international popularity is not invulnerable to this effect, and if there is even a slight perception of prices falling then bidders may stay their hands to watch and wait. Rather than a 'crash', these pauses represent more a form of artificial market interruption, and if taken advantage of can generate substantial returns.

Small scale crashes are not always artificial, however, and are particularly prevalent for those coins at the upper reaches of the market where the absence of one bidder can dramatically increase prices. Within the wider financial market, when the share price for a company rises too high, that company may introduce a stock split; this increases the number of available shares whilst decreasing prices proportionally. This allows smaller investors to participate in the market for shares that have otherwise reached an unwieldy value. Within real estate, should a property in a coveted area be too large to realistically attract buyers at market value, it can be split into apartments; once again, this splits up the total value of the asset among more buyers, thus decreasing risk.

Coins have no such options open to them. As a coin's price increases there is no measure to divide its value amongst several collectors, which heightens risk and the possibility of a steep drop in value. In 2018, an example of the exceedingly rare and popular US 1804 Dollar graded PR62 was offered at auction. In 2008, that exact coin had sold for $3.74 million, then once again in 2013 for almost $3.9 million – and then in 2018 it realised just $2.64 million, more than a million-dollar drop within five years. US coins are seen as essentially fully commoditised and so this was a slap in the face of the market; however, it had no bearing on prices realised for the wider US market, simply for this one coin. Unfortunately as there are no 'price ceilings' for coins, no maximum amount they can rise to before dropping, the collector is exposed to risk at this level of the market.

What is far more devastating is a wider market crash on a large scale. When a small scale crash occurs, a handful of collectors may see somewhat lacklustre prices realised for their coins and the original seller will incur a loss. On the other hand, a large scale crash will damage not only the profits of every market participant but also cause widespread loss of confidence in the industry as a whole. The crash of 1989 is the most famous example and the market took over five years and a major technological innovation to recover. Fortunately, crashes such as these are extremely rare as the market does not generally let an entire coin series overinflate in value, and a collapse of this level is unlikely to occur again.

Case Study – South African Numismatic Market

The South African market is a US-type market and has a reasonably strong collector base with several high-value coins. Accordingly, prices for South African coins are on average higher than in many other countries and certainly more than any other African numismatic material. But despite its apparent strength, this market is still on the recovery from a recent crash that occurred between around 2011 and 2013.

In the late 2000s TPG began to be widely used in South Africa and, just as occurred in 1989, collectors began to focus entirely on numerical grades. Prices climbed correspondingly and a bubble formed. The market reached its peak in 2010-2011 and then just as suddenly dropped off; this is demonstrated by price change for a particular South African rarity, the 1874 'Burgers' Pond. An example of this popular type graded MS66 sold in October 2011 for $178,000 hammer, but less than three years later in June 2014, an example of that same coin graded MS67, the finest known, realised a lesser price of $130,000.

South Africa, 'Burgers' Pond, 1874, MS67 NGC

Prices had climbed prohibitively high and simply became too much for most collectors to pay. Once the wealthiest collectors had their collections complete, they stopped participating in the market and all other prices dropped back to their pre-TPG levels or lower. Many South African collectors who bought at the height of the market are now left with collections worth 50-70 per cent of what they originally paid; many will simply not accept this loss and so much high-value South African numismatic material goes unoffered or unsold. Interestingly, South African Sovereigns represent an exception and have retained the majority of their bubble prices due to the comparatively strong international collector base for this type.

Finally, the numismatic market is slim and unregulated, and the actions of one or two unscrupulous individuals can have catastrophic effects on the trade. Everyone with an ear to the financial markets will have heard of Bernie Madoff. This former non-executive director of the NASDAQ stock market aimed to cheat investors through a massive Ponzi scheme which ran from the mid-1980s up until the crash of 2008; he is now serving a federal prison sentence in the US.

The Australian numismatic market's answer to Madoff is Robert Jackman, former managing director of the now-collapsed Rare Coin Company (RCC) operating out of Perth and Sydney. Jackman and his wife Barbara began RCC in 1982 with the aim to store and sell rare coins and banknotes on behalf of investors, and the company steadily grew from an annual turnover of $600,000 in 1997 to $44.3 million in 2010. However, supposedly due to the financial crisis of 2008, between September 2011 and July 2013 136 investors complained that they did not receive their funds. It transpired that Jackman had claimed that investors' coins had not been sold, but in truth they had been disposed of and the money re-injected into RCC. Additionally, reports came in that the same coins had been double and triple sold to multiple investors at once. By 2013 liquidators had been appointed and the scheme unravelled, and Jackman, like Madoff, is currently serving a prison sentence for 36 counts of theft. The Australian numismatic market is yet to recover from the shockwaves of RCC, demonstrating how it is possible for a crash to originate from just one individual's actions.

Every market exhibits swift peaks and troughs. This is a fact of financial markets, and the coin trade is no exception. The shrewd numismatic investor can learn to anticipate these vogues and crashes and protect themselves accordingly – or even use them to further their profits. By diversifying across countries and types in what you buy, you will be able to weather any market-specific crashes and potentially benefit from the formation of new vogues.

It is important to note that unlike most conventional securities markets, presuming you have bought through trustworthy channels the value of your rare coins will never truly drop to zero. Unlike the 1989 collapse, the accessibility of auction records puts out a safety net protecting the majority of your capital. The slow heartbeat of the numismatic market means that investors and collectors are incapable of 'rushing for the exits' unlike any other stock or share market, and prices can never plummet quite so severely. On the worst of days your $3.8 million coin might sell for $2.6 million, but you will not have lost everything. As long as you practice discipline and are not swept up with the excitement and fear that causes dramatic rises and falls in price, you stand a better chance than most in generating a profit.

4. Find and Forgeries

For any financial asset or security to command reliable value, the quantity of available units must be known to the market. Consequently two of the main factors allowing coins to enjoy their status as investments are their finite supply and their often well-documented mintage figures. This control of numbers allows for a confidence-filled purchase, as the market cannot suddenly be flooded by new specimens that lower the value per unit. There are, however, two main factors that can create a slump in a coin's market price without a change to the size of the collector base – an influx of genuine examples entering the market (Finds), or an influx of fake examples (Forgeries). New finds alter the balance of supply and demand, while forgeries extinguish collector demand altogether.

The invention of the metal detector in the 1920s by Gerhard Fischer (essentially by accident; his radio navigation system kept being distorted by metal ore-bearing rocks) absolutely revolutionised numismatics. Once the equipment began to be widely used, coins previously represented by only a handful of examples became relatively abundant as more and more specimens were found by amateur archaeologists. In some regards these finds boosted the market as pieces became more accessible to collectors, but equally they eroded the value per specimen as scarcity decreased. As such, the price of those types 'vulnerable' to this effect remain relatively low in contrast to those of the last two centuries with known mintages, such as hammered pennies and ancient coins. The price of many early British types (for example, pennies of Offa, 756-796 AD) have fallen considerably in the last two decades as more and more pieces are dug up and enter the market. Collector interest remains strong for these earlier pieces, but as the supply has increased, collector demand has been met and, in turn, prices have dropped.

On the other hand, 'hoards' (large quantities of coins in one assemblage) can have a contrasting effect on the numismatic market. The general public is ever-hungry for news of treasure being dug up, of ancient riches discovered by Joe Bloggs of Hertfordshire. As such, the press coverage of these finds can actually lead to higher prices being paid as more collectors enter the sphere. A hoard of 99 Saxon pennies was recently discovered in Suffolk which sold at auction for a total of £90,000 – three times its pre-sale estimate. The desire to own a slice of this treasure, and to own a coin with unbeatable provenance, bolsters their market value. Even BBC 4's television show "Detectorists" has generated interest in coins and produced higher numbers of metal detectorists allured by its enticing scenes of the English countryside.

The vulnerability of early coin types to potential new finds or hoards must be taken into consideration when making a purchase, as these are one of the few areas of numismatics where new supply can enter the market. Fortunately, only around one in every 100 metal detecting-found coins are of premium collector quality so supply will only increase gradually, and prices for the finest specimens will remain steady.

Forgeries, on the other hand, are far more toxic to numismatics than newly-discovered authentic specimens. While new finds only decrease the value of individual coins by dividing collector capital amongst a greater number of examples, forgeries dissuade buyers from participating in the market altogether. The former still contributes to the market, but the latter destroys it. Take, for example, the British 'Wreath' Crown of George V struck in 1934. This coin had a mintage of 932 pieces and is an exceptionally highly collected denomination – yet its price has dropped dramatically in recent years due to numerous Chinese copies entering the market, a quantity vastly exceeding its original scant mintage. The element of doubt introduced by these convincing copies entirely puts off potential buyers. Prices are now on the rise again, but only for those specimens in PCGS or NGC holders. This once again highlights the essential role played by TPG in the industry: salvaging the shattered confidence of collector-investors, providing a financially stable guaranty for otherwise spurious coins.

Authentic example of the George V 'Wreath' Crown 1934

Unfortunately, those types most commonly entering the market by way of metal detectorists also represent some of the easiest types to fake – hammered coins. Saxon pennies have seen a particularly large number of imitations enter the market in the last few years, leading to many high-profile coins being withdrawn from auction at the last minute and prices either exhibiting stalled growth or a downward trend. As hammered coins are often crude, used multiple die varieties and are poorly documented, it is fairly simple for forgers to produce fantasy issues and unleash them upon the unsuspecting market with no mint figures or comparable specimens to contradict them. After all, these early coins encountered significant counterfeiting problems even when still circulating. Their vulnerability is in stark contrast to the more recent coin emissions of the past two or three centuries, which are generally substantiated through Mint records and produced to very high quality with inbuilt anti-counterfeiting elements.

This specific targeting of hammered coins by counterfeiters means that a vital question must come into play when a coin previously unknown to collectors is discovered – is it a find or a forgery? Arguably the most famous example to undergo this scrutiny in recent years was the Coenwulf 'Mancus' discovered in Bedfordshire in 2001 and bought by the British Museum for $350,000.

England, Coenwulf, gold Mancus, 796-821

The prevailing industry-held opinion is that this coin is authentic; its style, dies and overall appearance seem in line with contemporary pieces. But being a unique, previously unknown type it has encountered significant doubts from collectors since its discovery to the present day. Having reliable and authenticated examples to which you can compare a newly-discovered coin is extremely important to the market when calculating what to pay.

Whereas market fluctuations and behavioural economics represent symptoms of an inefficient market, the reaction of collectors to new finds and forgeries is perfectly logical. If new authentic supply satisfies the majority of demand, prices will fall. If, however, a coin becomes widely counterfeited then collectors may find the risk too great for them to decide to purchase an example also leading to a drop in prices. Happily, TPG has largely assisted in reinstating bidder confidence and the majority of high-profile coin finds do, if anything, benefit the market.

5. Risk and Safety Nets

Risk in finance is, simply, the chance of losing money on an investment. It exists for every transaction no matter how large or small, but will vary considerably depending on how you choose to invest. The numismatic market has numerous un-systemic risks, those particular to the exchange of coins; these financial threats comes from the inefficiency of the market, the limited numbers of high-value buyers, the arbitrary nature of prices, possible influxes of finds and forgeries, market bubbles and more besides.

One must remain constantly aware of the possible shortfalls that await if you have bought unwisely or the market turns against you. However, there is one prevailing feature that protects coins - and coins particularly - from major losses of value: 'safety nets', the action of either investors or collectors swooping in to buy coins at their newly-reduced prices.

A summary of your risk exposure between buying and selling a coin is as follows: perhaps you bought a famous rarity for an unprecedented price, in which case there may be no other collector willing to pay the same as you. Perhaps you bought at a market peak, and the price has now dropped. Your coin may be a type which was previously one of three known but a hoard has just been found; alternatively, a thousand high-level forgeries may have entered the market. Or, finally, there may be fears that prices are dropping for your coin and so bidding activity is artificially subdued. Any of these factors would increase the chance of your sell price being close or even below your original buy price.

But, unlike a financial security, coins are not purchased solely to generate an income or to sell at a profit – they are bought for enjoyment. The true appeal of a coin is to collectors, and collectors will ultimately pay what they want. Despite discussions of 'intrinsic' value, coins do not share the vulnerability of securities in being solely money-making instruments.

Take, for example, a share in Apple. At the present price, one share costs $319, ten would cost $3,190. If I were to offer ten shares to passers-by on the street for $2,000, perhaps 10 per cent would recognise this as a bargain and accept (assuming they were willing to trust the strange stockbroker on the street). If I then offered these shares directly to active and knowledgeable investors, all of them would surely accept. However – what if the price suddenly dropped to $0 per share. Would anyone still buy my shares at $2,000, or any price for that matter? Certainly not.

Imagine instead you had a coin that had been trading at $319 before its market value suddenly plummeted. The coin suddenly loses its appeal as a financial asset, but those collectors who had not previously been able to afford an example will begin to participate, providing a form of safety net for value. You would only need two collectors to bid the price up and the value precedent is in the records; as such, the coin might still sell for

$200, 250 or even $300. These bidders would not be buying as a store of value, but simply as they want to own the coin. The actions of collectors such as these means that, particularly for mid-market examples, there is only a limited percentage that a coin's value can fall before it encounters a new tier of bidders.

By this same token, those buying and selling coins for investment will also be willing to pay a fair percentage of a coin's peak market value. Investors may see a coin's value dropping fast, but as collector interest was there before it may well be there again even if prices have reduced. As such, even in a worst-case scenario a coin's value is extremely unlikely to fall by more than 50 per cent between two auction appearances, especially if it was bought at a moderate market level. Dealers will provide a safety net and compete to buy it at a reduced price, meaning it will likely hammer somewhere between 60-80 per cent of its previous value.

In the course of holding any asset, investors run risks of losing their original investment should the market change or should their original venture be flawed in some way. The numismatic market does have its risks, its inherent inefficiencies and an ultimately unscientific approach to value. However, all in all the fact that its prices are based on supply and demand rather than an intrinsic perception of worth or income means that dealers and collectors are usually happy to speculate, and will provide safety nets limiting your potential losses.

6. Emerging Innovations

The fact that collectable coins can represent reliable stores of value is not a secret; indeed, this trend has been seen consistently over the last two decades and most collectors now expect at least some profit when they resell their coins. However, over the last 12 months, the traditionally established mind-set within numismatics has begun to shift at an alarming rate. As prices rise, the numismatic market continues to evolve to match demand and incorporate the increasingly prevalent investment mindset of its participants. Despite its unpopularity with more traditional collectors, TPG has aided the widespread commoditisation of numismatics through standardising grades and prices. Yet even this 'new-fangled' practice is being left behind in the dust by even more cutting-edge innovations within numismatics. The line between coins and more traditional asset classes has never been so blurred as it is currently. This section will briefly address some of the most radical moves recently seen in the numismatic and collectables markets, simply to allow the reader to 'watch this space' for further developments.

In June 2021, Sotheby's held their 'Three Treasures' auction consisting of just three lots: the two most valuable stamps in the world and the 1933 $20 double eagle. The 1933 double eagle sold to a private collector and ended up setting a new world-record price for any coin at nearly $19m. One of the two stamps – the unique 1856 British Guiana 1c magenta – also realised an immense sum, selling for $8.3m to the well-known philatelist company Stanley Gibbons. However, unlike the buyer of the 1933 double eagle, Stanley Gibbons announced immediately that they would be selling their stamp. Not to one collector - but instead to 100,000. The company has allowed collectors to participate in a fractional ownership scheme, in which shares in the stamp are offered at £100 each. The stamp will reportedly stay on display in their London office, while ownership is distributed globally amongst thousands of collectors.

For the best part of a year, this scheme was limited to this one stamp. But, with precedent set for shares of high-value collectables to be offered to collectors, it was only a matter of time before coins followed suit. In February 2022, it was announced that the shared ownership website ShowPiece.com would be assisting with offering shares in an Edward VIII pattern Penny of 1937.

Edward VIII pattern Penny, 1937, graded PF63+ RB by NGC.

This rare coin had been purchased in 2019 for an impressive £133,200 and had remained with the buyer for over two years. Now valued at £200k, the penny has been split into 4,000 shares costing £50 each, with buyers limited to owning 400 shares per person - ie ten percent. With prices at an all-time high for many coin types, it is unsurprising that this practice has now reared its head within numismatics. It seems likely that shares in coins such as the 'Una and the Lion' Five Pounds will soon be released to collectors, while the coins themselves stay locked in bank vaults and the concept of private ownership of such items becomes merely a distant memory.

In later 2021, the TPG company PCGS announced in October that they had certified an unusual item - a 'Casascius' gold 1,000 Bitcoin piece. Although this 'Gold Cas' is simply one ounce of gold struck in 2012 with the Bitcoin symbol, it bears a hologram that, when removed, will reveal a code that can be used to access a digital wallet containing 1,000 BTC. As such, at the time of writing this is by far the most valuable numismatic item ever certified with a market value of $56m, three times that of the 1933 double eagle. Some may claim that this coin represents little more than a key that unlocks a fortune, and that its PCGS grade – PR70 Deep Cameo – is irrelevant to its price tag. However, no matter what proportion of its market value is derived from its BTC component, its numismatic value or its third-party grade, this Gold Cas still represents the first ever fusing of the cryptocurrency and numismatic markets.

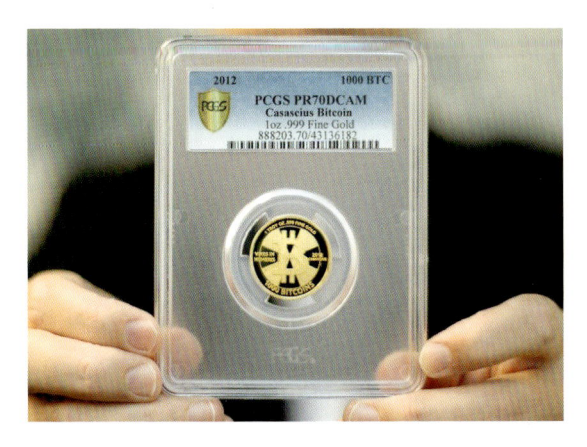

The 1,000 Bitcoin "Gold Cas" held by Ian Russell, president of GreatCollections.

And in the most recent development, January 2022 saw the London auctioneer Spink & Son offer a Henry III gold 20 Pence discovered by a metal detectorist in autumn 2021. This extremely rare medieval coin, one of only a handful known, sold for a world record price of £648,000. However, in an unexpected move, Spink also auctioned the digital property rights to the coin in the form of a non-fungible token (NFT).

Henry III gold 20 Pence, struck in 1257.

NFTs are currently sweeping through many other collectibles and art markets. In March 2021, the auctioneer Christie's sold their first major digital artwork - a collage of photos called 'Everydays: The First 5,000 Days' - for an unbelievable $70m using a NFT that supposedly confirmed authenticity and exclusivity, while protecting ownership and copyright. Not limited to merely art, in more recent news an NFT is facilitating the sale of the original files of the World Wide Web at auction, consigned by its inventor Sir Tim Berners-Lee.

The January 2022 auction is the first time a numismatic NFT has been offered. Despite widespread criticism at the decision, the NFT found a buyer at an impressive £15k, perhaps representing more dramatic changes ahead for the numismatic market. Sales such as this – and the fractional ownership schemes being offered by Stanley Gibbons and ShowPiece.com - are indicative of a major change within the collectables world: the thrill of ownership is being replaced by the prestige of ownership.. Instead of collecting for the joy of collecting itself, collectors now focus instead on the bragging rights they can claim from holding title to a rarity, while never physically taking possession nor for a moment losing sight of their intention to resell. It is clear that the changes apparent within the numismatic market have not begun to plateau. As the perception of coins as investments becomes more normalised, it becomes less and less of a reach to commoditise them further through similar innovations as seen in the examples provided. Fractional ownership, NFTs and cryptocurrency are a growing force within many collectables categories alongside coins, and despite resistance from traditional collectors, these new approaches may represent the future of the market as a whole. However, due to the novel and largely untested nature of these developments, it is wise to remember that the cutting edge of the market brings with it the greatest amount of risk.

Chapter 2.4.
Costs, Fees and Taxation

So you have arrived safely back in port. You have weathered the dynamics of the numismatic market and have successfully sold your coins. But have you made a substantial return on your initial investment?

Imagine you bid $1,000 for a coin at auction because you know of a comparable example being sold by a dealer for $1,100. You gleefully go to pay at the auction house, and are aghast when buyer's premium and VAT brings your charge to $1,360. Not to be discouraged, you re-consign it to auction right there and then at 10 per cent commission, but this time it sells for $900. After fees, you are left staring at the $810 in your bank account and wondering where your $550 disappeared to.

When evaluating the advantages and disadvantages of an asset class, the complexity of its purchase and resale procedure can be an important deciding factor as can the presence of numerous unwelcome costs and fees. In order to ensure you remain solvent while conducting numismatic transactions, you will need to factor in the initial charges involved with purchasing a coin as well as the fees you incur when you come to resell. This chapter briefly addresses the return you can expect weighed against the costs and fees associated with numismatic trading, as well as some beneficial tax implications provided by certain coins.

1. Capital Return

A central consideration of numismatic investments is how much return you can expect to make, and in what form it will arrive. Without this knowledge, you can be encouraged to make poor purchasing decisions. A rather unfortunate client once approached me with cautious optimism having bought a set of privately produced gold proof coins for somewhere in the region of £5,000. These were brand new unofficial coins which were being marketed exclusively at investors; they were still on sale, and yet he took them to an auction house in the expectation of immediately turning around and selling them for multiples of his original sum because he had 'bought early'.

It may seem obvious that successful coin trading should net larger sums than you initially ventured, but capital return arrives in different forms for different assets. Shares produce dividends and can be sold on after purchase, real estate generates rent but requires costly upkeep and repair, silver bullion sees only minor price fluctuations and incurs capital gains etc. An understanding of the numismatic market will assist you in buying well with the greatest chance of a profit – but what will that profit look like?

Contrary to what my client thought about his brand-new coin set, coins are not like shares; typically buying them when they are new and waiting for their price to double, triple, quadruple, is not a practical strategy[19]. If you buy well, you will achieve a profit when you resell, but this profit can vary hugely. A small minority of coins will dramatically increase in value within a relatively short period of time, but most will rise by a fairly steady percentage of their starting value. For the purpose of consistency and managed expectations, it is always safer to assume that this percentage will be small. Longer term investments will net larger returns, but short-term profits will usually have to be generated through a volume>margin model and by maintaining a high turnover. As this active investing approach is far more hands-on it is tempting to just buy, sit back and let the market do the work.

Unfortunately it may not be as simple as this. Unlike real estate or shares, coins do not generate any income whatsoever. Real estate investors can live on their tenants' rent and shareholders can live on their dividends but numismatists have no such advantage. If you have bought a superb coin for $50,000 and believe that it will be worth $100,000 in three years, you will have made a great purchase but you may have just tied all of your savings into one asset (that now needs insuring). Despite your inevitable gains, you will only net a return on your coin when you have successfully sold it – leading to the cash flow problems associated with high-level numismatic trading.

---

[19] Some modern coins are an exception to this rule when they are produced by an official national mint. My client's error was due to his buying an off-brand privately produced set.

Once you are familiar with the risk and liquidity issues coins carry, you can decide what your major motivations are for participating in the numismatic market. Some investors choose a passive approach and use alternative assets specifically to provide a long-term, stable form of capital as opposed to an appreciating yet volatile form. Through their steady and regular price growth, many coins do provide this stability while also gradually maturing in value. If, however, an investor would like to be active but try a relatively low-risk and low return approach, coins will also offer that option. If an investor would like to gamble even more and try for a high-risk high-return investment, coins offer that route also. It is always an equation of risk and cash flow to potential return, and if you are otherwise solvent and able to potentially lock away a lump of capital in coins for an indeterminate amount of time then you are in good stead to participate in the numismatic market.

> *It is essential to keep in mind the 'maths of the investment'. Capital return is a very achievable goal when buying and selling coins, but the percentage return must be worth the time and effort you put into your investment. You must remain aware of the form in which this capital will arrive and be able to weather the associated issues with buying and storing coins. And, most importantly, every transaction within the numismatic market will have some form of commission or mark-up; you must remain aware of these various fees and taxes in order to ensure your dealings are profitable.*

2. Costs and Charges

The 'buy side' of numismatics, ie the purchasing of coins, brings with it several associated costs. In some instances, these extra charges can drastically alter your purchase price and thus potentially cut into your profits. Some of these costs are invisible, represented by the margin a dealer or collector adds to their sale price to ensure a worthwhile return. As it is impossible to anticipate quite what this margin will be, this section will only cover those set percentage fees associated with buying coins. In every case, these costs and charges must be factored in to the sum you choose to bid in order to ensure ongoing solvency.

I. Buyer's Premium

An auction-specific cost involved with purchasing coins is called the 'Buyer's Premium' (BP). This is a percentage added to the sale or 'hammer' price for a coin sold at auction alongside whatever the auction house is charging the seller themselves. Over the last few decades the average BP percentage has been creeping slowly up; at time of writing, it is typically 20%. Accordingly, a collector who buys a coin with a +20% BP for $1,000 will actually pay $1,200 plus additional fees. Anything less than this percentage is favourable, and anything greater unappealing. Sometimes when reviewing auction records or reports you will see prices described as 'hammer', in which case they have omitted the BP, or 'all-in', which generally means BP inclusive. It is beneficial to keep aware of this difference to ensure your research is accurate.

The BP can catch new bidders out as an unexpected charge. It would be fair to ask why anyone buys coins at auctions at all with such a lofty fee to pay; however, despite its being the largest cost by far to the numismatic buyer, for the most part the BP is factored into the sale price. When bidding it is essential to not get swept up into an irrational and competitive mind-set, and to remember that whatever sum you are putting forward will incur BP on top.

II. VAT

VAT (Value-Added Tax) is an extremely widespread levy and represents essentially a form of sales tax charged on the price of goods or services. The majority of the developed world employs some form of VAT except for the US, which has its own specific sales tax. VAT is applicable to the total purchase price of a coin including its BP and is typically in the region of 5 per cent; a coin bought for a hammer price of $1,000 will accordingly have a final purchase price of $1,260.

A notable advantage of gold bullion is that it carries no VAT charge, an element limited to gold; silver or platinum will incur a VAT charge, potentially hurting profits. The VAT-exempt status of gold applies also to coins considered 'investment gold', generally any of those less than 200 years old. As many of the world's most valuable coins have been struck in this recent period, it is extremely beneficial to the investor to be able to avoid this 5 per cent tax.

An additional benefit in place for UK collectors and investors is that legal tender currency is not subject to VAT in Britain, no matter from what metal it is produced. As such, legal tender coin types are some of the most enticing prospects for British numismatic investors as their potential market is extremely strong and their tax exemptions desirable.

III. Sales Tax

Sales tax will come into effect for coin purchases made in the US and is its own equivalent of VAT. This tax varies from state to state and from year to year; a handful of states (Oregon, Montana, New Hampshire, Delaware and Alaska) have no sales tax whatsoever, and for the remainder it can be anywhere from 5 to 8 per cent. This tax is applicable to the total purchase price for your coin, BP inclusive. As such, the final price for a coin bought in a state with a 6 per cent sales tax for $1,000 hammer will be $1,272.

Sales tax is destination-based, and you will incur the sales tax of the state where you take delivery of a coin; accordingly, auctions held in higher taxed states such as New York often have very few bidders collecting their purchases in person and prefer to have them shipped to states or countries with a lower sales tax.

IV. Importation Duties

For the majority of purchases, importation duties will not apply. However, some auction houses may occasionally offer a collection of coins based outside of the country in which it is being sold. In these instances, the auctioneer will pass any importation duties on to the buyer – usually this cost is around 5 per cent. Typically such charges are clearly marked, and can be factored into your purchase price alongside any other charges.

V. Shipping

Shipping and handling fees are always unwelcome as they are perceived as being entirely outside of a coin's intrinsic value; whereas taxes and charges are all part and parcel of a coin purchase, shipping fees are seen as directly hurting profit margins. Some buyers are able to circumvent this cost by collecting the coin in person, but in the present international and internet-focused market this is often either impractical or impossible.

If shipping is required, in most cases the charge will be minimal; coins are easily transportable and even for the most valuable pieces of $100,000+ shipping costs will rarely exceed $100-200. Unfortunately the percentages shift dramatically when assessing the costs of lower value coins. If you are buying a coin for $100 then your buyer's premium is $20, your VAT $5, but your shipping may be as much as $30 – a very unwelcome +30% charge. This effect is amplified in further-flung locations such as Australia and New Zealand; in these countries it is standard to pay as much to ship a coin to you as it was to purchase it in the first place.

It is essential to research potential shipping costs prior to competing in an international auction and to take these into consideration when choosing what to pay.

VI. Insurance

Alongside the charges involved with buying coins is a major ongoing cost in keeping them – that of insurance. One of the greatest advantages of coins as an asset, their portability, also makes them highly vulnerable to theft. Even if not easily portable, coins are still common targets; in 2017, thieves broke into a Berlin museum and managed to escape with a 24 carat gold Canadian coin weighing 100kg and worth $4.3 million by wheeling it away in a wheelbarrow. This coin is still unaccounted for, and was presumably melted down soon after its theft. Having a comprehensive insurance policy in place to protect your coins is not just wise, but absolutely vital. Accordingly, between buying and selling you can expect to run up charges for the protection of your coins.

Alongside insurance, coins should be kept in a secured home safe or a safe-deposit box in a bank (if you can bear to keep them apart from you), and these options will incur further costs. The potential losses from theft of uninsured coins are so great that it is always cost effective to spend on enhanced protection for your assets.

Insurance is such an integral component of numismatics that the majority of coin shows now have stands for insurers available to discuss various coverage policies. An advantage of TPG and price standardisation is that insurance values for your coins can be quite precisely estimated. As a side note, it is important to exercise caution when attending these coin shows; thieves operate and occasionally follow attendees out to their cars or residences. In every situation where one makes a public appearance at a coin show or discusses their collection in an open forum, due diligence must be practiced.

If you are buying a coin with the intention of a profitable resale, you must be aware of the costs and charges involved and keep vigilant with your equations. An auction I attended earlier this year had not only a 24% buyer's premium, but also 5% VAT and 5% import duty. Accordingly, £1,000 bid would equal £1,340 paid. On top of these costs will be whatever shipping charge was applied and ongoing insurance fees. Most of these charges will not appear in auction records, meaning that the value precedent would not be reflective of what you actually paid.

4. Taxes and Fees

After buying coins with their associated charges and holding onto them for a period of time - racking up insurance costs and storage fees - you will eventually decide to liquidate them and hopefully achieve a return on your investment. This 'sell' side of numismatics has its own associated fees which must be factored into any transaction; some of these fees occur before the sale, some at the moment of sale and some arrive in the form of taxes after the auction. By remaining aware and tracking these fees you will be able to ensure the 'maths of the investment' will work in your favour.

I. Certification Fees

Depending on their type and the market you are operating in, when you decide to sell your coins it may be wise to have them certified. The benefits of TPG to wider market appeal and consumer confidence are numerous, and some auction houses will actually require your coins to be certified before they will offer them for sale. Certification charges are generally paid by the consignor themselves but some auction houses do offer to pay these costs as an added incentive.

TPG fees vary and are calculated based on the declared value of the coin. For the most part, NGC and PCGS's fees are fairly similar. Certification costs are divided into various tiers split depending on whether your coin is US or world, gold or non-gold, modern or antique etc, but overall certification for US or world coins of value up to $3,000 has a fee ranging from around $16 to $35. Up to a coin value of $10,000 the fee will be $60 or $65, for coins up to $100,000 the fee is around $150-200, and anything over $100,000 has a fee of $300 plus 1% of 'fair market value'.

This latter fee may be rather worrying as this 1% could feasibly be several thousand dollars. However, for coins at this value level TPG is extremely beneficial and this fee will be worthwhile. It is also worthy of note that grading costs for coins are far cheaper than for other collectable categories; the premier certification service for collectable sports cards, PSA, charges $3,000 to certify cards worth between $50,000 and $100,000 – a minimum of 3% of value and 20 times the fee for a coin of comparable value.

For the most part, certification costs for coins are minimal compared to their benefit at auction and only represent a trivial fee. Nevertheless, if you are operating on a model of volume>margin or are selling gold coins close to their bullion value, even a $16 fee can hurt your profits considerably and so TPG costs must always be included in your investment calculations.

II. Auction Commission

If you are selling a coin through an auction as opposed to directly you will likely be charged commission by the auctioneer. Auction commission is typically in the region of 10-15 per cent for coins; any higher than this and you should probably find a different auction house. At 10 per cent commission, were you to sell a coin that realised a hammer price of $1,000 you would be due $900.

Depending on the value of your consignment and the number of coins within it, auction commission can be subject to negotiation. If you have a $1,000,000 consignment which consists of 1,000 coins, this will represent a huge amount of work cataloguing and photographing for the auction house and so the fee will remain a standard 10-15 percent. If your $1,000,000 consignment consists of three coins, your consignment will be extremely desirable and you will be in a good position to negotiate.

III. Buyer's Premium

Alongside auction commission, buyer's premium represents both a buy side and sell side cost. On the buy side you must pay an additional 20 per cent on top of the hammer price, and on the sell side bidders will pay less than they otherwise would in order to balance out the buyer's premium. Accordingly, if you sell at an auction commission of 10 per cent plus a 20 per cent buyer's premium, then you will lose approximately 30 per cent of your coin's actual value to the auction house. This may once again raise the question: why transact through auction houses at all considering the sums they extract?

Despite their charges, auction houses and their ability to let buyers compete with one another do generate some of the highest prices for coins. If these firms consistently generated a net loss for their consignors then they would have no benefit, nobody would use them and their prices would be impossible to justify. However, their continued existence is testament enough to the contribution they have to the numismatic market. Auction houses will work with you to achieve the highest price possible for your coin – after all, their payday is a percentage of your payday. Accordingly, they are on your side and will discuss reduced fees, advances and other benefits to ensure they have your business.

IV. Capital Gains Tax

Assuming that after the buy and sell side costs of trade you have netted a profit, the final consideration to make in your numismatic equation is how much this profit will be taxed. Capital Gains Tax (CGT) applies whenever you dispose of an asset for more than you initially paid and is a levy on this positive difference. In the UK, the percentage will vary based on your tax bracket but for higher earners CGT is 20% of the profit produced from selling an asset and 28% for residential property. In the US, CGT will be 0%, 15% or 20% depending on your income, and long- and short-term capital gains are taxed differently. If you have incurred any capital losses within the same tax year then these can be used to offset CGT. By familiarising yourself with your country's tax laws you can ensure you have paid the appropriate amount for your trading – and choose whether to proceed in the first place if you regard it as too steep.

There is currently one exception to CGT for UK investors that makes the numismatic market rather enticing indeed: legal tender coins incur no CGT whatsoever. This effect not only covers modern coins but also any Sovereigns, Two Pound or Five Pound coins struck after 1837, coins which already have relief from VAT. This would mean that every UK collector to have bought and sold an Una and the Lion Five Pounds would have avoided an additional 5 per cent of the purchase price and would be off the hook for a 20 per cent CGT tax when they come to resell. This happened to one of my clients a few years ago; he had bought an Una and the Lion Five Pounds in around 2001 for £20,000. He then sold this in 2018 for a hammer price of just under $300,000 (around £220,000). His capital gains were £200,000, but as the coin was considered legal tender, he avoided a £40,000 haircut on his profits.

The buying and selling of almost every asset and security involves a considerable number of associated costs and fees, and a successful venture will incur additional taxation. These are unavoidable truths and ones which need to be accepted and considered early on and their presence factored into the maths of the investment. For your numismatic investments to bear fruit, a realistic perception of the profits to be had balanced against the costs they incur is essential.

Chapter 2.5.
Coins in Context

The final questions to ask when considering a new investment are, of course, "Why this investment?" and "Why not another?" For the potential investor, numerous asset options are available, each with their own advantages and disadvantages. After gaining an understanding of the numismatic market, the research involved and the potential risks versus potential return, why would you choose to invest specifically in coins rather than in another, more traditional asset?

It behoves the investor to regularly weigh up the security and performance of their investments, and to ensure that they form a comprehensive portfolio. By evaluating the expected return against risk exposure, the investor can determine how much of their capital should be stored in each asset for maximum returns and minimum risk. Alongside the comparative performance of assets and securities, the extent to which their returns correlate should be noted; eg the rise in gold value when traditional securities markets dip. This way, investments can be hedged against one another to ensure the greatest chance of consistent returns and capital stability. This chapter will place coins in context within wider markets and compare their performance as a store of value against that of some more traditional tangible and financial assets.

The most successful investors diversify across industries and types of asset. Accordingly, the purpose of this discussion is not to imply numismatic investments completely outweigh any others and that you should abandon all of your investments in favour of coins. Rather, this discussion will attempt to emphasise the positives of coins in contrast to more traditional classes of asset alongside any correlations the two might have. Using this information, the investor can decide whether or not to add coins to their portfolio alongside their other investments.

1. Financial Markets

When asked for an example of a type of 'investment', the layman will most often give a stock, share or bond as their answer. All of these are financial instruments, which - alongside futures and derivatives - are types of securities that are traded on stock exchanges (organisations facilitating the trade of financial instruments). Stock exchanges are a form of financial market, a term referring to those markets aimed solely at the generation of capital, split into 'capital markets' for long-term finance and 'money markets' for short term finance. Rather than an asset class themselves, these financial markets are a resource for traders and investors to buy blocks of shares in companies, trade foreign currencies and cryptocurrency, exchange commodities and participate in a vast trade of financial instruments.

The financial markets are the behemoths of global finance, the powerhouses of economy that determine the health of markets worldwide. Due to the centralised physical and virtual locations of financial markets, overall impressions of global market strength can be gleaned from market indexes, groupings of share prices for representative companies. By their nature, financial markets provide the easiest means of building an investment portfolio and undoubtedly offer far greater returns than the majority of other investment means. They have the largest numbers of participants, the greatest liquidity, they cover every sector and commodity and are essentially the platform for global trade. Accordingly, why would investors choose to operate outside of this convenient central marketplace and buy off-road assets such as coins?

It is not a question of which particular route you choose but rather a question of how much you choose to limit yourself. Despite the numerous advantages and conveniences offered by financial markets, they are subject to extreme volatility and introduce forms of risk that coins do not suffer. Additionally, alternative assets provide a measure of capital security when global financial markets experience turmoil. As such it is wise to expand your portfolio beyond financial markets and evaluate the merits of alternative assets, of which coins are an excellent representative.

One of the major advantages of the financial markets, their interconnectivity, can also be one of their major downfalls. Should one industry or sector begin to fail, it can drag market after market down with it in a domino effect. Accordingly, if you choose to operate exclusively within the capital and money markets, you have put all of your eggs in one basket - no matter how diverse your securities portfolio. A key benefit of coins as assets is that they are nowhere near as reflective of the economy as more conventional securities. During a bear market (period of decline) on the wider stock exchange or periods of major political turmoil, those securities plugged into the global economy will all experience value losses whereas coins are actually considered safe havens for investors in these troubled times. Tangible, physical assets not linked to wider financial markets become far more appealing, and thus coin prices can rise (alongside bullion prices). Accordingly, the purchasing of coins and bullion alongside traditional securities represents an attractive form of hedging.

But perhaps most significantly, increases in coin values can also correlate with prosperous times in the financial markets. Due to their occupying a rather unique market niche - being seen as both a form of investment and as desirable collectables in their own right - in a favourable economic climate collectors will have more disposable income to spend on coins, meaning prices can rise. During periods of economic unrest and low interest rates, investors turn to coins for their function as stores of value; during periods of economic prosperity, collectors turn to coins to buy as luxury items. This dual appeal considerably strengthens coins as an asset and helps keep prices relatively stable and consistent.

This strong market position has helped coins measurably outperform the wider financial markets during recent economic instability. In the US between 2007-2008, subprime mortgage lending and excessive risk-taking by US banks triggered a global financial crisis. This shockwave volatilised Asian markets, spurred a banking crisis in Europe and ultimately caused a global economic downturn referred to as the Great Recession. Were it not for colossal bail-outs of financial institutions there was a real possibility of a collapse of the world financial system during this period. As values dropped across the entirety of the financial markets, coin prices stayed steady; hardly a blip was exhibited in most numismatic markets as investors turned to this isolated asset class for safety. This effect was not uniform within numismatics, however: for lower value coins of below $1,000, demand sharply dropped off. This was due to coins in this value range owing the majority of their demand to lower-income collectors who were unable to justify their unnecessary spending in troubled times. Prices remained stable for higher value coins that were considered to be investments.

In a more recent example, during the Great Lockdown of 2020 caused by the global coronavirus pandemic, markets saw turmoil comparable to that of the Great Recession. The New York Stock Exchange had to close its trading floor for two months and the economies of almost every country suffered considerably from the cessation of face-to-face interaction. Between January and May 2020 two major Western indexes, the FTSE 100 and Dow Jones both lost 20 per cent of their value whilst Asian markets shrunk in kind. And, once again, coin prices flourished. An Una and the Lion Five Pounds sold in Japan for $930,000, a US 1804 Dollar sold in California for $1.8 million and across the board coin prices either stayed steady or grew - even for lower value types. Yet again, coins stood firm during global market turmoil.

What distinguishes coins from other safe haven assets such as gold is that due to their value precedents, coin prices do not drop sharply between crises; accordingly if you buy during a market peak you are less likely to lose capital when markets recover. Care must be taken to select those particular coin types with enough of an investment appeal to retain a buyer base during troubled economic circumstances, but in any case numismatics undeniably offers a secure investment alternative.

With or without market disruption, coin prices consistently trend upwards. Unlike the array of motivations and contributing factors behind the value of securities, coins only have two factors that dictate their value: either collectors want them, or investors gamble that collectors will want them. Accordingly, unless there is a significant disconnect between collector desire and an investor's perceptions of collector desires then coin prices generally remain stable with incremental growth over longer periods of time. As touched upon earlier, in early 2016 several articles reported that the British coin index GB 200 had outperformed the FTSE 100 in 2015 by producing a return of 6.2 per cent while the FTSE 100 lost 4.9 per cent that year. Coin values, being heavily influenced by previous results, tend to slowly grow in every numismatic market.

The fact that at base level collectors only buy coins because they want them means that their value can only sink so far before lower level collectors and dealers jump in to buy and prices begins to rise once again – their 'safety net'. You can very easily lose money through trading coins, but unless you have bought a forgery you will not lose all of your money. If prices drop then the value precedent may reset to whatever lower sum the coin has most recently fetched, but it is very rare for a coin's price to drop twice in succession. On the other hand, the value of securities has no such floor and outside factors can cause them to drop to zero. If this occurs and your position is significantly leveraged then you may end up owing more than you can possibly repay, while a coin can be exchanged or resold to repay a debt. A poor numismatic investment will cost you something, but a poor security investment may cost you everything.

However, with higher risk comes higher returns, and just as there is no floor to the value securities can drop to, there is no ceiling to which they can rise either. The nature of the numismatic market means explosive value growth is unlikely and generally unsustainable, unless you have been fortunate enough to buy a coin which later receives unprecedented international interest. On the other hand, share prices can skyrocket in reaction to market news and instantly generate significant returns for their owner, a phenomenon essentially absent from numismatics. Additionally, whereas the buying of coins involves potential cash flow problems and any profits are only achieved when selling, shares offer dividends to their investors on a regular basis generating income even before they are sold.

Alongside the possibility of greater and more regular returns, the speed and ease of trading on the financial markets makes for significantly increased liquidity in comparison to coins. The sheer numbers of buyers and sellers in financial markets means that assets can be liquidated almost instantly – and meanwhile transaction costs are substantially lower than the various fees and costs involved with numismatics. Capital gains achieved from trading shares will incur CGT, a tax not applicable to a slim number of British coins, but for the most part the purchase and resell procedure for coins is far tougher than for commodities and securities on the financial market, and the profit margins are generally much slimmer.

And finally, unlike securities traded on the financial market, coins must be physically taken ownership of. In some instances coins can be bought and sold sight-unseen, but at some stage down the chain a collector will want to own the coin and it will need to be shipped and delivered. Coins are portable but this still makes for an interruption of liquidity. During the Great Lockdown of 2020, larger auction houses continued operating and saw prices remain strong, but lower level collectors and dealers were unable to access post offices to ship their coins off to buyers. This meant that many had to halt their coin trading for the duration of the crisis leading to a grassroots loss of liquidity entirely unrelated to the collector base.

But are these factors truly disadvantages? Coins are comparatively illiquid and their prices less prone to swift rise, but what this owes itself to is the slow heartbeat of the numismatic market – an aspect which makes them the perfect accompaniment assets to conventional securities. In financial markets, the lightning-speed at which securities can be traded means that markets react instantly to news and trends and prices change accordingly. On Black Monday of the Covid-19 crisis in March 2020, the Standard & Poors 500 Index plummeted 7% within the first minutes of market opening, triggering an automatic 15-minute trading halt for the first time since October 1997. These 'circuit breakers' are built-in to prevent hysteria tanking market values, and allow investors to breathe, reflect and reconsider. More than anything, this demonstrates how linked financial markets are to human emotion and its corresponding irrationality.

Contrastingly, the numismatic metabolism is not fast enough to react instantly to market trends or news; the 'stock market of numismatics', major auctions, are spaced out over the course of a year meaning that there is a built-in circuit breaker after every auction closes and before the next one begins. While the financial markets enter arrhythmia easily – for example in 2020, Tesla founder Elon Musk tweeted that Tesla stock was "overvalued in his opinion", share prices instantly fell and $14 billion was wiped from Tesla's value - coins, with their far slower trickle of data points, cannot experience such immediate and dramatic reactive swings. Should a coin type start to lose value, this effect will likely be spread slowly over time giving ample opportunity for investors to liquidate their coins and reinvest. In this way, the numismatic markets and their steady progression exhibit a strength entirely absent within the financial markets and, despite their lower returns, are a perfect complimentary asset to traditional securities.

2. Real Estate

In the diminutive Micronesian island of Yap there is a very unique system of currency in place. Yapese 'money' is held as Rai, large donut-shaped stones carved from calcite ranging from just over an inch to 12 feet in diameter. These stones were quarried from the neighbouring island of Palau in ancient times and the money supply is now fixed with no new Rai entering circulation. 'Circulation', however, is something of misnomer for Yapese currency, as most of these stones stay put. Rather than physically exchange the Rai themselves (which are far too impractical to actually move), the Yapese simply keep track of who owns what stone. Title is exchanged but the stone stays where it is. Even when a particularly large Rai was lost to the sea between Palau and Yap it remained in circulation; the Yapese knew it was down there, somewhere, so it was still used in trade.

Rai stone money at the village of Gachpar on Yap.

The Yapese Rai is a unique monetary system – but its money works in much the same way as property. People can't physically move the properties they own but they are satisfied knowing that title has changed and transactions can continue. Yapese Rai are the only currency to share the immobile nature of property, but the trade of antique coins also resembles that of real estate in other respects. Coins are portable but both coins and properties are bought for leisure as well as being considered investments; both typically increase in price, and if your property or coin is now worth less than what you paid it is generally considered that you must have chosen poorly. Both properties and coins incur a cost of liquidation, either by realtors' fees and stamp duty or by auction commission and buyer's premium. And, most significantly, both coins and properties have to sell to truly realise their value yet oftentimes have substantial gaps between their appearances on the market. Accordingly there may be a general market perception of value, but only sales will truly show what buyers will pay.

There is no correlation per se between the market trends of coins and real estate; both are distinct industries that serve entirely different purposes. There are doubtless comparisons between the two and both share challenges and benefits. However despite their similarities, both coins and real estate have particular advantages and disadvantages over one another that makes them worthy of separate consideration.

First and foremost, everybody needs a home. The real estate industry will always be far larger than the numismatic market; it is an ever-growing Hydra, more properties being built every day and prices constantly rising. Together with the motivations of desire and profits that fuel both property sales and coin sales, real estate has an additional factor driving demand – functionality. Real estate is among the most illiquid of the tangible assets but nonetheless has a much wider market than coins due to its being a fundamental day-to-day necessity. The sheer numbers of potential buyers in the real estate market outweigh those of the coin market 100,000 to one. Accordingly, in some respects there is greater risk within the numismatic market as the bulk of capital is wielded by a far smaller buyer base.

Alongside the greater demand for real estate come potentially greater profits. Properties, although being subjective tangible assets, echo financial markets considerably more than coins do. This means that external factors can lead to sudden rises in price, such as the announcement of a train station being built in a previously remote area or a company establishing its new headquarters nearby. While in numismatics the only effective short term method of generating a profit is volume>margin or through successful value investing, you can purchase a property at market price and resell it a relatively short time later for significantly more. This is far harder to achieve within numismatics.

On the other hand, a larger market means that buyers have more options open to them, and unlike stocks or shares houses can have a very subjective appeal. Many properties will have differing vantage points, proximities to local resources, noise levels, foundation stability etc., and despite the size of the real estate market, the large cost for even the cheapest properties means that the demand base is high but the buyer base proportionally low. As such, if you are selling a property without much appeal in an area with several other units available you may struggle to find a tenant or buyer, as those in a position to buy will choose the choicest properties first. It may eventually be the case that you must repeatedly slash the price of your property until it finds a buyer at your level; people are hesitant to place such large sums into less optimal properties. Similarly, some coins may be less appealing than others, but the on-average lower values means that the chance of selling them for your intended price is far greater. The vast array of low-level coin collectors creates multiple buying tiers which offer some price protection for coins, and create a more accessible and liquid market overall.

Aside from the Yapese Rai, it is the matter of portability that spells the most significant difference between coins and real estate. If you cannot sell a coin quickly, you are left with a large amount of your capital left in a small portable disk which can be kept in a safe or bank vault for the duration. If you cannot sell a house, you are loaded with an elephant-sized responsibility of upkeep tied down to a specific location. If it is a foreign property it may be impossible for you to regularly attend to it thereby leaving it vulnerable. Coins are stable assets which require little more than security to protect them, and their size makes storage comparatively cheap. Properties on the other hand are stuck where they are, exposed to the elements and to vandalism. As such they will require constant maintenance and repairs to keep them functional, and will need modernisation every few years to retain their market appeal. If you have wealth distributed over several properties without tenants, you will be actively losing money over time.

Furthermore, for the most part those coins you have kept in your safe will likely rise in value; their mintages are limited and no more examples will enter the market and so numbers will only decrease as time passes. Real estate, on the other hand, does not have this security. Should more houses be built around your property then its value may well be eroded, both by decreasing scarcity in the area and by reducing its appeal. You cannot simply pick up your house and move it to a less populated and wealthier area.

Despite the limitations provided by immobility, real estate has some intrinsic advantages that coins do not. While they may be difficult assets to move (both physically and financially), properties can generate income and serve as collateral for large loans. Coins do not generate an income until they are sold for a profit, whilst property owners can rent out their buildings for a steady stream of revenue thus softening any associated cash flow issues. Additionally, despite the possibility of using coins as collateral in smaller loans, owning property - large tangible assets which cannot get up and walk away - provides a significant measure of confidence to banks and financial institutions when issuing loans, unlike the very condensed and portable value provided by coins.

Real estate carries weight. It represents wealth and generates income, it is a market we all must participate in sooner or later, and its profits can be large and quickly attained. As discussed, real estate trends mirror the workings of financial markets more than most tangible assets - certainly more than coins - leading to potentially greater profits. But this possibility of prices swiftly increasing correlate with the inverse: prices swiftly decreasing. If markets turn against real estate then prices can stagnate and fall. The dependence of property value on its location brings a myriad of issues. Distinct from their being an immovable assets, if the value of an area or associated industry decreases then so will the houses within it. The coin market is vast, international and centreless. Collectors who buy coins can bring them home with them – while real estate buyers either need to want to go to their properties themselves or be sure that others will want to go there. When doubt is cast on an area's prosperity, property prices can fall across the board.

To illustrate this effect we can look at one of the world's most expensive real estate markets – that of London. Between 1989 and 1995, house prices in Britain dropped by 18%, or in inflation-adjusted terms, 37%. In London, this drop was nearer 47%. In the 90s, it was possible for an average worker in London to enter the property ladder. But growing popularity of using London property as assets meant foreign investment entered in a landslide, leading to today's property market in the city being worth over £1.5 trillion and most London citizens struggling to afford property in the capital. After the Brexit vote of 2016 was passed, growing fears of international divestment in the UK led to house prices instantly stagnating. London's housing market is now the slowest growing out of any of the UK's top ten cities. This is because, as bloated as prices have become, buyers are nervous to commit the huge outlay necessary to obtain a London property title.

When an empire begins to fail, its denizens move inward to the centre; like blood rushing to the vital organs during hypothermia, when barbaric invaders threatened the Roman Empire in the 5th century AD the Roman peoples abandoned their satellite states and retreated to Rome. Only in prosperous and calm times were such empires able to persist and spread themselves so thinly, but when faced with aggression they were forced to flee with their wealth to those locations they could be sure to defend completely. Similarly, when economic turmoil hits, real estate becomes more of a burden than a boon. A portfolio of properties without tenants spread across countries will quickly incur costs greater than returns; additionally, in extreme circumstances and times of civil unrest, properties and their titles cannot be defended. Contrastingly, coins with their condensed value can be transported and hidden far more easily.

At the time of writing, millions of workers are conducting their business from home and many companies are extending remote working for months or years beyond the expected decline of Covid-19. House prices are already projected to fall by 20 per cent and some believe that the impact of the disease on the real estate market will be long-term, as no longer will workers be forced to huddle around cities to find jobs and compete for a limited number of properties. Real estate has for years formed the backbone of traditional 'wealth', but cannot be seen as an infallible fail-safe as a store of value. Its reliance on location and vulnerability to market trends and increase in supply means that in many ways it carries more risks than numismatic investments.

The market will always be strong for property overall, as will potential profits if investors choose prudently. Real estate prices are more likely to suffer in times of economic turmoil than coins; as such, property may be something to buy during harder times, while coins may be something to buy in preparation for harder times. In any case, you cannot go wrong if you buy an appealing and well-located property and proceed to fill it with appealing coins.

3. Bullion

A stock will be worth nothing if the company it belongs to is bankrupt. There will be no buyers for a luxury house in the middle of a barren desert. Supply and demand creates a perception of value but 'value' itself is nowadays fairly meaningless, no longer referring to those items needed for survival but instead solely to those which can be exchanged for other goods or obligation. Most securities and assets derive their value from some underlying factor such as company performance or a buyer base. If value truly exists in any intrinsic form it is in bullion, and for the sake of this discussion predominantly gold bullion[20].

Precious metals have represented the wealth of society for millennia, from the first moment that a food surplus required a non-perishable transferrable form of asset. Even today, despite the myriad of more useful materials and resources available we still carry on the practices of our ancestors and treat gold as the most intrinsically 'valuable' substance on the planet for no other reason beyond convention. Like the US dollar, gold is almost the true currency of finance, the measure against which all other currencies and assets are compared. Of all the tangible assets traded on the financial markets, gold is one of the most widely exchanged.

Gold bullion is the 'conventional' asset most closely linked with coins. Indeed, the accruing of one is often mutually inclusive with the other; often bullion is issued in the form of coins, and many antique gold coins are still considered 'investment' gold. Many benefits to investors are shared by both gold bullion and some collectable coins. Investment gold is VAT-free and refers to any gold coins younger than 200 years old, and many UK gold bullion coins are technically legal tender and so their resale bears no CGT. It is common for those who keep large stores of gold to supplement their bullion with collectable coins and vice versa. Both gold and collectable coins tend to increase in value during times of economic or political uncertainty, making them popular physical assets to supplement those purely virtual. Once again however, there are specific reasons why both gold and antique coins should be considered

---

[20] All precious metal bullion besides gold incurs VAT making them less favourable as stores of value, and accordingly this discussion will focus primarily on gold.

separately as part of any investment portfolio.

The chief superiority of gold bullion over collectable coins is undoubtedly its liquidity. Gold is perhaps the most liquid tangible asset of all, in some cases even more so than cash; this is because whereas cash can be specific to whichever country you are in, gold will almost always be accepted as payment anywhere. Coin transactions tend to be for more subjective sums and must take place through auction or those professionals or collectors who know their value, while there are far more options to sell gold. Every establishment that trades bullion will have an up-to-date and precise market price and will typically purchase gold at one or two per cent below this figure and sell at a few per cent above. Transaction costs are thus relatively low. Additionally, as the gold you buy is objective and no more superior or inferior to any other gold, buyers will waste no time comparing bullion as they may with coins and will instead likely be far quicker to purchase. For swift transactions at current market price, gold outstrips all other tangible assets.

Where gold leaves something to be desired in comparison to coins is in its reaction to prosperous economic times. The liquidity of gold and absolute precision in its market price means that when conventional securities are performing well, gold price will quickly sink in favour of other more profitable ventures – an effect we saw in late 2020 and through 2021 as Covid-19 vaccines rolled out across the globe. This effect is not so prevalent within the numismatic market. Value precedents set for coins during a less favourable economic period remain in the record once the markets recover and do not often exhibit significant dips afterwards. This means that whereas gold bought at its peak price can lose value quite quickly, coins bought at market peaks are less likely to encounter such significant losses, and certainly not so swiftly.

In addition, gold is not a vessel with which to generate significant riches unless traded in massive quantities; rather than using it to produce profit, investors merely place capital in gold to keep it stable and to weather uncertain economic times. This means that although its price will increase with demand, it will never experience the significant price growth that coveted stocks, shares or assets can. Many investors enjoy owning gold, but will not pay over the odds for it like they will for particular coins they desire as they are not 'collecting' as it were. As such, gold cannot be relied upon to generate considerable returns unless the original investment was sizeable.

Gold bullion is a comparatively dense asset in that it has a relatively large value for the space it occupies. At the time of writing, 1kg of gold is equal to around $55,000; as such, realistically one could carry 10-20kg, or roughly $500,000 to $1,000,000 worth of gold, without much issue. This transportability makes bullion an appealing prospect, as it means your wealth can be taken with you. Portability is also a chief advantage of coins but to an even greater extent than gold bullion. Should you have invested in rare coins instead of bullion, then that 20kg could feasibly represent a sum as much as $50 million. The condensed value of coins is comparable to very few other asset types.

But in some scenarios where you would be forced to physically carry your assets with you, the value of gold would be more likely to persist than the value of your rare coins. Coins are fortunate in that they are seen as investments and also boast a strong collector base. However, were there an absolute societal collapse (eg war, mass disease, alien invasion!) and chaos descended upon the world it is likely that the value of coins would sink to solely the weight of their metal. Much like stocks, shares, bonds, currency and even property, coins derive their value from an underlying factor, ie their collector base, and in a global catastrophe coins would cease to be widely considered valuable as collectors would have more important things to worry about. Meanwhile bullion is seen as an emergency holding and a portable mark of true value and would be far more likely to be accepted in transactions.

Unlike most other asset classes to which one can compare coins, compared to bullion coins are comparatively less secure. However, while society remains intact enough for coin collectors to go about their normal business, coins offer greater returns to investors than gold and retain their market values in both prosperous and uncertain times. Gold is only a means of generating substantial profits when traded in enormous quantities, and even then their margins are razor-thin; a gold refinery I visited in late 2020 informed me that to protect their profit, every year they go so far as to burn their doormats and employees' overalls to ensure that all gold dust is extracted.

It is wise nonetheless for investors to ensure that gold makes up a sizable portion of their portfolio as although the price growth will be slow and steady, few other investments are as secure or allow for as effective market hedging.

4. Alternative 'Collectable' Assets

The technical definition of an alternative asset is any investment type that is not a share, bond or cash. This is an immensely broad umbrella category that encompasses a range of both tangible and financial assets, but typically there is a scale of just how 'alternative' alternative assets truly are. For example, bullion and certain real estate investments fall under the category of alternative assets, but their strong links with the financial markets make them comparatively more conventional.

Within alternative investments there is a specific subset of collectable tangible assets of which coins are one, alongside other groups such as stamps, art, jewellery, wine and cars. It is these similarly veined investments that will be evaluated in this discussion as opposed to the various other financial instruments technically considered as alternatives. Every group of collectables has their distinct advantages and disadvantages, and to assess each individually would require a far longer discussion. Accordingly only wider comparisons will be drawn between types based on their performance as commodities.

Alternative collectable assets all have similar buyer bases made up of both collectors and investors. Most of these collectables only began to be considered as economic assets when their collector bases grew and became wealthier; as prices rose, investors stepped in. The dual motivation of collectors and investors means that collectable assets tend to have reasonably strong market positions. The desire of collectors actually fuels the trade, while a healthy base of investor capital keeps prices steady. Many of the more prestigious collectable assets are those with the longest history such as coins, stamps, wine, art and books, yet there are still many modern types – like US baseball cards - that bring enormous sums at auction.

Alternative tangible assets all have a similar appeal for not being tethered to the financial markets, making their prices slower to respond to wider economic trends. This has led the London private bank Coutts to establishing an index of popular collectable types, their 'passion' index – so-called for its subjects being usually bought from a place of passion instead of investment - to track their performance over time.

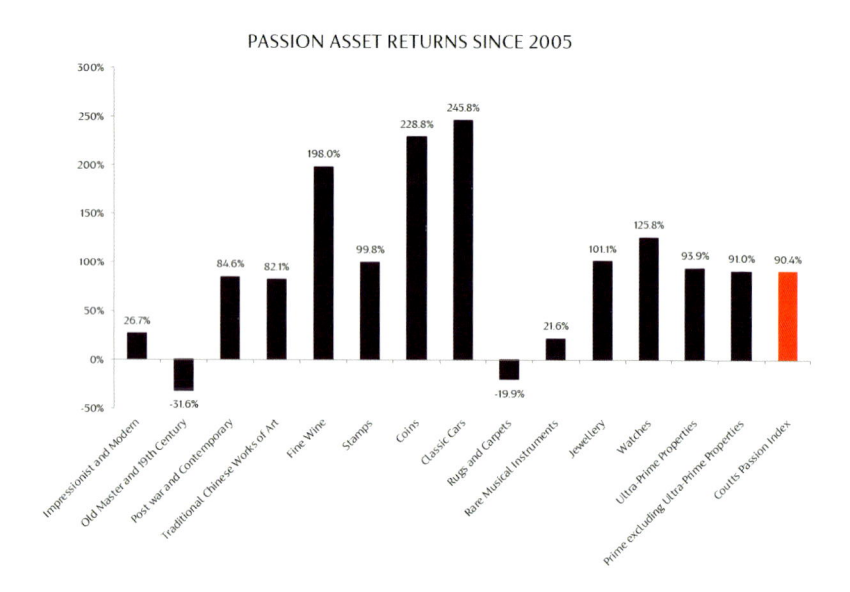

PASSION ASSET RETURNS SINCE 2005

Impressionist and Modern	26.7%
Old Master and 19th Century	-31.6%
Post war and Contemporary	84.6%
Traditional Chinese Works of Art	82.1%
Fine Wine	198.0%
Stamps	99.8%
Coins	228.8%
Classic Cars	245.8%
Rugs and Carpets	-19.9%
Rare Musical Instruments	21.6%
Jewellery	101.1%
Watches	125.8%
Prime excluding Ultra-Prime Properties	93.9%
Ultra-Prime Properties	91.0%
Coutts Passion Index	90.4%

The Coutts passion index covers a range of collectables from broad groups of art to smaller collectables such as stamps and coins and other popular types of antique. Since the index started in 2005, values have risen almost uniformly for the various tracked collectable groups; coins are the second fastest-growing asset after vintage cars with a 228.8% increase in value. Overall, the passion index has seen a 90.4% overall increase since 2005. This index is useful for a cursory comparison of different classes of alternative asset, but despite their inherent similarities, the performance of collectables as investments varies hugely from type to type.

Firstly, the level of accessibility is significantly greater in some collectable categories than others. It is far easier to break into coin collecting with some low-level examples than it is to buy a cheap Old Master painting. Collectors often need to have built up a foundation of items before their hobby truly picks up momentum, and so coins, stamps and wines have an advantage over, say, high-level art and classic cars in that there are lower value types available for beginners to whet their appetite. The comparatively lower values mean that there is a healthier grassroots collector base to contribute capital to the hobby which considerably reduces market thinness and thus reduces risk.

Alongside price accessibility, space requirements are another limiting factor for various collectable types. As discussed previously, coins are among the most condensed assets available and a vast collection need only occupy a cabinet in the corner of a room. A similarly impressive collection of furniture would need considerable floor space, as would the display of a number of artworks or rare rugs and carpets. The need for a large home or storage area to house one's collection is enough to dissuade some from participating in a given industry and touches upon an even greater issue – that of upkeep.

Just as in ancient Lydia, there is still a desire today for the most stable and secure assets. Investors enjoy tangible assets as they can be touched and stored and so represent something more 'real' than many traditional securities; but cars rust, stamps bend, art fades, wine spoils and rugs get slowly eaten by moths. Many tangible assets require painstaking care in their protection and storage; this means that for many collectors, there is a real risk of alternative investments losing value if stored improperly. Coins, being made from mostly unreactive metals are some of the most hard-wearing assets with possibly only diamonds their superior in stability, yet diamonds – being a naturally-occurring mineral with an uncontrollable supply – have their own disadvantages. The compact nature of coins means that an impressive and high-value collection can be stored and maintained with relative ease.

And, once again, the major appeal of coins as an asset of choice is the extent to which they have been commoditised and their prices standardised. Most collectables on the Coutts index have very subjective values – art pieces tend to only exist as unique items, as do many pieces of furniture and jewellery. The fact that coins exist in multiple units means that their appearances at auction are far more regular and thus the market can settle on more precise values for each type. The unique and subjective nature of many other collectable types means that they do not suit third party certification thus hindering their performance as assets, while coins have fully embraced encapsulation and professional grading. Even for those other collectable types that do offer TPG possibilities, certification costs will significantly exceed those for coins.

Coins have comparatively stable and established market prices, their value is compact and their upkeep simple, the hobby is accessible to new collectors and the markets correspondingly strong. These factors all coalesce to put coins at the second highest returns on the Coutts passion index since 2005 after vintage cars – but what exactly makes cars superior to coins as an asset class?

Case Study –Coins vs Cars

The Coutts passion index reports that vintage cars are the sole alternative asset class presently beating coins with a +245.8% increase since 2005 against +228.8% for coins. Here follows a brief glance at the attributes of cars as an asset class and why this data may bear further scrutiny.

I. Price Standardisation

Cars, similar to coins, are produced in multiple, known numbers. Numerous resources exist to help investors and enthusiasts track market values; price guides such as Parker's echo similar guides within numismatics. Buyers will choose cars based on similar values as numismatists such as eye appeal, originality, extent of 'wear' (mileage); most will buy coins and cars in spite of some aspects and because of others. And, like coins, it will be those limited edition or ultra-high quality cars produced in small numbers that are most likely to increase in value. In this way coins and cars enjoy similar status as standardised assets.

II. Storage and Upkeep

Coins are relatively easy to keep, but to physically store your collection of vintage cars will require considerable space and security and the cars themselves will require constant maintenance. Even then, your cars will be vulnerable to theft and damage. It would be possible to hide a coin collection in a safe or hideaway in your home, but cars are far more difficult to store discretely. Should you ever want to actually use any of your cars you would run considerable risk, and with every usage you would be potentially detracting from their value.

III. Accessibility

Despite their arguably wider appeal, the classic car market is prohibitive to lower-level buyers. Almost every car will drop in value after being bought and it is only vintage or high-value models that appreciate year on year. This means that the possibility of engaging new collector interest is far more difficult as it takes a considerable amount of capital to purchase just one classic car, let alone a whole collection of them. This tallies with a thinner buyer base from the bottom to the top of the classic car market, increasing risk considerably.

IV. Market Trends

The bar chart form of the Coutts passion index paints an incomplete portrait of comparative market performance; the accompanying line graph helps to further analyse price trends for alternative assets over time.

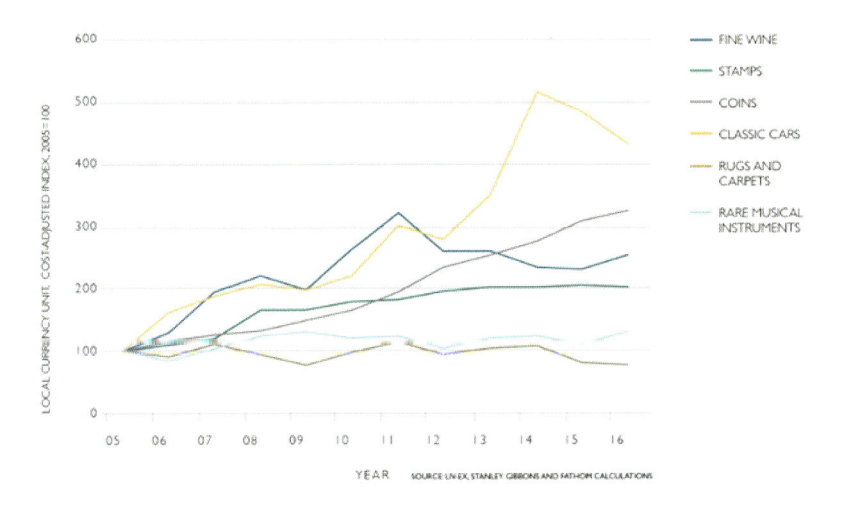

Coins still come in second to cars, but the growth of classic car values instantly stands out as being sporadic and exhibiting sharp peaks and troughs. Had you decided to invest in classic cars in 2014, by 2017 you would have potentially lost a significant portion of your initial investment; meanwhile, coins are the sole asset to appreciate steadily year on year within the index. Accordingly, the purchase of classic cars may have netted greater capital gains had you bought and sold at optimal times, but your risk would clearly have been significantly higher.

We must often part with capital out of necessity, but desire is our number one motivator for spending. We want the item on the menu, we want that new outfit, we want that holiday or that house. On the other hand, when we invest we may not want the security or asset just for itself but instead we want a capital return when we come to resell. Accordingly, it is only logical that the collectables markets with the strongest buyer bases will combine both collectors' desires for items coupled with investors' desires for returns. Confidence is crucial in such instances, otherwise the feeling of 'investing' will be lost; this means that those collectables with effective price standardisation and trackable performance will have the most confident buyer base and correspondingly secure values. Coins stand head and shoulders above most other collectable asset types for their numerous advantages, but as always it is advisable to buy a cross-section of alternative assets that you are passionate about.

Section 3
Trading Coins

AVAILABLE FROM
SPINK BOOKS

SPINK
Where History is Valued

COINS OF ENGLAND
AND THE UNITED KINGDOM 2022
PRE-DECIMAL ISSUES
57TH EDITION

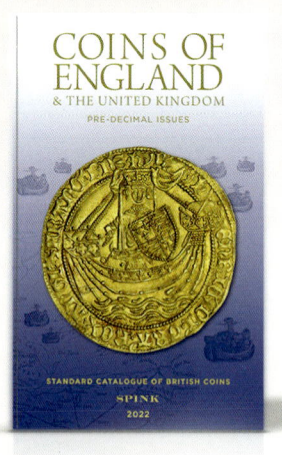

This historic reference work for British coins is still the only catalogue to feature every major coin type from Celtic to the Decimal coinage of Queen Elizabeth II, arranged in chronological order and divided into metals under each reign, then into coinages, denominations and varieties. All decimal coinage since 1968 is listed in a separate volume, available as an independent publication.

The catalogue includes up-to-date values for every coin, a beginner's guide to coin collecting, numismatic terms explained and historical information about each British coin, from our earliest (Celtic) coins, Roman, Anglo-Saxon and Norman coins, the coins of the Plantagenet Kings, the Houses of Lancaster and York, the Tudors and Stuarts, to the more modern Milled coinage, minted for the first time in 1561 during the reign of Elizabeth I.

From the earliest of times, coins have been used by states or monarchs to communicate with people; Coins of England is therefore not only a reference book for collectors, but a fascinating snapshot of British history, illuminating its economics, technology, art, politics and religion. As always, the content has been updated and improved throughout by the editors, with numerous new images and revisions of key sections.

Hardback
216 x 138mm
648 pages with colour illustrations
throughout
RRP £30
ISBN: 978-1-912667-70-3

COINS OF ENGLAND
AND THE UNITED KINGDOM 2022
DECIMAL ISSUES
8TH EDITION

The Coins of England and the United Kingdom Pre-Decimal and Decimal volumes comprise the Standard Catalogue of British Coins, with the pre-decimal issues under Elizabeth II (and all previous coinage) listed in a separate volume.

This volume of Decimal issues under Elizabeth II gives a comprehensive overview of all individual coins and sets issued by the Royal Mint since 1971 (and in circulation since 1968), offering an authoritative catalogue of modern British coins. The revisions and updates completed in 2021 have been built upon to provide a completely comprehensive guide to decimal coinage in the year of its 50th anniversary, and the volume is published in hardback for the first time to celebrate this milestone.

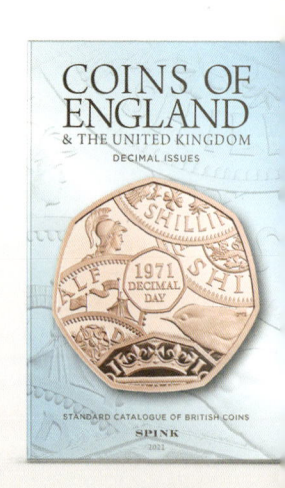

Hardback
216 x 138mm
360 pages with colour illustrations
throughout
RRP £15
ISBN: 978-1-912667-71-0

Order at
WWW.SPINKBOOKS.COM
or contact us
books@spink.com | +44(0)20 7563 4119

SPINK UK | 69 Southampton Row | Bloomsbury | London | WC1B 4ET
LONDON | NEW YORK | HONG KONG | SINGAPORE | SWITZERLAND

#SPINK_AUCTIONS

WWW.SPINK.COM

The numismatic market is vast and truly international with demand for coins coming from every corner of the globe. Far be it from being merely an antiquated hobby, coins can also consistently offer buyers a substantial return on their investment - even if this was not their main intention going in. The final stage of your journey through numismatics is, of course, participating in the trade yourself. Once you have familiarised yourself with the nuances of the global numismatic market and are aware of the risks and return possible, you can begin to hone your knowledge in the interest of buying your own coins. But even if you feel comfortable with the aspects that govern coin values and are entirely familiar with how the numismatic markets operate, to be successful in numismatic trading you must know how to recognise those coins with a resale potential, know how to buy them and know how best to sell them on.

The identification of potentially valuable coins comes from both research and examination. When a coin is being offered at auction, research can tell you that coin's mintage figures, how many examples were subsequently melted down, the strength of the collector market and how desirable it is. This will allow you to establish a coin type's rarity and its demand. Meanwhile, examination will tell you just how appealing an example of that coin it is, its condition and eye appeal and whether it stands out amongst others of the type. These factors directly determine the value of a coin, and by using both research and examination in conjunction you can often quite easily isolate the best buying opportunities. It is always wise to aim for the finest coins you can afford, as these have the greatest chance of a profitable resale – after all, if you own the best, then other collectors must come to you if they too want the best.

When buying coins, collectors have an abundance of options open to them. Auction houses, dealers, private individuals and mints all offer opportunities to purchase coins. Once you have identified an appealing piece offered by any one of these participants, the next stage is to decide whether or not their price is affordable and acceptable to you. If the coin is truly exceptional, there is no issue in paying more than previous examples have sold for; if you have recognised something unique about its appeal, the chances are that other collectors will too.

However, when buying it is vital to always adhere to the principle of *caveat emptor* – 'buyer beware'. In numismatics, much of the onus of assessing coin quality and price falls to the collector rather than the dealer or seller. Third party grading has assisted in increasing buyer confidence for coins, but even when encapsulated it is important to be able to establish a coin's individual quality in order to decide what to pay. The more knowledge you can bring to a transaction, the greater the chance you will operate wisely.

Selling coins also requires appropriate research and consideration. Collectors can take many paths to liquidate their numismatic holdings, each with their own distinct pros and cons; however, what it ultimately comes down to is whether a speedy sale is preferable to potentially higher returns. It is always wise to pursue your most trusted route, whether that is with an individual or company you are familiar with to ensure full transaction transparency. Be that as it may, it also behoves the collector to be always weighing up his or her options for sale to ensure he or she is maximising profits.

The process of identifying, buying and selling coins is relatively simple but must be known inside and out to ensure the best possible outcomes from your numismatic trading. This final section will detail the research necessary to build your knowledge base, the best practices to observe when participating in the market and the range of advantages and disadvantages regarding each option for buying and selling.

Chapter 3.1.
Conducting Research

Before anyone parts with their capital for a product or service, proper research should be undertaken. Only through research can buyers determine how the price they are being quoted compares to the market in general, thus preventing them from spending more than they need to and unnecessarily losing money. This is especially true of investments; research sheds light on the past performance and market health for an asset or security and plays an instrumental role in deciding whether or not to invest. Without thorough research it would be extremely unwise to 'invest' in anything.

Likewise, research is vital in numismatics and contributes to one half of the illustrative equation given earlier: *Coin Value = (Number of collectors / number of surviving examples) x Grade*. By conducting thorough research you can hope to establish the rarity of a given coin type, the strength of the collector base and how prices have fluctuated in recent years. The first step is to isolate which area of numismatics you will choose to focus on, followed by three major means of gathering data: numismatic books, advice of industry professionals and use of internet resources. Each of these methods can be conducted prior to purchasing any coins. It is imperative to focus on research when considering numismatic investments in order to address the *caveat emptor* attitude prevalent throughout the market.

1. Finding Your Niche

Knowledge is power within numismatics, but there is an awful lot to know. The world of coins is extraordinarily broad and most countries have a rich and diverse history of coinage - nobody can be expected to retain all the possible information about every coin series and type. You could spend your whole life working in this field and you will still come across things that surprise you. It is impossible to know every numismatic market intimately, meaning it is vital to specialise early on and to find your collecting or investing niche. This way, you can foster a comprehensive working knowledge of this niche market affording you a strong ability to recognise buying and selling opportunities when they arise.

It is advisable to begin where your interest lies so as to fully engage with a market you will need to know it thoroughly. You will naturally retain the most knowledge about an area you find interesting, so it is advisable to try and concentrate your research on those coins you like the most. If you are passionate about the history of a particular country, you should consider collecting coins produced there; if a time period or empire fascinates you, you should buy those coins relevant to the era or reign. Your numismatic niche must feel like your own, and every coin should capture your imagination and enthusiasm. Coins are at their heart a hobby of passion and building your collection should be an enjoyable process.

After your interest has dictated the field you will concentrate on, within this niche you must practice sensible buying practices. Buyers should always intersect their passion and market knowledge to buy the finest available coins from within their interest base.

Rather than buying middle-range and common pieces with extremely standardised values, it is better to focus on the rarest pieces you can afford with the most unusually high eye appeal. This is where your in-depth research will assist you: your comprehensive knowledge will ensure that when a particularly favourable coin is offered for sale, you will be able to recognise it and compete aggressively for it. Choice coins such as these will afford you the strongest chance of turning a profit when you come to resell.

However, you must also pay attention to the pulse of the market you have chosen as your niche. If your area is too obscure and has too small a collector base, you could feasibly afford all of the rarest coins of the series but will have likely strongly contributed to price changes at the top of that market. You will thus struggle to resell at a profit. This is especially true if your interest becomes especially academic. You will find scores of numismatists out there who are quite happy to spend hours comparing dies and writing up lists of varieties and will tell you which ones they have found are the rarest types (sometimes with only a few examples known). But applying logic to this situation, if the only collectors who recognise the rarity of these types spend their entire waking lives examining coin varieties, then they probably will not have had too much of a chance to generate any real wealth, and as such, there is not a huge amount of money behind these parts of the industry. Meanwhile, collectors who have worked hard and made a lot of money in their life do not necessarily want to search through scores of low-grade coins to find the rarest; they want high quality, beautifully engraved and well-preserved high denominations, an effect substantiated by the immense prices such coins command. You must always ensure that there is a healthy pre-existing market for whatever you choose as your niche to ensure your activity does not alter the balance of the collector base too much.

For most collectors, their numismatic niche is predetermined by whatever first coins capture their interest. A young collector may happen upon a Roman Denarius and become a lifelong collector of ancient coins. Many collectors start large scale and will initially collect, say, every single ancient coin that crosses their path. Gradually, however, collectors will scale down to an area they can comfortably understand and specialise on obtaining the finest examples they can afford within it, such as exclusively Roman Republic Denarii in high grade. Coin collecting should be interest-led with capital return a secondary consideration – but this potential profit should always be considered within any purchase. Within your chosen niche you can buy the coins you truly desire, but ensure you always observe prudent buying practices and give yourself the best chance of a profitable resale.

2. Books and Reference Guides

There is a mantra used by numismatists: "buy the book before you buy the coin". Collectors are encouraged to enhance their knowledge of a numismatic area before they attempt to participate, and used correctly, numismatic reference guides can be the collector's best friend (sometimes literally if you are a nerdy teenage numismatist). Books remain the most respected learning resource within numismatics and there is an impressively wide selection out there covering almost every facet of numismatics, each book offering a unique insight into its specific area of the market.

Books are used primarily for two main purposes: to assist with identification of specific coin varieties and to give an idea of their value. Since the early 16th century reference guides have been an essential part of the hobby, initially designed as a catalogue of types for the benefit of collectors. As the market progressed and the collector base grew, these books evolved to give an idea of rarity and basic prices for each coin. Nowadays, numismatic books fall into a few broad categories but very few omit to mention coin values, and the collector has come to expect this price guide aspect. You can find books specifically detailing the coin types of a country or era, or those expanding on the history behind the currency itself, and as such when starting out in the discipline reference guides can be exceptionally useful in identifying coins and finding out their historical significance. But there is one vital lesson to keep in mind: do not rely on books when it comes to estimating a coin's value.

The benefits of books to collectors are many and their place within numismatics is steadfast, but the price guide aspect is quite frankly archaic and outdated. Several times per week I will hear clients exclaim that the 'book value' of a certain type might be, say, $3,000, to be met with utter shock when I tell them that the coin is actually worth perhaps $2,200. Equally, I have heard even seasoned professionals express disbelief that a coin that is priced at $2,000 in a book would sell for $20,000. To be fair, why would these values be printed if they were incorrect or irrelevant? Surely if it is written in black and white, it is gospel?

In short, the responsibility to accurately document a coin's market value is unfair and borderline impossible. As comparatively liquid as the numismatic market is, it is not a stock market and you cannot tell people what to pay for a coin; only they can decide that themselves. Coins do not have intrinsic values, and, like the catch of the day, they will always sell for their 'market price'. As such, books are always by nature running to catch up with the latest auction results, and thus are out of date from the moment of printing.

Fleur de Coin Cafe

MENU

Appetizers

1. Great Britain, Victoria, Sovereign 1838, Very Fine..................... MP
2. France, 20 Francs 1857, MS65 NGC................................... MP
3. USA, $10, 1801, Good Very Fine, Cleaned............................ MP
4. Brazil, 4000 Reis, 1703-R, MS62 NGC................................. MP
5. China, Dollar, Year 22 (1933), Extremely Fine .... MP

Entrées

6. USA, $20, 1933 Double Eagle, MS65 PCGS........................... MP
7. Great Britain, Edward VIII, pattern Five Pounds, 1937, PF67 UCAM NGC........ MP
8. Germany, Württemberg, proof 3 Marks, 1912, PR63 DCAM PCGS........ MP
9. Great Britain, Anne, Five Guineas, 1713, Extremely Fine............... MP

Most price guides rely on recent auction results to update their figures, so should no examples of a particular coin type appear at auction for years, its guidebook value would then appear to stagnate compared to other coins listed - simply as there is no up-to-date data to include. This means that the writers of some price guides tend to increase coin values by a small percentage across the board year-on-year even without these prices ever actually being achieved. This effect is especially true of higher value types with perhaps just one or two know examples - many of these prices are entirely fictitious. Numismatic reference guides can tell you almost everything you need to know about coins themselves, but it is only through consulting past prices realised that you can reliably assess their market values.

However, it is important to keep in mind that despite the fundamentally flawed analysis of written price lists, books are still highly respected within numismatics. What you are reading, everyone else will be reading too. Accordingly, at lower levels of the market where coins are priced below $1,000, collectors tend to adhere to the prices listed in guides. It ultimately works backwards as the books do not necessarily document the sums that collectors are paying; rather, collectors pay what the books suggest, and either way it means the values at this level are more accurate. Price guides can also be useful in giving a proportional idea of values for certain coin types. Even if the values are imprecise, should one book value be significantly higher than another for a coin variety you can be relatively assured that that coin is of considerably greater value. Books allow for an insight into market prices which can then be researched further using up-to-date resources.

In some isolated cases the impact of books can create market bubbles. In 2014 a book was released in Japan detailing what was essentially a list of coins to invest in. It is not advisable to follow such lists within numismatics as they are rarely accurate. However, accurate or not, the impact of the book was that prices for each coin type listed within it shot up soon after publication, supposedly substantiating the author's claims. Prices dipped for many of the coins a handful of years later. Books should be used as instruments of learning around your chosen numismatic field, but should not be used as your major guide to market prices or which coins to invest in.

It is wise to buy as many books surrounding your chosen numismatic topic as you can; as public knowledge in your field, it is the guidance that every other collector will also be following and can dictate buying practices and market trends. Books can dramatically affect the market as collectors derive their maximum bids from catalogue values, serving to standardise the lower value pieces. But when evaluating outstanding coins with an affluent but thin market, you can entirely disregard guidebook values as collectors will simply pay what they want and not one penny more or less. As such, numismatic books and reference guides should form a strong component of your knowledge base from which you undertake further research but should not represent your sole source of market information.

3. Internet Resources

Numismatic books provide an essential base of knowledge for the collector; few other resources are as valuable for researching individual coin varieties and types or for reading up on the history of a coinage itself. However, for the most cutting edge information - on coin values in particular - we must once again turn to the internet. The revolutionary interconnectedness brought by the World Wide Web that so transformed numismatics did so in part through awarding every numismatist the power to research their coins and their true market prices. There are numerous websites dedicated to offering information about particular coin types which can supplement book learning, but it is ultimately through market analysis that the internet proves its true worth. By using books and the internet in tangent, one can learn both the extent of a coinage's denominations and rarities as well as its up-to-date values.

Most auction houses will publish the prices realised for their recent auctions online. Facilities for research vary from auctioneer to auctioneer; some will offer extremely slick means of searching past results, and some provide less sophisticated lists of prices realised. Either way, the information is public and offers the most current market values for coins. The prices realised made available by auction websites will tell you the sale prices – but only for whatever coins they themselves have auctioned recently. If a dealer offers you a coin that you have never seen at auction, it can be difficult to know where to begin looking.

This is where CoinArchives comes in – a search engine designed exclusively for research of recent auction results for any and all coins. Rather than having to search reams and reams of old auction catalogues, you can simply enter your coin's details in CoinArchives to pull up comparable examples and what they sold for. You and all other subscribers are viewing the most current prices worldwide allowing you to assess market values, thus contributing significantly to value standardisation.

CoinArchives Pro

Currently archiving 5,246,391 records from 5,928 auctions

Auction Lot Search

Search options ▶

Search only in auctions from:

See **Search Tips** for more information.

Browse and Search Lots by Firm/Auction

Choose a firm: Go

Should your coin not be in the database, you can assume it is rare. This being said, CoinArchives is an exclusionary search engine and so just one incorrect word or spelling will omit potentially relevant results. This is especially troublesome considering that CoinArchives pulls results from various countries and thus results are often in multiple languages. I developed a reputation in a previous role for being able to find anything on CoinArchives through what I called 'trawl fishing' – essentially just putting in as little detail as possible and searching through the mass of results it returns. If you only put catalogue numbers or dates, you should eventually be able to find what you seek as these figures are uniform across descriptions and languages.

Despite its extraordinary usefulness, CoinArchives also has its limitations. Its memory only goes back at the very earliest to the late 90s, meaning older auction results are inaccessible. It only lists the hammer prices for coins rather than including buyer's premium meaning you are not seeing the precise figure the coin sold for. It has a comparatively weak following of US coins, and for research on this market other US auction websites are far more useful. Finally, the price of subscription is not cheap at $600 per year. For many this sum is prohibitive, and so a CoinArchives subscription should be used only by serious collectors or investors to ensure it is cost effective.

The grading companies PCGS and NGC offer their own online resources for research in the form of their aforementioned population reports. If you cannot find a coin on CoinArchives after thorough searching, you can assume an example has not sold publicly since 2000. You can then turn to the population reports to see how many examples have been certified to give you more data as to its rarity. If the grading companies have also not seen an example then it is quite likely that your coin is extremely rare[21]. Additionally, population reports can supplement data gathered from auction results. If, for example, you see a coin upcoming at auction graded MS62 and find the grade rather uninspiring, you might check the population report to find that 100 have been certified but no others are Mint State. You can then assume that that MS62 piece is rather special and worth a strong bid.

Beside the highly specialised internet resources available to numismatists, there is an open secret that much of what one desires to find out about a coin can be obtained through generic search engines - provided you input the correct search terms. If you have a coin and have simply no idea what you could be looking at, searching part of the legend, the date or a rough description can often be enough to show you images of comparable examples. You can then take this data and research more thoroughly using books or auction records. Search engines should not be your primary method of research but do demonstrate just how much the internet has transformed numismatic research. In times gone by a collector would have to pore through book after book or track down experts in the hope of identifying a mysterious coin.

The internet can be a fantastic resource, containing auction records, coin information and helpful advice. But a word of warning – stay vigilant and do not take anything you read online at face value. Several legitimate-seeming websites or organisations might offer numismatic tips and show you what to buy, but many are not to be trusted. Numismatic books will usually have a respected publisher (many boast an academic society or auctioneer's name) and can generally be assumed to be trustworthy, whereas it is the work of a moment to establish a legitimate-looking website and offer advice to collectors. Unless you are very confident in your knowledge base, it is far better to become comfortable with a

---

21 However, do note that if a coin is especially low value it is unlikely to have been listed on CoinArchives or have been certified in significant numbers as this would not be cost effective.

handful of trusted websites and dealers and build up a relationship rather than believing everything you read online.

4. Industry Professionals

Industry professionals are a resource just waiting to be called upon, and there is no substitute for the opinion of an established numismatic specialist. It is unrealistic for the novice collector to be expected to distinguish even a genuine coin from a replica, let alone to be able to correctly estimate a coin's grade and identify any minute varieties. As such, the opinion of a seasoned numismatic professional is invaluable to quickly identify and evaluate your coins, and it is the work of a moment to give them a call or email through photographs of what you have. Even within the numismatic industry external specialists are consulted, either when coins are submitted for TPG or shown to museums for authentication. The specialist you choose to contact could be a grading service, an auctioneer, dealer, museum or mint; each participant offers a different viewpoint on numismatics. Museums and mints have a vested interest in the spread of information and research of coins while auctioneers and dealers will be careful to assess a coin's value in case they can make an offer for it.

When consulting professional numismatists or numismatic institutions, you should consider the element of bias that your chosen specialist may have. A lesson I learnt very early on in this market is that numismatics is heavily polarised between those who are 'academics' (ie are very clued in as to coin varieties, numismatic history, reference works etc.) and 'businesspeople' (great at selling, excellent at spotting trends and price fluctuations but less confident on subject matter). Professionals from these two viewpoints thus might give you conflicting information regarding the significance or value of certain coins; for example, a coin might be of high academic importance but have a comparatively small collector base.

More academic-leaning numismatists or institutions will tell you everything about your coin but little about its market value, while numismatic businesspeople will tell you market value but nothing about the coin itself. Early in my career I worked with a very active numismatic salesperson who was very efficient at cajoling clients into parting with their coins, but knew so little about coins themselves that he was forced to bring me along to all of his client meetings to field any questions about coins the clients had. The most successful numismatic market participants are those who manage to straddle both the academic and business mind-sets and keep a profit-focused perspective in what is at heart an academic field. As such, you should choose the specialist you consult wisely to ensure the comments you receive are informative both in an academic and market sense.

Alongside the harmless academic to market bias, there are also differences in standards between the largest and smallest dealerships. Some industry professionals are used to seeing the very finest coins on such a regular basis that they may be overly dismissive of coins worth a few hundred dollars that smaller dealerships would compete fiercely for. The position of your chosen consultant within the market should be taken into consideration when seeking advice.

And remember – only act on advice regarding value or selling when it comes from a trusted source. There are those 'professionals' who prey on the uninformed and either buy coins at unreasonably low prices or sell at unreasonably high prices. The largest firms and most well-established dealers are almost always going to be trustworthy, as unscrupulous dealers operate far more surreptitiously. Organisations such as the American Numismatic Association (ANA) and British Numismatic Trade Association (BNTA) exist to help identify reputable dealers and auctioneers, and should your chosen numismatic professional be a member of one of these associations it is usually a sign that they can be trusted. Nonetheless, it is usually wise to get at least a second opinion – if not a third - when offering a coin for sale to a dealer, or use only a small group of trusted individuals and institutions.

To make one thing perfectly clear, which I tell every would-be consignor: never be embarrassed about your questions, and always ask a professional about your coins if you suspect them to be valuable. It might take the specialist all of five seconds to look through your coins and announce that they are all worthless but at least you will know for sure.

Case Study – Bermuda 'Hogge' Penny, c.1616

When confronted with a coin outside of your chosen niche, in-depth research is essential– even for numismatic professionals. In late 2019, I was contacted by a metal detectorist who had found a strange looking coin on farmland in Kent. It was corroded from its time in the ground and looked at first to be a 17th century trade token, but unusually it showed the image of a wild boar on one side and a ship on the other. In its appearance, it resembled the early 'Hogge' token coinage of Bermuda, produced in 1616 for the first British settlers of the island. These coins all bore representations of the wild pigs that ran rampant on the island; the animals had originally been released in Bermuda from a 16th century Spanish shipwreck and were there to greet the first English settlers of the Virginia Company on their arrival in 1609. However, the designs of the Kent specimen did not match any known types in this rare and popular colonial series.

Bermuda, Sommer Islands Company, 'Hogge Money' token or coin, c17th-18th century

Bermuda, Sommer Islands Company, 'Hogge' Twopence, c.1616

As I had very limited knowledge of the early Bermudan numismatic record, I had to conduct as thorough research as possible before offering the coin for sale at auction. Initially, I consulted internet resources. I compared the images of my client's find in the Portable Antiquities Scheme database against recently sold examples to see how far it differed from the accepted norm. I could see that it was roughly the size of a Twopence, but lacked a mark of value above the pig and had different portholes on the ship on the reverse.

Next, I turned to books and journals to try and explain the differences in design. An article in the 2009 edition of the Colonial Newsletter postulated the existence of two extra denominations in the Hogge series: a 'Penny' and 'Fourpence', neither of which had ever been seen. This theory was echoed in 'The Coins Of The British Commonwealth Of Nations, Part 3: West Indies' by F. Pridmore. As such, the possibility that the coin was the previously lost 'Penny' denomination began to emerge.

The metal detectorist who discovered the coin had submitted it to NGC, who returned it with no formal decision made. NGC did, however, provide a full metallurgic breakdown of the coin that they had undertaken during their examination. Armed with this information I was able to contact numismatic professionals in the early Bermudan series, namely M. Sportack and C. Simpson. These two specialists provided a wealth of information on the Hogge coinage and were able to place the information I had in context. The metallurgic data suggested that the Kent specimen was produced prior to the 19th century as its copper contained no modern impurities such as silicon or cobalt. Due to the levels of bismuth in the copper, Sportack was able to establish that the metal used was likely Swedish in origin rather than Cornish (as was used for most original Hogge pieces). As such, the prospect of the coin being a recent copy was thrown out, and the likelihood that the coin was either authentic or a near-contemporary tribute piece to the original Hogge coinage became more realistic.

With the research I had conducted, I was able to place the coin in an auction in April 2021 with all of the available data, raising the possibility that the coin was a tribute piece but also that it could potentially be the missing Penny denomination. This wealth of data – alongside the coin's appearance in the Bermudan national newspaper – piqued the interest of the collector base, ultimately causing the coin to jump from its pre-sale estimate of £5,000-8,000 to its final price of £33,600.

No matter the resource you choose, research is an integral part of numismatics that cannot and should not be avoided. By making use of books and internet resources coupled with expert advice you will put yourself in a strong position from which to begin buying and selling coins. However – in most cases you can only safely involve industry professionals when you already own a coin, as it is obviously unwise to go around seeking advice on a prospective deal in case you unwittingly generate competition. You must already be relatively sure of yourself when buying coins. Consequently, the final skill you must learn before you begin trading is that of evaluating the quality of individual coins to ensure you are purchasing only genuine and high-standard pieces

Chapter 3.2.
Quality and Authenticity

Research can tell you a great deal about coins. It can allow you to identify the rarest types, those least seen at auction and those that have recently exhibited either a rise or drop in value. Through proper research you can potentially isolate extremely profitable buying opportunities - but this, as discussed, is only half of the equation. The second - equally important - part is coin grade, how the quality of an individual coin compares to others of its type. This essentially means every aspect from the coin's production standard through to its level of wear or damage. Just imagine; you see a coin offered for auction, bid sight unseen and win at a price you think is cheap. It arrives, and it then transpires that the coin has been cleaned, is significantly worn, is damaged or worst of all – it is a copy.

Alongside your in-depth market and numismatic research, you must also familiarise yourself with what original and untouched coins look like in contrast to improperly handled and inauthentic pieces. This is true across all of numismatics; non-specific to any one area, it is always valuable to be able to identify issues with a coin's surfaces or detail, or to challenge its authenticity if need be. Through close analysis and experience you will be able to recognise the difference between an entirely original piece and one with surface alteration or significant wear. The presence of these detractions should certainly not stop you from buying, but rather should simply affect how much you will pay and allow you to make as accurate comparisons as possible with other coins of the same type.

If you are limiting your buying to TPG coins then grading analysis will already have been undertaken by the grading company of your choice. However, some of the greatest profits in numismatics are achieved by recognising problem-free and high grade coins while they are still uncertified, buying and encapsulating them and then re-offering for sale. As such, it is undeniably beneficial to be able to assess coin quality and authenticity yourself.

You will need a high-powered loupe for detailed analysis of coins. The most useful means of educating yourself is to examine multiple examples of original and damaged coins; in lieu of that, this chapter will instead cover the theoretical elements to look out for and offer a base from which to conduct further research.

1. Production Standard

One of the main factors by which you can judge a coin is the quality to which it has been made - its standard of production. The importance of a well-made piece has already been emphasised; collectors will always prefer coins with good-quality metal, sharply-struck devices and an overall pleasing appearance. Even cursory examination of a coin's planchet and strike will evince its comparative quality, particularly when directly compared to others of the same type. Major mint errors can also be identified when assessing production standards.

Production standard is especially useful to assess in conjunction with TPG-certified coins. Two coins may be technically of the same grade, yet their visual appeal can be worlds apart due to the conditions of their manufacture. Here are two James II Shillings, both struck in 1686 and both graded MS62 by PCGS. It does not take an expert to determine the difference between these two coins; the left-hand example has far less detail, more pronounced die deterioration and an overall loss of eye appeal, while the right-hand piece is perfectly struck with fresh dies and is well-centred on the flan.

The grade may have been the same for these two coins, but their prices were markedly different. The left-hand piece sold for a $1,440 while the right-hand piece achieved $5,700. Unless you pay attention to production standard, you might well be buying a crudely-produced and weakly struck example of a type which, despite its technically high grade, will not be of significant interest to collectors.

Much regarding coin production standards was covered earlier, and thus this chapter will merely provide further instruction how to distinguish a well-made coin from an inferior one through examining its planchet and strike. For the most part these scrutinies should only be applied to ancient, hammered and early milled coins, as from about 1800 onwards coin production became so standardised that most finished coins were essentially identical. Preservation is far more important for these later pieces, as well as any varieties and errors.

Engraving standard will not be covered here. Despite its importance to collectors, the quality of die engraving is intrinsic to a given coin type and is an aspect that relates more to the quality of the type itself rather than to individual coins within it[22]. The same is true of metal quality; rarely do coins vary in their alloy composition within the same series (as otherwise the face value will constantly fluctuate) and so although collectors prefer coins with a higher precious metal content, this is again a factor specific to a given coin type. Remember, you should always compare coins with others of the same series when evaluating production quality, as some coinages are notoriously poor and even the finest example of that type may well look inferior to that of another coinage.

The three main aspects of a coin's production standard to evaluate are its Planchet (I), Strike (II) and the presence of any Varieties and Rarities (III).

I. Planchet

a) **Shape and evenness.** The first aspect to evaluate is the shape of the planchet itself. Many ancient coins have fairly well-regulated round flans, a factor also true of Arabic Dinars and hammered pennies circulating in

---

22   An exception is true of ancient coins, where some pieces are famous for having far finer engraving quality than others within the same type due to being the work of a more accomplished artist.

the later 1st millennium AD. However as denomination and coin size grew, production became less regulated and many coins began to lose their round shape and instead focused solely on having the correct weight. When examining a hammered or ancient coin, the shape and evenness of the flan directly contribute to its appeal to collectors. Look for those pieces with the most circular appearance (as most dies were engraved with circular designs, these round coins also have the greatest chance of bearing the most detail), comparing with others of the type for accuracy.

Coupled with their irregular shape, many hammered coins also have a poor distribution of metal in their blanks and this unevenness can lead to thin edges that are prone to cracking; sometimes entire chunks of the coin can separate and leave ragged edges which are very off-putting to collectors. Many coinage types are more irregular than others, but by comparing with other examples you can quickly identify how your piece compares against the general standard of that coinage.

Two Anglo-Saxon Pennies of the King Baldred of the same type both offered at auction in 2018. The 'ragged' piece on the left sold for a hammer price of $575 whilst the round and complete piece hammered for $5,400.

b) **Adjustment marks.** These marks are left when an overweight coin blank was produced and subsequently filed down to remove excess metal and standardise weight prior to striking. Adjustment marks will almost always be on the face of the coin rather than the edge. If only minor, then the strike can sometimes obscure these marks entirely, especially in the field where the dies impart the most pressure on the face of the coin. If deeply adjusted, then there will almost always be a trace of ugly filing marks across the face of the coin obscuring the designs and affecting the desirability to collectors.

A pair of France Ecus both struck in 1792, the right-hand example showing adjustment marks

Adjustment marks are most often found on milled coins from the mid-17th until the late 18th century, and can be distinguished from post-mint filing as they will have been flattened and softened by the strike. As a mint practice they will never affect value in the same way as if a coin was filed after striking, but collectors nonetheless prefer coins with little to no adjustment marking.

c) **Annealing marks**. Annealing marks are common on the large Taler or Crown-sized silver coins from the late 14th century through to the 17th century, and manifest themselves as groups of soft-edged cracks on a coin's surface usually corresponding with areas of striking weakness. Almost exclusively found on hammered coins, these marks are inevitable in many series. Although not as obtrusive as adjustment marks, once again collectors will pay more for examples not bearing these annealing cracks.

Close-up of annealing marks on an Elizabeth I Crown struck in 1601

d) **'Haymarks'**. Also called 'flecking', these are marks that occur mostly on European milled coins of the 17th and 18th centuries, and numerous theories exist as to quite what they are. Their name comes from a belief that the planchets of early milled coins struck in screw presses had to be hot to take the strike fully, after which the still-hot coins were placed in hay to cool down. Sometimes, it is said, the hay would ignite from the heat and leave black pits on the coin. This theory is now mostly disregarded, as fire-damaged coins have a very specific appearance and burning hay would not leave such precise marks across the surfaces. Additionally, one would think that after starting numerous fires the moneyers might cotton on and consider changing their system. Another theory says that this flecking is simply the remains of extremely rough adjustment marking which has been otherwise obscured by the strike. However, the most widely accepted theory states that when the metal alloy was poorly mixed, impurities would show at the surface as haymarks; silver and gold coins of the 17th and 18th centuries were alloyed with Welsh and Midlands tin, and the corrosion of tin impurities over time would leave black streaks on the coin. Again this theory has problems, as tin has a far lower melting point than silver or gold and so it would be unlikely for clumps of tin to remain together at the coin surfaces, but it would seem that some form of alloying issue is the most likely cause of these marks. Whatever their origin, these flecks can undoubtedly hurt the appearance of a coin.

Anne Shilling, 1703, exhibiting haymarks

As they are less obtrusive than bona fide adjustment marks and rarely impact a coin's sharpness, haymarks are among the least significant production issues of all. This being said, if they pass over the portrait of a monarch such as the Anne Shilling illustrated above, they can reduce the eye appeal and give collectors an excuse not to bid.

If a coin has been produced on an even and solid piece of metal of the correct weight (thus removing the need for adjustment), it will certainly have the best-quality planchet possible. The next element to examine is, of course, just how well that planchet has been struck.

II. Strike

a) **Highpoint sharpness**. The most deeply-engraved parts of a coin's dies are the least likely to reach the planchet of the coin they are striking. If a die has been overly engraved and there are slight irregularities with the thickness and regularity of blanks then there may be considerable variation in striking sharpness between coins. If the stars align and the coin is struck perfectly on a perfect planchet, then the design will have detail all the way to its very highest points. No matter if your coin is ancient, antique or modern, a sharp strike is certainly a most desirable feature - particularly if these well-struck design highpoints have also been minimally worn.

If a coin has been softly struck then the highest points of the design will appear flat and featureless. This can be difficult to distinguish from circulation wear in some respects, but a generally safe method is to look at the colour and texture of the surfaces. Handling removes the original surfaces of a coin and so, whilst those untouched areas in the recesses develop a patina, the worn highpoints will appear lighter where hands have removed the upper layer. If a coin has flat highpoints but a uniform tone and colour across the planchet it has a good chance of being merely softly struck. The two 1689 William and Mary Halfcrowns illustrated were both certified as Mint State by NGC and neither has any circulation wear, but the right-hand example is considerably better struck and thus has far more highpoint detail.

b) **Localised weakness.** Should the planchet of a coin be uneven and not flat then, when struck, those higher portions of the planchet will hit the die first and be disproportionately sharp whilst the lower-lying portions will hit the die last and be weaker. Sometimes this effect is so pronounced that entire portions of the design are lost and there appears to be a 'bald spot' of localised weakness on the coin. This is prevalent throughout hammered and early milled coins. If the coin is clearly as struck and has lustre shimmering across the sharp and soft aspects alike then it will still be desirable to collectors and befitting of a high grade, but this effect can offer a distraction from a coin's eye appeal. Even if a coin is technically the highest graded it may be passed up in favour of an evenly struck piece, so it is usually better to ensure the design is as complete as possible.

c) **Centring and double striking.** Where ancient and hammered coins are concerned, production standards were not uniform enough for off-centre or double struck coins to be enticing as errors. It was rarer for a coin to be produced perfectly than imperfectly, and so it is these pristine pieces that now command the greatest premiums amongst collectors. Buyers will look for those coins that have a well-centred design on a large flan. If the first hit was unsuccessful then the moneyer may have struck the coin again, giving a blurred doubling of the designs. This is generally unappealing and so collectors will seek those coins struck once, definitively, to give sharp and clear detail.

Left: Double-struck hammered Quarter Angel of James I. Right: Double-struck milled Shilling of William III.

As discussed, the later the coin the more appealing double striking and off-centre strikes become, but for the majority of coinage types these are undesirable traits.

d) **Age of dies.** The extent to which the dies have been used prior to striking your coin determine how the finished product looks. If dies are nearing the end of their life then the coins they strike will have somewhat weakened detail, sometimes exhibiting blotchy lumps where the die has rusted or corroded over time. Some collectors consider this as adding character and take no issue with it, and indeed if die rust is light it can give a pleasantly matt texture to a coin's surfaces. However, at its worst it entirely obscures and distracts from a coin's visual appeal and will lead to weaker results at auction.

Two Anglo-Saxon Pennies of the King Edward the Martyr both offered at auction in 2020. The far more rusted piece on the left sold for £3,968 whilst the sharper right-hand example sold for £11,160

III. Varieties and Rarities

Evaluating the production standard of coins is probably the easiest form of numismatic analysis for the novice collector to understand. It takes but a moment to compare your coin with another example of greater detail or grade, and this comparison enables you to quickly assess how well-made your coin is. However, a more difficult area of analysis regarding a coin's production concerns errors and varieties. You should always look three times at a coin: once to see what it is, once again to evaluate its quality, and one more time carefully to look for errors, varieties or other value drivers. Varieties and rarities can dramatically contribute to a coin's sale price, and it is those numismatists who examine each coin as if it is the first of the type they have seen who will pick up the most minute elements that can spell the difference between a $100 and $1,000 coin.

Mechanical errors will not be covered here; in general, issues with a coin's fabric or production can be quite easily identified even without any expertise. This will only cover those error types that are considered as varieties in their own right and carry an associated premium for their rarity.

a) **Overpunched numbers and letters.** These elements are the main determiner of a coin 'variety'. When first assembling a coin die or re-punching a worn one, a die sinker would sometimes punch an incorrect letter or date number. For earlier coins, literacy of mint workers was a rarity and so these errors would often go unnoticed. If however they did not escape scrutiny, the die sinker would then have to punch the correct letter or digit over the incorrect one. This also occurs in the final one or two digits of the date when the die sinker reused an outdated die that had not been yet worn out. These elements can appear as an extra serif, loop, diagonal or other element visible beneath a letter or digit on the coin. Many collectors consider these coins as types in themselves and, due to their rarity, some error varieties can command significantly higher prices than more common normal issues.

For many coins there is a comprehensive list of known varieties to which a potential error coin can be compared, but if handling a newly-discovered error then you should compare with other letters or numbers on the coin to identify the specific over-punched character. It is generally the rule that a coin will only have a letter that is also present in the legend struck over another.

b) **Die varieties.** Within a short but heavily collected coin series (such as within a UM), sometimes analysis will have been conducted on every die combination for a given coin type - even without notable errors or marks. The saturation of collectors within these market types means that, even if heavily worn, collectors will compare a coin's visible features to establish which specific pair of dies struck that coin. If it transpires that it is rare, it can sell for many multiples of a common die type. This trend is prominent within early US cents as well as amongst other American coins.

c) **Numismatic or historical intrigue.** Sometimes a coin will encounter alteration after it is struck; generally this is always considered post-mint damage. However, in rare cases what appears at first to be damage can turn out to be something else altogether. An ex-colleague of mine bought an 1843 proof US Cent at auction which had been considerably scratched and graffitied meaning it was in a PCGS 'details' holder. A coin with such damage was less popular than undamaged examples and so the price he paid was reasonable. This numismatist then conducted research on the coin and discovered that the scratches precisely matched up with the engraving for the following year's US Cent design; in fact, the coin was none other than a trial engraving piece by the US chief engraver Christian Gobrecht. As a result, the coin immediately had a greater value for its numismatic significance.

Simply put, a coin's production standard comes down to three main elements: how much of the die design has been applied to the coin, the quality and shape of the metal to which it is applied and the presence of any errors or varieties. Once you have established these factors, the next stage is to determine the quality of your coin's surfaces – a somewhat more challenging process.

2. Scanning Surfaces

A coin's 'surfaces' specifically refer to the top layer of its metal, the finish on the planchet itself; the term incorporates anything regarding the coin's colour, toning, metal quality and deliberate surface alteration or cleaning. It is often used to refer to specifically the fields (the space between the designs of a coin) as these empty areas offer the clearest view of the coin's surface quality. Being able to accurately appraise a coin's surfaces is one of the most fundamental elements of numismatics. Surfaces, and how appealing they look, can define the difference between a $1,000 coin and a $10,000 coin, if not more.

Being able to accurately judge a coin's surfaces takes time and experience, but here follow the basics split into four main groups: how a coin's surfaces should look (I), how they should not look (II), how a coin's edge should appear (III) and how planchet colour can change either naturally or unnaturally (IV). By acquainting yourself with the intricacies of coin surfaces you will be able to avoid accidentally picking up a cleaned or overly handled specimen, circumvent forgeries, and buy the absolutely best coins possible.

I. Original Surface Textures

These are simply the main surface textures associated with uncirculated coins, those you would expect to find on a Mint State piece. There are several types of authentic surface texture; if the dies or planchet are in any way irregular it may leave a different effect on a coin's surfaces, but these are the four main appearances an uncirculated coin will have.

a) **Lustre**. Caused by microscopic metal striations in the surface of the planchet from striking, lustre causes an attractive satin effect on a coin's surface. Rather than being shiny like, say, a pool of water or a polished gold ring, lustre appears as a shimmer, a shifting mass of white luminescence on the surface of the coin. Authentic lustre is caused by a metal from the centre of the planchet flowing towards the edges when struck and forming a thin layer of particles, and so lustre patterns should also generally follow this outward direction. When tilting the coin in the light you should see a 'cartwheel' pattern emerge, two opposing wedge-shaped patches of lustre spinning around the coin. As discussed earlier, lustre is extremely delicate and even moderate handling will cause it to fade. Accordingly, lustre is a better indication than almost any other that a coin will have original surfaces.

Even a circulated coin can have lustre, but you will never find an authentic coin with lustre on worn central surfaces; after moderate handling, lustre is limited to the fields and recesses, those areas that will have been touched less. Due to its being a dynamic and motion-dependent effect, lustre is sometimes difficult to capture in photographs – but it quickly becomes obvious to the trained eye when a coin has lustre, even from a picture. As mentioned earlier, the most common form of forging lustre is through 'whizzing'.

b) **Reflectivity**. Coins are sometimes naturally struck with clear, reflective surfaces as opposed to the satin sheen of mint lustre. These mirror surfaces can be deliberately applied to proofs through polishing of the planchet prior to striking or are sometimes simply a quirk of a particular coinage's production. The majority of today's coins issued from mints tend to have a reflective finish as opposed to a lustrous one. Often, proof coins are produced with matte designs and mirror fields giving a pleasing contrast, while circulation coins that have reflective fields tend to also have reflective devices.

Reflectivity is a popular trait with collectors for its eye-catching and dazzling appearance, but natural mint brilliance should always be distinguished from polished coins.

c) **Die polish lines**. These are striations on a coin's surfaces that were left when the die used to strike it was itself polished. Die polishing rarely has any impact on a coin's devices as it would impact only the highest area of the die - that which strikes the field of the coin. Die polishing manifests itself as numerous raised lines in the field (scratches and hairlines will always be incuse). These lines are most often parallel and of equal depth in more modern coins, but on hammered coins die polish lines can spread seemingly randomly throughout the field and be of varied size.

Often die polish lines are associated with coins from older dies, the polishing performed to remove rust. As such, if they are extremely pronounced these lines can potentially dissuade buyers and usually correlate with a loss of die detail. For the most part, however, die polish lines are minor and offer a pleasant matte effect on a coin's surfaces.

d) **Die rust**. As mentioned in the previous section, dies can rust and this impacts the finished coin they produce. This effect varies in severity; die rust can either leave a subdued matte gleam to a coin's surfaces through a light speckled texture, or it can be incredibly prominent and entirely obscure a coin's devices.

From top left to bottom right: a Canadian 50 Cents exhibiting mint lustre, a proof gold US $20 showing reflective brilliance, a hammered Charles I Triple Unite with prominent die-polish lines and a Sovereign struck with a rusted reverse die.

Many dies exhibit rust, an intriguing element considering it would take a reasonably long time for the iron die to oxidise and dies did not have a long lifespan (the prolonged hammering would eventually cause them to split). Either way, they are an undeniably common feature in older coins. Die rust mostly appears as numerous bumps on the surfaces of a coin, some of which might be larger than the others but importantly they will all be raised - die rust can occasionally be mistaken for corrosion which instead leaves shallow pits in a coin's surfaces.

II. Modified Surface Textures

These are the most common textures that coins develop from both normal handling and from deliberate alteration. Again, there are numerous ways a coin can have its surfaces altered but these are the ones you will see most frequently.

a) **Scratches, hairlines and circulation wear.** These effects are almost always found on coins to some degree unless the coin has never been handled. Even then, technically Mint State coins can exhibit scratches as some occur in the mint itself or in bags as they leave the mint. 'Hairlines' is a term used for light, long thin scratches caused by friction with a cloth or abrasive and is most often used to describe parallel scratches on the reflective surfaces of proofs. Circulation wear is as it sounds, areas of the coin being flattened from handling.

Collectors are perfectly happy to accept coins with circulation wear, scratches or hairlines – these are associated with normal wear-and-tear and so are not seen as damage - provided they are incidental and not deliberate. Scratches should appear to follow no uniform direction or pattern. Circulation scratches and hairlines happen over time and from impact or friction with a variety of items, and so the scratches will appear random and dispersed over the planchet. A heavily worn coin will appear smooth at first but closer examination will reveal countless small scratches that have built up on top of one another. Circulation wear is also an incidental effect and should begin at the highest points of the designs and work its way down; if every element of the devices is worn equally, it is likely that the coin has been sweated (deliberately worn). Due to the ubiquity of scratches and wear on almost all coins, having fewer marks or hairlines has a strong positive correlation with higher prices paid at auction.

It is beneficial to take the type of coin into consideration when you examine hairlines. Some coin types such as matt proofs have swirling hairlines on their surfaces as part of their production which leads the grading services to give them lower scores. On the other hand, Canadian 'specimens' also have swirls of polish lines on their coins; if you were to compare one of this issue with a regular Mint State piece it would surely appear polished, but these swirled types will regularly find themselves in SP67 or SP68 (near-perfect grades) holders. There are exceptions to the rule, but in general it is always better to identify hairlines and scratches and aim to purchase those coins with the least marks possible.

b) **Cleaning and polishing.** By far the most common surface modification for coins to have encountered, cleaning has been a blight of numismatics for thousands of years. It is only logical; everybody knows that shiny coins are better, and so what do you do if that shine dulls? You do what you can to restore its brightness, right? Wrong! Cleaning is any action intended to enhance the appearance of a coin or to remove dirt and patina and usually is attempted with a cloth or abrasive. Even the lightest wipe will leave clusters of hairline scratches across the face of a coin which immediately impacts its value. As opposed to normal wear and tear, hairlines from cleaning appear as numerous parallel striations which can give an unattractive brushed look to the metal when caught in the light. The image below shows the centres of two William and Mary Halfcrowns (similar to those discussed in the previous section). The left-hand example has been cleaned and the right hand example has been scratched and worn from circulation wear. Notice how the field in front of Mary's face on the cleaned example shows parallel striations, while that of the right hand example has no such brushmarks and instead shows numerous small scratches of varying direction.

Cleaning can be immensely subtle, but it is best to assume that brushmarks of regular direction such as this are always indicative of cleaning. Some die-polish lines will also be parallel to each other, but these will always be raised and not incuse.

Polishing is a far more dramatic form of cleaning and describes a coin that has been abrasively rubbed until its features are blurred and it is bright and featureless. These coins are immediately distinguishable by even the untrained eye, and are essentially worthless no matter their rarity. As far as surface alteration goes, polishing is the most sure-fire way of obliterating a coin's originality.

c) **Smoothing, repairing and plugging**. These three surface modifications reflect deliberate attempts to modify coins and often intersect with one another; a repair is manifested by smoothing of a coin's fields or flat portions of the design, and plugging is technically a form of repairing a previous hole. Although these activities were often undertaken by collectors in antiquity who were innocently trying to improve their coins, the truth is that these modifications are now mostly intended to deceive collectors into thinking a coin is undamaged.

Plugging is fairly easy to spot as an area of surface disruption. This can vary depending on how skilfully the hole was repaired, but generally the eye is quickly drawn to the discoloured or featureless patch of metal where the hole once was. Smoothing and scratch repair can be more subtle; generally, you should look for an area of the field or design that shows a disproportionately concentrated amount of hairline scratches, far more than the rest of the coin. If you look carefully in the light, you may see the blurred outline of a scratch beneath this smoothed area of hairlines. This is where the metal was repeatedly rubbed to obscure a deep surface mark. For the impact that repair and smoothing has on value, it is better to leave a coin with its damage and offer as-is.

Field tooling is sometimes classed as repair, intended to level the fields and obscure a scratch. Tooling is not so much smoothing as it is roughening, however, and can leave numerous furrows in the field distinguishable from die-polish lines from being dug into the metal rather than raised above it. Design tooling occurs when someone has attempted to re-engrave the devices of a worn coin to make it appear sharper; this activity can be easily identified through comparison with genuine pieces.

d) **Whizzing.** To recap, this practice is intended to emulate mint lustre on an otherwise dull coin and is particularly prevalent in the US market. Whereas smoothing and repair was sometimes undertaken by collectors of old before the market for originality existed, whizzing is a more recent activity and one that is purely intended to deceive. Whizzing involves the use of a circular brush to polish and literally melt the highest surface of the metal and redistribute it, and a whizzed coin may at first appear lustrous; however, once you have examined just a handful of coins with authentic lustre, that whizzed piece will begin to appear odd. The lustre that whizzing creates is random and does not follow the circular 'cartwheel' pattern of a genuine piece. Additionally, examination of the surface will reveal a strange texture appearing as minute speckling to the devices and fields alike. Finally, the motion of the brush will leave tiny ridges of metal on the devices that follow the direction that the metal has been pushed. The skill of the 'whizzard' will vary hugely and the highest tier pieces may be difficult at first to distinguish from those with genuine surfaces, but comparison with original coins will quickly draw attention to the inauthentic surface texture of the whizzed coin. Whizzing dramatically impacts coin value as it has removed the entire original surface, and so when in doubt it is sensible to have a piece third-party graded for certainty.

From top left to bottom right: a George IV proof 5 Pounds with a repair in front of the portrait, a Charles I Pound with heavily tooled fields, a plugged US $1 of 1795 and a whizzed US $1 of 1847.

III. Edge

These are specifically those elements to look for on the edge, a frequently overlooked but important area of the coin. Generally the edge of a coin should either be plain (in ancient, hammered and some proof coins), 'reeded' with parallel grooves, struck with an incuse or raised legend, or otherwise marked with some other pattern. The edge is an important determiner of coin authenticity as will be covered in the next section, and also can exhibit subtle mishandling that will impact coin value.

a) **Mount marks.** As they sound, these are marks left from a coin being included within a piece of jewellery. For the most part a coin that has been in jewellery will also show heavy cleaning or polishing, but occasionally the only evidence will be a small lump of solder or metal disruption at the top, bottom or elsewhere on the edge of the coin. These are common on gold coins and mostly those above 200 years in age. If a coin has been in a circular 'swivel' mount it will have two small holes drilled into its edge at 12 and 6 or 3 and 9 o'clock; these are often plugged but usually leave areas of discolouration behind. Using a loupe and tracking around the edge and rim of a coin will usually reveal any hint of Mount marks.

b) **Clipping.** This is prevalent on only hammered and ancient coins, and describes the removal of metal with tin snips from the edge of a coin to extract a profit. Clipping was easy for irregularly produced hammered coins and was such an issue that it formed the chief reason for lettered edges beginning to be applied to coins in the 17th century. The common inscription on the edge of British coins even up until the present day reads DECUS ET TUTAMEN, meaning "an ornament and a safeguard (against clipping)".

Clipping will appear as a flan shortage, and will either be rounded where the clipper has cut around the edge of a coin or may appear instead as sharp diagonal slices. The best way of determining if a coin has been clipped rather than merely poorly made is to check its weight against full-flanned specimens. If it still weighs correctly for the type then its appearance will likely be as-made rather than clipped.

c) **Filing.** This is a more difficult element to evaluate. Mostly impacting hammered and ancient coins (yet present on early and even later milled coins), filing was another means of removing metal from a coin by applying a rasp to the edge. Edge filing appears as parallel scrape marks on the edge or rim of a coin, much like adjustment marks as they use essentially the same method. As filing would leave a rounded finished product, it was intended to be more subtle than clipping. However, some planchets were adjusted around their edge with a file before striking to regulate their weight; if not struck in a collar or with an edge legend, these pieces will appear to have edge filing and the grading companies could potentially deem this filing to be unscrupulous. As a rule, you should try to avoid pieces with this element unless it is definitely an intrinsic aspect of the coin type.

d) **Edge knocks.** These are the simplest form of edge modification to look for – those areas of the rim where the coin has hit a hard surface. Edge knocks are very noticeable and hard to disguise, appearing as sharp digs into the metal which catch the eye and the finger. Generally, small edge knocks are treated much the same way as scratches, they are associated with regular wear and tear and so do not detract from value as much as deliberate alteration. But, as usual, the collector should aim for those pieces with the fewest edge knocks.

IV. Colour

The final point to cover in brief is that of a coin's correct colour. Metal naturally tones in predictable patterns over time, and any diversion from that course can indicate a coin that has had altered surfaces.

a) **Authentic patina.** An original and attractive tone is always a desirable feature in a coin, and each metal tends to have its own distinctive colourations based on its reactivity. Copper and bronze coins generally turn a dull brown over time but can sometimes tone to vivid purples and reds – however, as a metal highly prone to severe oxidisation, tone on copper can be more of a warning sign of growing verdigris rather than an attractive characteristic. The widest range of colours are found on silver coins, which can range anywhere from cobalt to red, magenta to gold, yellow, green, orange etc, and the more appealing the combination the generally greater the value. Gold coins are the least reactive but can still occasionally tone to vibrant reds and oranges, and these rank amongst the most valuable of patinas for their rarity. Patina corresponds with areas of increased stress to the planchet, and so it often follows the pattern of a coin's devices and 'cloaks' them in colour. This means patina can provide shadows emphasising the designs and increasing the eye appeal of an otherwise relatively worn coin.

Patina forms slowly and colours should blend quite seamlessly into one another. If a coin is left in unfavourable conditions too long it may develop an unattractive tone which impacts its value, but it is usually more sensible to leave a coin with unappealing tone than to attempt cleaning it in any way. Numismatists do always favour originality.

b) **Artificial and natural re-toning.** If a coin has been cleaned, unscrupulous individuals may attempt to artificially re-tone it to appear as if it has original surfaces. The technique can vary in sophistication anywhere from treating a coin with a cocktail of chemicals to placing it in a bag with some smashed-up boiled eggs (the sulphur reacts with silver coins and causes them to tone). Fortunately, artificial toning is relatively easy to distinguish from genuine. As it has usually been formed far more swiftly, fake patina will appear blotchy in comparison to authentic tone and its transition from colour to colour will be far more abrupt and jarring to the eye. The chemicals used for artificial toning can cause damage to a coin long after they have been applied and so artificially toned coins should be purchased only with extreme caution.

Even if not artificially re-toned, a cleaned coin will eventually re-tone by itself. This is definitely preferable to artificial re-toning, but the surfaces of these coins will always appear unusual and overly reflective even with a layer of colour above it. As toning – like lustre - follows those areas of the surface that experienced the greatest stress from striking, genuine patina will blend with lustre and cloak the devices of a coin, beautifully accenting the designs. However when a coin is cleaned, that layer of redistributed lustrous metal is stripped away. Accordingly, a distinctive feature of re-toned coins is a flat expressionless wave of colour which flows indiscriminately over the fields and devices alike.

Left: US pattern 50 Cents 1869 which has been cleaned and artificially toned; note the overall polished look to the highpoints and the unbroken blue colour. Right: China $1, 1912 with authentic toning over lustre. On this coin, the gold and red tone blend together and the central portrait (where the planchet experienced the highest pressure) has most of its original colour.

c) **Dipping.** In contrast to artificial toning, a dipped coin generally appears as too bright and perfect for its age and has had its (presumably unappealing) toning removed. Dipping uses chemicals to strip surface dirt or patina from a coin, and gentle dipping is hard to detect; indeed, in some ways gentle dipping can be relatively harmless. If a coin is over-dipped, however, its mint lustre will be destroyed and its surfaces will appear 'lifeless' and with a dull gleam instead of a satin effect. Additionally, close inspection may show minute pockmarks on its surfaces. These coins will also re-tone in the manner of cleaned or polished coins with indiscriminate colour across the planchet.

Collectors prefer original coins with original colour. There are some occasions in which dipping in particular substances (acetone, ammonia) can enhance a coin without damaging its metal, but these should not be attempted by novices. Where possible an expert should be consulted to ensure you do not unwittingly destroy your coin.

Many new collectors underestimate the importance of a coin's surfaces. They feel that the chief motivation for collecting coins is history, and so surely if your example is recognisable and has clear details it will be as valuable as any other specimen of that type. On the contrary, a coin's surfaces are the canvas for natural tone, lustre, sharp details and all of the other aesthetic elements that collectors develop a taste for as they continue through the numismatic hobby. Developing an understanding of coin surfaces is absolutely imperative for a successful foray into the numismatic market - but have patience. It may take time to properly understand the intricacies of altered and original surfaces, and with repeated comparisons and examination you will eventually be able to accurately evaluate these elements and buy accordingly.

3. Identifying Forgeries

There are masses of fake coins in the global numismatic market. Apparently this is common knowledge, as on seeing an old coin nearly everybody asks first "how old is it?" followed by "how much is it worth?" and finally, "how do you know if it's real?" The simple truth of it is that if you assign significant trade or collector value to a small and often crude metal token, it only makes sense to try and produce your own copies for profit. For this reason, coins have always encountered forging. For the vast majority of their existence it was contemporary coins which were counterfeited to be used in trade, and it was likely within a year of the first coins being struck in Lydia that the first copies began to be produced.

Money was forged even in those cultures that did not use coins; the Aztecs of South America traded cacao beans, and some unscrupulous characters would fill empty cacao husks with mud, reseal them, and then mix them with genuine cacao pods to fool traders.

As coinages lost their intrinsic metal value the benefits of forging them dwindled, and only with the rise of collector demand in the last couple of centuries have antique coins also been forged. Nowadays, the balance has shifted. Barely any currently circulating coins are worth copying - besides those stronger currencies such as the British pound - and counterfeiting has moved instead to the larger-denomination banknotes. Accordingly the flow of fake coins being churned out daily by numerous Asian and European counterfeiters are all pretending to be antique, intended to deceive collectors and not everyday traders; and, as the potential payday is far greater, copies are becoming increasingly more sophisticated.

In October 2020, Roma Numismatics of London sold an extraordinary coin – a gold example of the Ides of March Denarius (considered to be an Aureus) struck under Brutus in 42 BC. Silver Denarii bearing the same dual dagger design are known and always highly popular at auction, but just three examples of this type are thought to exist in gold. One is in the Deutsche Bundesbank collection, one is on long-term loan to the British Museum (discussed earlier), and the third was the piece offered by Roma.

Rome, Marcus Junius Brutus "Assassin of Caesar and Imperator" Aureus, 44-42 BC

Since the first appearance of an example at auction doubt has been cast on these pieces; they were too enigmatic, too unknown, and too obvious a target for deep-pocketed collectors. Gradually through die analysis and substantiation from museums the market has come to accept them, and the example offered by Roma had one additional accolade – it had been certified by NGC[23]. This instilled such confidence in bidders that when the lot opened the price climbed, and climbed, and climbed, eventually reaching the unprecedented heights of £2.7m hammer - £3.24m with buyer's premium, and a new record for any ancient coin sold at auction.

Doubt still remains among some collectors, but decades of work and research have assured the wider numismatic community that these gold Ides of March pieces are likely genuine. What the Roma auction has shown is that, genuine or not, the possible payday for selling a convincing forgery is immense and entirely justifies advanced forging techniques.

The advancement of coin forgeries has led some to believe that casual collectors will soon be unable to distinguish genuine examples from fake and will fall by the wayside, meaning that numismatics is on a 'death march' – but the situation is not so dramatic as this. It is true that collectors must be vigilant and check and double check their coins, but it is perfectly possible to observe careful methods of detecting fakes and avoid being burned by forgeries. The same methods of ascertaining coin quality coupled with a range of additional techniques can quickly weed out counterfeits. And similarly to assessing for coin quality, coin authentication can be outsourced to the grading companies for absolute certainty.

As always the best means of familiarising yourself with the differences between fakes and genuine coins is in-hand inspection, but this section will provide at least a starting point and will cover the major diagnostic features of fake coins split into simple and sophisticated forgeries. This way you can hope to successfully navigate the numismatic market purchasing only genuine and as-described coins.

I. Simple Forgeries
The vast majority of fake coins are very simple; this is not to say that they are not deceptive, only that they would not fool a numismatist with even moderate experience. Fortunately only the bare minimum of analysis and research is necessary to distinguish these fakes from genuine examples, and so such copies are generally limited to bazaars, flea markets and the

---

23 It is important to note that NGC offers no guarantee of authenticity for coins certified through its Ancients service.

like, ie anywhere they can be bought by non-numismatists.

a) **Die comparisons**. Many fake coins - particularly copies of rarities where originals are near-impossible to locate – use entirely fabricated dies that differ significantly from genuine pieces. Some are even so-called 'fantasy' pieces bearing designs that never existed in history, types that throw together a few enticing elements (an early date, a famous monarch and a dramatic-looking design). It is the work of a moment to compare these pieces to genuine examples and conduct a die comparison, ie comparing elements of the genuine design to those of the suspected fake. This is the first hurdle where most fakes fail, and frankly these fantasy pieces have been doomed since the internet allowed real-time comparison with photos of genuine examples.

b) **Surface texture**. If a forger has made a cast copy of a genuine coin then the fake may pass the die comparison test. Cast coins are produced by making moulds from two sides of a coin, filling them with molten metal and joining the two finished casts together. Once again surface analysis comes to the rescue on these examples, as cast copies have an entirely different surface texture to that of struck coins. Cast coins are the result of cooled molten metal while coins that have been struck are solid pieces of metal impressed by two dies. Accordingly the former method produces tiny air bubbles at the surface where the metal cools, an element absent on struck coins that have remained solid throughout the process. Cast pieces also typically have softer details. The presence of surface bubbles and weak design detail is almost always indicative of a cast copy.

Left: Cast copy of a 1653 Commonwealth of England Crown. Right: Genuine example

of the same coin. Notice the air bubbles in the centre of the cast piece, as well as the generally weaker details.

c) **Living on the edge**. If a cast copy has been made well, it may be difficult to pick out bubbles on the surface. Fortunately, as these copies are produced by creating each side of the coin separately then joining them together lengthwise, the process often creates a seam that runs around the edge of the coin. No genuine coin will ever have a seam such as this, and its presence always implies a forgery. As many coins have edge reeding or an edge legend, successfully obscuring an edge seam is one of the most difficult elements for a forger to achieve and therefore one of the most effective methods of identifying a fake.

d) **"Clunk"**. If a coin forgery has been produced with accurate designs, a relatively clean surface texture and its edge seam has been obscured, then it can be trickier to identify it as a copy. However, one of the most basic percussive methods to determine whether a coin is inauthentic is to drop it on to a (wooden) surface and listen to the sound it makes. A few years ago I was examining an 1861 Victoria Halfpenny in about uncirculated condition; I had not looked at it closely because the coin's value was so low, only about $100 or so. Then I happened to drop it on to my desk, and was met with a distinct 'clunk' where a solid disk of copper should produce a bell-like jingling. Sure enough, closer analysis showed it to be a Chinese copy. Similarly, a silver, gold or copper coin can be balanced on one finger and gently tapped at the edge; a genuine coin should produce a clear continuous note that gently fades. If a coin has been cast, it will clunk once and then fall silent.

It is important to note that this element is not so effective on ancient and high-relief coins; the irregularity of the metal disk creates a sound more similar to the clunk that a fake will make. However, a cast coin will still have air cavities within it that will produce a different noise to a solid piece.

e) **Weight watching**. A forger may have produced an excellent copy of a coin with an invisible edge seam and minimal evidence of surface cooling, but in trying to perfect all of these visual components will almost certainly have neglected one key aspect – coin weight. As discussed, coins were historically struck to precise weights of precious metal, often at the expense of their shape, in order to regulate their value, and so if a coin varies even five per cent from its standard weight this may well mean that it is a forgery. The single most effective means of proving coin authenticity is to weigh it and compare it with the usual weight range for that type.

II. Sophisticated Forgeries

With the rise in market prices coupled with the gradual advancement of technology, some counterfeiters are getting really quite inventive. Coins are being scanned and new dies laser engraved, circumventing the primary means of identifying fakes; additionally, entirely new dies are being fabricated for hammered coins and masquerading as new and undocumented types. It is sophisticated forgeries such as these that are able to fool even experienced numismatists. I was recently given a Polish copy of a hammered penny, which I showed to coin specialists from three separate London auction houses. All of these professional numismatists were fooled and gave auction estimates ranging from £800 to £2,000.

Distinguishing sophisticated forgeries from genuine coins is a difficult skill to master and one which takes time; a specialist should be consulted where possible and if there is any doubt on a coin's authenticity you should ask questions first and buy later. If a deal appears too good to be true, it almost certainly is. These are the most effective ways of identifying sophisticated fakes.

a) **Striking detail.** To produce laser-scanned coin dies, forgers require an example of a genuine coin or a high resolution photograph. When produced from an authentic example, the likelihood of a forger getting their hands on an immaculately made coin is slim, and so most will produce their fakes from a specimen showing evidence of circulation or handling. Even if their reference specimen is flawless, often highpoint detail is lost in the counterfeiting process on either the legends or designs. As such, fake coins may show a loss of definition to the design yet without evidence of friction or circulation. Additionally, when dies are produced from photographs of authentic coins, the designs can be rendered too low-relief as their depth has to be estimated by the forger. Comparison with authentic pieces can help judge the level and depth of detail on a potential forgery.

b) **Mirror marks.** If a coin is forged based on an original and circulated example, it may show tell-tale marks or scratches that then become present on every copy. For example, fakes of the 1763 Shilling of George III are common, but most of these show the same horizontal scratch in the field in front of the King's face that featured on the original coin used to produce the forgeries.

Top: Great Britain, authentic example of a George III 'Northumberland' Shilling, 1763, showing no scratch in front of the portrait. Bottom: Forgery of the same type, showing distinctive scratch in front of portrait, softer design details and incorrect rim.

It is inefficient to produce just a few examples of a fake coin, and so generally copies of a given coin type will exist in substantial numbers. This means that there will usually be internet resources showing similar fakes to which suspicious pieces can be compared. If they both feature circulation marks and scratches in the same locations, it is likely that both are inauthentic.

As an aside, this applies only to incuse marks on the coin's surfaces. Dies often show scratches or marks which have then been rendered on every coin they produce, but these show up as raised lines as opposed to being dug into the coin.

c) **Metal analysis.** Archaeological science is a wonderful thing, and offers us an opportunity to analyse not just the elements of the coin we can see but also those invisible to the eye. Metal alloys can be analysed using XRF (X-Ray Fluorescence); when bombarded with x-rays, atoms within a structure become ionised and as their electrons re-shuffle they release their own secondary x-ray radiation. This radiation can be used to assess the atomic structure of the metal and can thus give an idea of whether it is refined or alluvial, its trace contents, and help to determine its origin.

By subjecting a coin that is considered suspicious to XRF along with a contemporary piece thought to be genuine, the trace components and makeup of both can be compared to judge how closely they match. If the suspicious coin has a vastly different alloy to that of the genuine piece and shows modern refining techniques, it can be safely assumed to be a copy, while if the two match closely it will suggest it is genuine. XRF analysis is not infallible as some of the most sophisticated forgeries actually involve the melting of genuine pieces to produce fakes, but the method provides a valuable insight nonetheless.

d) **Stylistic analysis.** When confronted with a piece with no comparable specimens such as a 'newly discovered' die variety of a coin, stylistic comparison can be used to assess its likelihood of being genuine. If a coin masquerades as being, say, from 9th century Britain but is a type previously unseen, that coin can be closely compared to other 9th century British coins to assess its production style and imagery. Even if unique, too significant a stylistic variance from contemporary coins will count against its chances of being genuine. It is useful to consult with an expert in the given field for a precise analysis of a coin's designs and production.

e) **Slab forgeries.** As mentioned, the grading services are invaluable to numismatics through the confidence they provide to inexperienced buyers. It follows logically that sophisticated forgers will not merely make the coin but the slab as well, and it is not uncommon to see a forged coin within a forged slab. Fake slabs often have minor font or label inaccuracies which are quickly evident to those familiar with genuine pieces, and so familiarising oneself with the various models of slabs over the last few decades can help quickly identify possible fakes. Additionally, by using the barcode provided you should be able to pull up images of the correct coin attributed to that number on PCGS or NGC's website (although unfortunately for some older slabs there are no photographs available). Finally, you can circumvent fake slabs simply by closely examining the coin within to see if it matches the assigned grade and attributions listed on the holder. It is always safer to examine a slabbed coin as if it is un-encapsulated, and treat it with the same caution.

f) **Provenance**. There are numerous sophisticated methods to ascertain whether or not you have a forgery in your hands, but technology is catching up. This is why it can substantially add to a coin's value if it has an extensive provenance, as the longer you can prove a coin has existed in the market the less likely that it is a recent advanced forgery. For some of the greatest - and most commonly forged - numismatic rarities such as the 1804 US Dollar or 1933 British Penny, a complete corpus (list of known specimens) exists which has a record of which coins reside in which collections. As these generally incorporate the original mintage figures, it is impossible for a newly-discovered authentic piece to enter the market, and so a provenance would be vital to sell any of these rarities. If you can confidently list where your coin has been for the last 10, 20, 50, 100 years it will add a substantial premium to its price at auction[24].

The numismatic world is a minefield of fakes, and to truly know that you are buying a properly described and fully original coin you must closely examine it in person before paying any reasonable sum, and seek expert advice if possible. Numismatics is not, however, on a 'death march' - if you buy from trusted sellers, auction houses and dealers you are likely to be buying authentic pieces and, should they turn out

---

24 This is far more applicable for coins of significant value or high quality as a record of provenance is not expected for lower-value coins.

to be fake, you will be issued a refund. Third-party grading can also provide confidence that you are buying authentic pieces even without having any expert knowledge yourself. The resources exist to forge coins to an immense degree of sophistication, but fortunately so do the tools to identify such deceptive copies. By acquainting yourself with authentic pieces and learning how to distinguish them from fakes, you will be best equipped to participate in the numismatic market without fear of being burned.

Chapter 3.3.
Buying

There is no point at which you will know everything about coins, or even everything about your chosen field of specialisation. Even the most seasoned numismatists are learning and gathering new information about their niche. That being said, once you are comfortable with the methods of assessing individual coin quality and have a rough idea which types you want, you can finally look at dipping a toe into the numismatic market and buying coins for yourself. After all, the best way to learn is to have coins physically in-hand to examine.

When buying coins, several options are open to you. You can buy from a coin dealer who maintains an active stock; you can wait and buy from auction; you can buy directly from collectors through online auction sites, or buy coins brand new from a mint. Each source brings with it its own advantages (and some their own disadvantages), but for the most part it makes sense to pick and choose where you buy from according to your own collecting habits. If you intend for your collection to hold or increase its value, buying is one half of that journey. You cannot hope to sell your coins for a price you are happy with unless you have bought wisely. As such it is wise to understand the variety of sources through which one can obtain coins, and the costs and fees associated with each.

As always, it is important to remember to buy the best coins you can, but chiefly to buy what you love. Coins can demonstrably retain and increase their value but are first and foremost bought for enjoyment. Proper buying practices can ensure you stand the best chance of buying at realistic and sustainable levels with the best chance of a profitable resale, but think of the journey and not the destination whenever you can.

Buying. 1. Dealers

By far the swiftest and securest means of buying coins is from a reputable dealer – and I do not say that simply because I work for one! As I have previously covered, dealers are the original form of numismatic professional, those individuals or companies who maintain a stock of coins available for purchase. When it comes to buying, dealers offer the easiest means of obtaining coins and there are numerous advantages to purchasing from a dealership over other coin sources - along with possible shortcomings that should also be taken into account.

Firstly, as 'dealer' is a vague term, the most important step to remember is to research your coin seller thoroughly before transacting with them to ensure that they are of good repute. Dealers come in all shapes and sizes, from the antique trader who keeps a small stock of overpriced coins to the large dedicated numismatic firms with millions of dollars of turnover; the larger and more established the dealer the greater the reputation they will need to protect. The ancient coin seller on a flea market stall probably would not care too much if an angry customer returned claiming that they had been sold fakes, whereas a prominent London or New York establishment would do all they could to resolve any customer complaints satisfactorily.

As industry professionals with a vested interest in retaining clients, reputable dealers are one of the most trustworthy sources of coins, particularly when you are just starting out and are unsure of what to buy. Dealers carry an active stock of coins at all times which you can peruse at your leisure, letting you become familiar with different coin types and identify what you like. Unlike auctions, you can transact instantly without waiting for a sale date and with the comfortable knowledge that prices are all-inclusive with no additional fees or taxes. Additionally, unlike anonymous online transactions you can buy from a dealer with full confidence that your coin is as-described and with the safety net of a refund should it turn out to not be.

The basic model for coin dealers is to buy from individuals or auctions and then resell at a profit, and as such there will always be a mark-up on the coins they offer – otherwise, they would never be able to afford a hot dinner. This does not mean you are overpaying for coins offered by dealers, however, provided that your dealer is reputable. Competition between dealerships and widespread price standardisation means that it is difficult for dealers to obtain too hefty a profit margin on their coins, as their stock would then move extremely slowly and exacerbate the inevitable cash flow issues of numismatic trading. Accordingly, dealers base their prices on the latest auction results and tend to operate on the aforementioned volume>margin model. This aspect, coupled with the avoidance of the auction competition that can push prices to unrealistic heights, means that there is a minimal risk of price inflation when buying from a dealer.

However, just as prices can be competitive at auction, they can also be extremely favourable when coins fly under the radar. Coins offered by a dealer will always have been seen by a professional and so will likely be suitably priced, while it is possible to obtain a bargain at auction that has somehow escaped the notice of other collectors. Auctions offer some of the only occasions to obtain coins below their 'market price', while it is fair to assume that coins you buy from a dealer are offered at the current going rate or, in some cases, slightly above that rate.

Despite the fact you are paying the dealer's price, they do know the quality and value of their stock and will have priced their coins accordingly. You do not risk the element prevalent on online auction sites where common coins are given ridiculous prices in the hope that inexperienced collectors will buy them without price comparison to other examples. In addition, during the Covid-19 pandemic and its associated supply and demand issues, auctions became heavily saturated by collectors and prices swiftly began to climb (in some cases exponentially), whilst dealerships became the more attractive option to buy coins at reasonable levels.

It is not always the case that coins offered by dealers have been painstakingly researched, either. I heard a story a few years ago about a particular coin that sat in a coin dealer's tray in various UK shows for a year, a 1928 South Africa Sixpence priced at £80 ($110). This type is not regarded as particularly rare or interesting and a 1927 South African Sixpence might be worth around $70, but 1928 happened to be an unusual year, unlisted in all reference guides. This brought it to the attention of the owner of a UK auction house who suggested selling it at auction as a rare date, where it realised an amazing £4,200 ($5,600) two months later. The coin was then bought by another dealer who offered it at a US auction two months after that, where this time it was described as a Specimen and sold for an unbelievable $155,000. It behoves the individual numismatist to know their subject area, and to never assume that a coin is what it seems just because it has had one or two cursory inspections. A coin's value is, as always, what collectors will pay for it, and dealers do sometimes miss things.

South Africa, George V Specimen Sixpence 1928, sold for $155,000

The greatest advantage of working with a coin dealer is the individual professional attention you receive in building your collection. When beginning in numismatics it is wise to gather as much information and intelligence as you can get, and there is essentially no one better to turn to than an experienced dealer. Not only can they advise on the quality of their own stock, but often they will be happy to offer an opinion on other deals you may have ongoing or offer a cheaper option if they have one available. The longer you maintain a relationship with a dealer, the more likely they are to offer you choice coins first, or potentially discount their stock for you. You essentially hire an expert consultant to help you to buy wisely and learn about your chosen field for the simple cost of doing business with them.

For a stress-free and instant transaction with a secure return policy, reputable dealers offer one of the best buying options available to collectors. You can handle and view coins instantly, negotiate a price and leave with your prize in hand. Additionally, in the course of building your collection you also make a valuable ally who will assist you in any way possible in furthering your numismatic interest and education. But the question still remains: if dealers buy their coins from auction houses and individuals, why should you not cut out the middle man and do the same?

Buying. 2. Numismatic Auction Houses

If it is both a transparent and confident transaction you seek, then a preferable method of buying coins for you may be to compete in a numismatic auction. Prevalent throughout any market and industry is a desire to get a 'deal' on a product or service; we hate buying at somebody else's price, but knock off any small percentage and we will feel that the transaction is far more on our terms. In this way, auction houses provide the most reassuring means of buying items we otherwise know little about, as it allows buyers to make purchases at a price that they choose - and one dictated by market demand. For almost three centuries these establishments have represented one of the premier means of obtaining coins and have helped to show the entirety of the market the maximum that collectors are willing to pay for all types of numismatic material (as well as all other forms of art and antique). Being experienced in their subject matter, numismatic auctioneers act as an effective arbiter between buyer and seller, adding a measure of confidence to numismatic transactions conducted through them and adding a guarantee that their offerings are genuine and as-described. Numismatic auctioneers are an invaluable means of obtaining coins and offer many advantages to the buyer, but should not be treated as a perfect source for building one's collection: some warnings must be heeded too.

First and foremost, one of the most advantageous factors of buying a coin, or indeed anything, at auction is that the price is set exclusively by the market as opposed to an individual. A dealer can price a coin at whatever level they choose based on their perception of market strength, and happily sit and wait until the right buyer comes along to purchase at the price they set. Meanwhile, auctions tend to offer coins starting at competitive sums and wait for collectors to bid them up. At worst, this aspect means that when you buy a coin at auction you have the underbidder right there below you who was willing to pay almost as much as you – while at best, you can actually hope to obtain coins for below their accepted market value. So, like premium bonds, the lottery, betting and all other forms of gambling, auctions offer something intangible that contributes dramatically to their popularity: hope. No matter how high the price you pay, the fact that you decided what to bid means you feel like you still may have bought below the market level, and you have the underbidder right there to prove you did not overpay by much. Some auctioneers are actually doing away with pre-auction estimates for this very reason – value is arbitrary, and so the market has complete discretion to decide prices.

This ability to tap into the beating heart of the coin market is a double-edged sword, however. Auction houses are usually where new trends and changes in the market come to light, hence their being considered the 'stock market' of numismatics. While this does mean that you can buy at the correct current market level and even occasionally hope to buy beneath this level, it also means it is harder to get ahead of the market and buy a coin cheaply when its prices explode elsewhere. When a dealer offers a coin, the price they set may be out of date compared to current auction results (such as the example of the 1928 South Africa Sixpence), while it is rare for prominent auction listings to slip through the net.

Despite the strong market connectivity shown by auctions, by their nature they are not scientific. We cannot completely replicate the conditions of any one auction as that is the only occasion that that exact combination of bidders are in attendance and actually concentrating. As such, all we can do is analyse one auction at a time. A coin may have sold for a certain sum in one auction, but unfortunately there is no guarantee that it would sell for more at the next auction or even reach the same price it did previously.

More importantly still, you have to consider your own contribution to the auction and how your presence has changed events. Auctions allow each and every collector to have a meaningful impact on the global price perception of a coin; by default, if you buy a coin at auction it is safest to assume that you are technically paying more than anyone else in the world was willing to at that point. What this means is that when you bid, you will always have raised the price above what your underbidder would have had to pay. Say you win a coin in a sale; nothing is saying that you did not get it cheaply, that the market may increase etc. However, what is certain is that it would not have sold for that much had you not been participating. If you had refrained from bidding, it would not have necessarily sold for just one increment less, either. The element of competition can supersede logic and reason in the auction room, and lead buyers to go further than they ever normally would in order to 'win'. The same capriciousness can be true of those staying their hand out of fear or being put on the spot by a time limit, only to regret their restraint later. It is certainly the case that your immediate underbidder would not have reached the price height you have taken a coin to by bidding; indeed, I have heard of many situations in which the winner of an auction did not pay, the coin was thus offered to the underbidder at the price they had bid and the underbidder refused, stating that they did not know what they had been thinking. So: always assume that when you win a coin at an auction you are the most motivated buyer in the world, and never try and place it straight back into auction (at least, not the same auction) as the market will be fully aware of the price you have recently paid.

While dealerships offer coins at an all-inclusive price, there are other considerations to take into account when buying at auction. For one, auctioneers have their own unique costs and fees that increase the total beyond the hammer price. The Buyer's Premium (BP) currently charged by most auction houses is around 20%, meaning that whatever hammer price you choose to pay for a coin will bear this additional cost; and unless your coin is investment gold - ie produced within the last 200 years - it will also incur VAT. Secondly, many auctioneers allow their consignors to place a reserve on their coin - a price below which the coin will not be allowed to sell. Most auctioneers will start bidding on the coin at this price and incorporate it within their estimate, but some offer private reserves. This means you may think that you have bought a coin at a competitive price, only to be informed after the auction that your bid did not meet the reserve and therefore you did not win the item. This obviously wastes the buyer's time and also breeds discontent in the auction system.

But do not be dissuaded from competing at auctions! They are so undeniably valuable within the numismatic market that their positives speak for themselves, but I would be remiss not to mention their undesirable aspects too. Provided you observe best buying practices, you should minimise your risk and be able to take full advantage of this vast global bazaar.

First, have a clear idea in your mind of what a coin is worth and what you would be willing to pay for it inclusive of BP and any other taxes. Then, when bidding, it is advisable not to bid too early - the earlier you bid, the more time you give the other party to think about it. But remember: major auctions are not like online auctions, and the lot will stay open as long as there are bidders, so you cannot 'snipe' coins. Try not to go overboard with your prices, but remember my previous advice that buying the best you can is never a bad decision. If you buy something truly special and unique you may pay far over estimate for it, but you will also know that people will have to come to you if they too want the best. You may have paid a premium, but the likelihood is that somebody else will down the line, too.

Auctions have swiftly become the platform through which the best coins available to commerce are offered, as it is common knowledge that they provide the widest audience and best chance of explosive yet transparent price growth. For higher level collectors or investors, participating in at least some numismatic auctions is a necessity to obtain the pieces you seek. As much as there are inevitable risks associated with buying from numismatic auctions, there are also easy methods to ensure you manage these risks. Remember to assume that you are paying the highest price anyone else is willing to, so decide your maximum level before the auction; and if all else fails, you are still able to point to your auction result as a value precedent for your coin when trying to resell at a later date.

Buying. 3. Mints

Much of the discussion thus far has focused specifically on the buying of antique coins – but this omits to mention the bustling trade of modern coins worldwide, those pieces struck recently and many of which were designed exclusively for collectors. Novices often carry contradictory views that a coin's value is predicated on its age, yet see all modern coins as 'investments' to be hoarded for future profit. In reality, some of the many modern issues struck today by mints around the world are likely to increase in value while some are not – just like any antique coins. Mints provide an opportunity to purchase newly-made coins directly from the source, which can lead to extremely enjoyable collecting while also providing opportunities for profitable resale. As I have already mentioned the advantage of modern issues is that they catering to some of the main themes of today's numismatic markets: they are made in limited numbers with excellent engraving quality, and, as they are brand new, they will be immaculate and thus perfectly suit TPG. Once again, which coins you buy should come down to careful selection based on supply and demand, and mint purchases should be balanced with other sources of obtaining coins.

The importance of the new, circulating coinage released by mints has already been emphasised; these modern issuances help to capture the imagination of new collectors and start them actively participating in the market. New coin types are constantly being introduced by mints around the world, issued sometimes as circulating coins (for example, the extensive British 50 Pence series or the US State Quarters) that can be rescued from your change, and sometimes as Proof-only pieces that you must specifically order. As most circulating coins cannot be bought directly from the mint, this section will concern those products actually offered for sale to collectors – usually brilliant uncirculated examples, proofs or proof sets. Products such as these have been popular with collectors ever since the first sets were struck in the 18th and 19th centuries as historically, these special issues were produced in extremely small numbers and have always commanded significant collector attention. Nowadays thousands of coin types are issued by mints around the world each year, produced to mark various anniversaries and events and celebrate the lives of significant national figures, so there is a plethora of varieties to choose from.

By far the chief advantage of buying modern coins is that mints are creating new and untested products that are not priced according to their popularity or existing market level. In some cases this means that the initial mint price for a coin may be above what the secondary market would actually pay, but for the majority of coins offered by a mint the initial price is extremely favourable. As such, for more popular types you must act very fast to buy new coins before they sell out, and generally speaking you need to be fortunate to buy coins directly from the mint itself. In most cases the majority of the potential market must buy their new mint products from dealers and auctions where the price will then be dictated by market demand. Referring back to the example given in Chapter 1.5, the 2019 'Una and the Lion' gold 2oz coin had an original retail price of £4,150 ($5,525) when offered by the Royal Mint. The 205 coins produced sold out instantly and, one year later, perfect graded examples are now selling for £60,000 ($80,000) – more than 14 times their Royal Mint retail price. If you choose your modern coins carefully, you can hope to achieve significant profit margins.

When selecting which of the abundant modern mint issues to purchase, it is better to search within popular markets such as the US, UK or China. These strong national markets have large collector bases for new mint products, making their resale potential stronger than in weaker markets. And, like most coins, the popularity of products from these mints comes down to a combination of three factors: their metal, their design and their technical quality.

Firstly, the metal from which modern coins are made makes a significant difference to their potential price growth. This is partially because collectors are more likely to buy coins produced from precious metals than from base metals, but mainly due to fact that these pieces are struck to far smaller mintages, thus decreasing the supply to demand ratio. Gold is the most popular metal for collectable modern coins, partially due to its VAT- and CGT-exempt status and partially because of its traditional appeal. Many of those modern types to have skyrocketed in price recently were gold – but not all. The Royal Mint's first 'Great Engravers' line included a silver version of the 2019 'Una and the Lion' Five Pounds, 3,000 of which were produced. Despite being initially offered at £150 ($200) each, perfectly graded examples are now selling for as much as $13,000 at auction. You should always make an assessment based on the mintage figure of a coin and its potential collector base.

Secondly, as the regard for the artistry of individual coins begins to increase, many modern Proofs are attracting significant premiums if they feature coveted designs seen as particularly attractive. Take, for example, the British 1989 'Sovereign Anniversary' gold proof set. 10,000 of these 4-coin sets were produced including a Five Pound, Two Pound, Sovereign and Half Sovereign coin, all with a Tudor-style design to commemorate 500 years since the first Sovereign coin was struck under Henry VII. Immediately popular, prices continue to climb for these coins with the most recent auction results for just the Five Pound coin realising over £8,000 ($10,720). Additionally, these old-established gold denominations in particular are popular with collectors as they form part of a longer series that starts in historical coins and ends in the present. As such, collectors wanting to complete their Sovereign or Five Pound collection must keep abreast of modern issues.

Elizabeth II, Sovereign, 1989, PF70 Ultra Cameo NGC

Thirdly, to an extent even greater than historical coins, the numerical grade that modern coins receive will entirely dictate their value. As modern coins have been recently produced there is a far greater expectation that they will have a high grade and no signs of handling, with a 70 on the Sheldon Scale representing absolute perfection. However, 70 is an elusive designation and one that not just any coin receives. Even if it appears perfect to the naked eye, any minute scratch or flaw will land a coin firmly within the 69 category and it is perfectly acceptable for new mint products to be as low as a PR68 level, so it is certainly not a given that a new coin is perfect. If possible, handpick (but don't touch!) the modern coins you buy and examine them with a high-powered loupe, as top-graded coins can carry a hefty premium. The conjunction of modern mintages with TPG has gained official status in recent years; the British Royal Mint has just recently partnered with NGC, and other Mints also now offer their coins graded, particularly in the US.

As with all coins, the intersection of supply and demand can push popular, high-grade modern issues to high prices. However, a word of warning – while official mint products can increase or decrease in value depending on their popularity, there are several off-brand companies who purport to be official mints and strike their own coins that almost always fall in value. A key identifier of these firms is that they specifically refer to their products as investments. If a new coin is marketed publicly as an investment, then its entire consumer base is made up of people buying the coin as an investment. Its consumer value is non-existent; everybody who has bought it has bought it in the hopes of selling it to an actual collector base. Thus, the moment that buyers start attempting to sell, the true lack of value is exposed and the framework collapses. These companies also aggressively try to sell their existing customers new coins as well as vintage pieces, usually at heavily marked-up prices.

Occasionally, one of these companies will produce a coin that does engage the wider market and jumps in value, but for the most part it is advisable to buy from official national mints. I have seen collectors who have bought exclusively from unscrupulous firms break down in tears after realising that their life's work, the collection they built as a legacy for their children, is worth just 10 per cent of what they paid. Never be pressured into a purchase; always conduct your own research and decide for yourself which coins are wise purchase choices, or consult with a trusted advisor in the field.

As grade consciousness increasingly takes over as today's collecting vogue, the part played by modern coins is steadily increasing. Reputable mints represent a trustworthy and reliable source of coins which, if bought directly, can sometimes rapidly increase in value - but you should thoroughly research the array of options available to focus solely on those pieces you believe to have a strong collector base. Due to their competitive pricing, you will require good fortune to be able to purchase directly from mints, but by buying regularly and forging a good relationship you may be able to request that particular pieces are put aside for you.

Buying. 4. Direct Purchases

Dealers, auction houses and mints offer the collector a wealth of avenues to purchase coins from a knowledgeable and reputable source – but the final method of buying coins is directly. Direct transactions involve buying straight from the owner of the coin; but in contrast to a dealer, whether they are the collector who bought it, the spouse who inherited it or the detectorist who found it, they are have not bought it for profit. Some of these coin owners may be collectors who know exactly what it is they have, while other owners may have no idea at all (or rather, claim they do not). You are essentially making a purchase that circumvents the involvement of a numismatic professional and the associated charges.

Nowadays these sorts of transactions are mostly conducted online, as those who offer coins physically tend to be some form of dealer. Even then, many online sales will ultimately be conducted by some form of industry professional. Platforms exist exclusively for coin dealers, such as VCoins, while other dealers offer their coins through existing online auction platforms or on their own websites. Major numismatic auction houses, too, have their own dedicated websites. As such, this section essentially encompasses all forms of buying, online or offline, that is not from a dealer or auction house - the wild west of coin buying, where you will need to keep your wits about you and know exactly what you are looking at or else have a reliable refund policy in place.

Many collectors will seek to avoid major auction fees or dealer's mark-up by offering their coins on online auction sites or through social media. In this way, they attempt to market directly to other collectors and cut out the middle men. These transactions can potentially be very advantageous for buyers. Firstly, collectors are not operating a coin business and are often merely trying to free up funds in the short term. By selling directly, the collectors avoid all fees and so are prepared to offer coins for close to their purchase price, something that dealers cannot feasibly do. Secondly, the online auction sites that they offer them on may provide an opportunity to buy them cheaply, as the audience for such sites is nowhere near as deep-pocketed as for major auctions that offer a guarantee of authenticity. Collectors may also have bought their coins some time ago and will unknowingly offer them at only a small percentage over their purchase price and below the up-to-date market level.

On the other hand, collectors with an eye on the market may actually be prone to overcharge for their coins in the hope that their coin will capture the attention of another collector. After all, collectors and dealers go hand in hand – it only takes a few coin sales for one to be indistinguishable from the other. Once you know the value of your coins, it makes sense to turn them over for profit where you can.

The expertise of collectors is not infallible, and I have seen many advanced collections that include a number of forgeries. Dealers turn over stock so regularly that they will quickly learn to identify forgeries, and their business will be dependent on their reputation so they will exercise caution when buying. Collectors, however, are unlikely to have familiarised themselves with the difference between forgeries and authentic pieces to the same extent. Their expertise will be less, and they are not immune to buying and re-offering fakes. You must therefore remain vigilant and treat each coin as a potential forgery!

In other direct transactions, the owner of the coin you are buying may have simply found or inherited it and have absolutely no market knowledge whatsoever. This has its advantages and disadvantages. For one, the owner may misdescribe their coin when listing it online and give it an arbitrary starting price, meaning that it can be bought cheaply. I once found a rare siege coin from the English Civil War online described merely as 'silver coin', and was able to purchase it for $250 then resell it for $1,100 later that month. However, by giving a vague description with no guarantee of authenticity this also means that the owner is absolved if the coin turns out to be fake or damaged. As such, you absorb all of the risk in the transaction.

More importantly, if the transaction is direct (ie you are personally making an offer to a clueless coin owner) and there are no other bidders involved, then you have a duty of trust not to underpay them. The industry is small, and all you need is one person to talk about you significantly lowballing them for your reputation to tarnish. Put yourself in their shoes and consider an offer that you feel to be fair by industry standards, whilst also giving yourself a decent chance of a profitable resale.

In both of these instances, whether buying from another collector or from an unsure owner, it is you personally who must act as the numismatic professional in that transaction in place of a dealer or auction house. You must decide a fair and realistic price above which you will not pay, and be in a position to competently assess the quality and authenticity of the coins for sale. Ideally, when buying in such a way you should hope for some form of refund guarantee should the coin be not as described. Direct purchases are the highest risk form of coin buying, and you do incur the possibility of losing money at some point or another. Therefore be confident in what you are buying and ensure that there is a fair refund policy in place.

When you buy from a dealer, auction house or Mint, you rely on the knowledge of the institution to tell you that it is genuine and to describe it correctly. You trust them that the sum being asked for is fair for the particular coin you are buying. On the other hand, when buying directly it is you who needs to have the market acumen and academic know-how to properly conduct that deal. After all, if neither you nor the seller had any knowledge about the coin, then the transaction would be entirely nonsensical. Online sources for purchasing coins offer some of the advantages of major auctions - such as the possibility of a cheap buy price - but without any assurances of authenticity and thus a highly increased risk. You should only attempt to buy coins directly when you have sufficient knowledge to do so.

* * *

Once you have gained the confidence to identify authentic and high-quality coins, you can make use of the worldwide network of auction houses, dealers and mints to build your collection. And if you feel particularly confident, you can buy directly from coin owners themselves. Buying a coin, no matter from what source, represents the opening of a financial position. The fate of your capital from that moment is tied to the whims of the numismatic market and the collectors who underpin it, meaning you should buy wisely with a mind for what coins may increase in value over time. Should you be buying coins solely out of enjoyment then you might not worry what happens to their value during your ownership, but whether for you or for those who inherit your collection, the value of your coins will one day be in question once again. Buying is the first half of any numismatic transaction; the second half is, of course, selling your coins once again – a step that requires as much forethought as choosing which coins to buy in the first place.

Chapter 3.4.
Selling

For a market as transparent and liquid as gold, it is always easy to sell. Banners adorn shops in every high street proclaiming that their owners buy gold, and it only takes a quote from two or three of these operations to establish the rough going rate for your old jewellery or bullion coins and to sell for the highest offer.

Numismatics is another matter entirely. The market is murky and often illiquid, and not every component - be it dealer or auctioneer - operates as efficiently as the next. You cannot simply offer your coin anywhere and expect the price to be identical each time. Even if you have bought wisely and the market for your coin is clearly increasing, selling your coin requires the same skill that you used to buy in the first place.

For one, your coin may not be suitable for auction; it may have too few interested buyers meaning its bid price would never climb too high, but will be suitable instead to directly market to a known collector of its type. Alternatively, there may have been a downturn in the market since you bought, and so placing your coin at a set price and waiting for a buyer who is slightly less up-to-date with market trends is also wise. Selling is not simply offering the coin at any time and place; it is carefully weighing up every aspect in order to ensure a maximum resale price.

In the same broad brush-strokes manner as I discussed the buying of coins, I will touch upon the various ways one can hope to sell. These methods mirror those of buying; dealers will always be happy to purchase coins, auction houses will vie to offer your collection, in some cases museums and institutions will even consider making purchases and, once again, the option is there to offer your coins directly. Each avenue offers unique benefits and possible considerations, and you should analyse each thoroughly before proceeding to a sale.

Selling. 1. Dealers

Just as when buying, dealers are one of the most obvious routes to turn to when selling your coin. The trade of coins is the bread-and-butter of these numismatic professionals and so for an efficient same-day transaction you can hope for no better option than a coin dealer. Their knowledge of the market and the coins themselves removes the barrier for significant umming-and-aahing, whilst their chequebooks are always poised, ready to pay out to sellers. But alongside the upsides of selling to dealers, there are the inevitable drawbacks to transacting with those who must also turn a profit, meaning any potential sale should be carefully evaluated to ensure you will maximise your return by selling to them.

One of the chief advantages of selling to a dealer is simply the speed of it all. As I have discussed, coin trading brings with it unavoidable cash flow issues yet when offering coins to a dealer you can expect to be paid within a matter of days. Most of these specialists have a large amount of capital poised at the ready to buy collections or individual coins (some even choose to advertise the specific amounts they have to spend in a given month), and are certainly clued-in as to the market and what your coins will be worth. If you have managed to buy a coin cheaply, you can likely sell it on to a dealer at a profit immediately and free up the cash to use elsewhere. As such, for a quick turnaround dealers represent a highly useful resource.

Alongside the speed of transaction, as numismatic market professionals dealers are generally competent when it comes to assessing coin values and will be able to provide a fair offer for your material where collectors may instead try to lowball you. Dealers are also well poised to speculate on the change in market value of a coin and as such are sometimes willing to pay more than the average collector if they perceive the market to be upturning for that type. And whereas auctioneers may be conservative with their estimates, dealers will sometimes compete aggressively for a coin should they have an interested client in mind. This direct form of collector 'matchmaking' means dealers may sometimes undercut the need for an auction and offer to buy coins at high auction-level prices.

However, to address the elephant in the room: when selling coins to a dealer, you are knowingly selling at less than the dealer believes your coins to be worth. As you are not selling to the end consumer, whatever price the dealer is paying for a coin will be less than they think they can sell it on for. What is important to keep in mind is that buying coins is a dealer's livelihood. They must build in a margin, a factor of safety where they know they will make a profit, or else they will go out of business; a direct contrast to selling directly to a collector who will simply spend what they want to own the coin. Accordingly, there are situations where it is sensible to sell to a dealer and situations where it might be safer to offer your coin by another means.

The question is really "just how much of a margin is my dealer making?" Reputable dealers must be competitive with one another in the prices they pay and so, as market professionals, they are unlikely to offer a price which is too unrealistically low. The generally adopted model of high volume, low margin means that dealers rely on a steady flow of coins in order to make enough to live on and so it is unlikely you are losing out on too much of an upside.

However, selling direct to a dealer is not necessarily your only option – you can also sell *through* a dealer. Many dealers will offer you the opportunity to sell coins at a commission, usually in the region of 10-20 per cent. They will offer these coins on their website and bring them to numismatic shows, allowing you the use of their reach and client-base to wait for the right buyer to come along. This allows you to factor in precisely how much the dealer is making on your deal and know exactly how much to expect for your coin.

In many cases, selling to a dealer even has advantages over that of selling through an auctioneer. At auction, you are at the whim of the bidding audience. Bidders may not be concentrating and many potential buyers will not have seen your coin in person and so may be unwilling to part with as much capital for it as a dealer who has had a chance to examine it. Additionally, selling to a dealer is as free of additional fees as buying from them in the first place. Say for example you are offered $1,500 for a coin by a dealer but have also been given an estimate of $1,500-2,000 by an auction house. Naturally you may decide to pursue the auction option, but for a consignment of that size you are likely to incur around a 10 per cent commission charge, and will certainly lose out on the 20 per cent buyer's premium if it sells for $2,000 all-in. This means that the auctioneer is making $600 while you are making $1,400 – and that is assuming collectors bid it up to that level at all. Had you sold to the dealer for their original offer, you would have saved time and saved money.

But, most importantly, prior to even considering a sale to a dealer you must ensure that you have done your research; make sure you know that your dealer is reputable, that you know exactly what it is that you have and, better yet, a rough idea of its value. Dealers are likely to take a shot at coins even when unfamiliar with them, but in these cases they will always pay extremely conservative prices to ensure that their upside is there. A few years ago I encountered a situation where a foreign coin had been offered to a dealer who bought it on a hunch for hundreds, and the dealer then placed it in auction where it sold for hundreds of thousands. Provided you are familiar with your coins and have done your research, you can shop around with dealers until you find one who is willing to pay you a fair market price.

To recap, selling your coins to a dealer offers the advantages of speed and efficiency, with the added benefits of transacting with a knowledgeable market professional. As long as the dealer you sell to is trustworthy, the widely used business model of low margin to high volume means you are unlikely to lose a significant percentage of your coin's value, and this method can offer significant upsides to selling coins at auction. That being said, auctions have their own prominent pluses which must also be weighed up when choosing where to sell your coins.

Selling. 2. Numismatic Auction Houses

In early 2020, I was browsing a coin group on social media when I saw an image posted of a coin that had been found by a metal detectorist – an Australian Half Sovereign of 1855, found in the Bay of Plenty, northern New Zealand. This was the first year of issue for the Australian Half Sovereign and also happened to be the rarest coin in the series. I made contact with the finder and asked him what he was hoping to get for the coin. The finder – let us call him 'Joe' - told me he had been contacted by numerous dealers offering various sums from $300 to $3,000. At the time I represented a prominent US auction house and so I advised him that for a coin of that significance a major auction was the only way to establish its value. He consigned the coin, and a matter of months later it had sold for $31,200 - far exceeding any offer he received from dealers and making New Zealand national headlines to boot.

Australia, Half Sovereign 1855, just after discovery

You can always choose to sell your coin through an auctioneer, and as in the case of Joe's Half Sovereign, for many coins this is by far the most suitable route available. The arbitrary nature of coin values cannot be better addressed than through public auctions: a platform through which collectors and dealers can decide what to pay, and the individual willing to pay the most wins. If an auction house has a strong internet presence, it has the potential to reach every interested collector worldwide and generate the maximum sale price possible. With their searchable sale histories aiding price standardisation and money back-guarantees for misdescribed items, auction houses successfully produce the buyer confidence needed for efficient transactions to take place. Simply put, auctions are among the best means of selling coins, and nowadays major auctioneers are the arbiters of most of the highest level numismatic transactions worldwide. But despite the popularity and advantages of numismatic auctions, there are always the right and wrong coins to sell at auction and you must make this assessment before considering this avenue of sale.

The auction process was touched upon in the first section; any coins accepted to an auction will be catalogued and photographed, presented to collectors for public viewing in advance of the sale, and then opened for bidding until all but one collector has dropped off and the maximum bid has been reached. During this process your coin will usually have received an auction estimate or starting price which is generally kept low to encourage bidding. You should not be too fearful if your coin is started at, say, half of what you believe it to be worth; if you think that price is low, there is a good chance that the bidders will see it as low, too. By placing low estimates on coins you entice bidders who otherwise would not have given your coin a second glance, and who then stand a chance of being sucked into the competition and raising the price of your coin further.

The main motivation behind selling through auction is that it is generating the largest possible audience for your coin and selling directly to the collectors with the deepest pockets. Alongside the number of bidders in attendance, the refund guarantee and expertise offered by auctioneers gives buyers worldwide the confidence to bid unrestrainedly. This means that, just as discussed in the 'buying' section, auctions are uniquely capable of introducing an element of competition that can drive prices beyond the realm of logic or sanity - the private hope of every consignor to any auction ever.

Auctions also allow you to take advantage of bubbles and boosts in the market in real time. In early 2020, as the coronavirus pandemic began to sweep the globe, many coin owners were fearful of the effect that Covid-19 lockdowns would have on their coin values. One consignor who had given me around $400,000 worth of coins for auction contacted me and asked what specific measures I was taking to ensure that his coins were protected. I assured him that if anything he should expect a higher price than normal as the uncertain financial times would drive investors towards tangible assets – but I did not know quite how right I would turn out to be. Throughout 2020 coin prices began to reach unprecedented heights, and the majority of these were achieved through auctions. Dealerships were able to increase their prices and sell their stock quickly, but it was only through auctions that consignors were able to ride the tidal wave of suddenly frenzied buyers to its maximum extent.

It would seem that, from their unique ability to reach wide swathes of the collector base in one go, auction houses would always be the logical option for selling your coins. But nothing is truly free in this world, and auctions are no exception. For the privilege of expert advice, marketing and the use of the auction platform you will incur the hefty fees discussed in 'buying' (a Buyer's Premium of typically 20 per cent on the hammer price realised, plus often a vendor's commission, generally in the region of 10-15 per cent). This amounts to as much as 30 per cent or more of the value of your coin ending up in the auction house's pocket, and for many coin types this is simply unacceptable. The lower and middle tiers of the numismatic market see quite steady price standardisation in general, meaning coin values remain relatively well established. The risk of disposing of these lower value pieces at auction is that, as the market is well aware of their going rate, this will be reflected in the final all-in price, including BP, and you will lose out on a significant portion of what you could have achieved from a direct sale to a dealer or collector. To reiterate, when considering an auction sale route, you should always factor in the fees you will inevitably have to pay.

The wait for the next sale date when selling via an auction house (to allow time for your coin to be catalogued, photographed, estimated and marketed) will also potentially affect your cash flow, versus a swifter method of sale. Any advances against consignments can certainly help your financial position, but these advances do often incorporate payment of interest.

If you have determined that you are able to wait, and that the potential upside of consigning your coins to auction outweighs the fees, then your next step is to choose an auction house through which to offer your coins. Generally it is wise to immediately disregard any auction house without a strong internet presence or existing numismatic following as you can essentially guarantee that the results they bring will be weak. Once you have weeded out these less appealing options, you will still be left with an array of auction houses all over the globe to choose from. There are auctioneers of all sizes specialising in all types of coins, all of whom will want your business and will try multiple angles to get it. Some will wave impressive results in your face, some will describe the strength of their platform and mailing list at length, while others will simply try to entice you through lower commission rates.

For the most part, there is no right or wrong choice to make when selecting an auctioneer, as in this interconnected day and age a coin offered for sale at any one reputable venue will usually be found by the same collectors and dealers it would have been elsewhere. There are, however, occasions where the choice of auction house will actually make a significant difference to the price realised for your coin. A particularly illustrative example I encountered early in my career is that of a 1792 Half 'Disme' (Nickel), a very rare American coin, discovered in early 2017 and offered in the US arm of a London-based auction house in April 2017. The coin was pierced - vastly reducing its value - but it nonetheless brought $15,500 at auction. This same coin was offered by a larger US auction house just four months later, where it sold for $37,600 in August 2017. Despite both auctions having an online component and both auctions taking place in the US, the reach and marketing of the latter auction house led to it almost doubling the coin's price. In this instance it was chiefly due to the latter auction house's reputation and large collector base for (specifically) US coins that helped to increase the price, but there is never a guarantee that re-offering a coin at another auction house will generate a higher price. When looking to sell a coin at auction, focus on the reach of the auction house itself, research its past prices realised and if possible talk face-to-face with a representative to get a feel for its operations.

US, 1792 Half Disme, sold for $37,600

A discussion you might inevitably end up having with your auction house is that of placing a reserve – the act of setting a 'price' below which your coin cannot sell in order to protect your peace of mind. Reserves are usually set by those individuals trying to protect their cost price, or those with particular expectations of how the market will perform. These reserves can either be public - published by the auction house - or private, where bidders will only know that they have not met the reserve after the sale. Some auctioneers are more than happy to place reserves if it means getting your consignment, while others can be very reluctant. In my experience, reserves are not a desirable tool to use when selling your coins as it removes the two most integral components of bidder mentality: confidence and autonomy.

Imagine you buy a coin for several multiples of its auction estimate. Even though it is a large sum, that final hammer price is built up and up and up on the shoulders of all the other motivated collectors out there; what you end up paying is thus only one increment over the second most motivated buyer. When you bid on a reserved coin, however, you are knowingly paying precisely what the owner wants for it. You are essentially buying it for a retail price, entirely counteracting the idea that you are buying something for what it is intrinsically worth as the seller may have set an entirely arbitrarily high reserve (they often do). For the lower and mid-tier of the market, prices are already fairly standardised; for the upper echelons, 2020 showed us that the price can go anywhere.

Whether they are public or private, reserves will typically put off bidders and at best lead to your coin selling at, or slightly over the price you set. If you have bought well, are happy with the prices you have paid, choose your auction house well and sell with conservative estimates, the market will competently decide the value of your coin.

What this discussion of reserves touches upon is perhaps the most important consideration of a sale at auction – managing your expectations. A dealer's price is matter-of-fact, a number that you can accept or decline, while consignors to auction nearly always have dreams of realising tremendous prices. After all, auctions allow bidding to increase to essentially any figure. The opening of a coin to public auction can cause excitement and trepidation in equal measures in the minds of consignors, and lead them to hope for the best but be terrified of the worst. This is the primary motivation behind placing reserves or requesting unrealistically high estimates. You must be ready to sell your coins and to present them to the open market, and provided you are dealing with a reputable auction house with a strong internet presence, your coins cannot fail to sell for precisely what they are worth at that moment. Remember, it is also in the best interest of the auctioneer that your coin sells for the most it can.

If you have bought a coin at a major auction recently and re-consigned it to another auction house without adding value (eg submitting it for third-party grading), bear in mind that every collector and dealer will have had the opportunity to see that coin offered recently. If possible, try to hang on to your auction-bought coins for a minimum of two to three years before re-offering so that the market does not recognise the same piece coming up again and again and become suspicious. A coin appearing at auction several times over the course of one year is a bad sign, and many buyers are very clued in as to which pieces are offered where.

On the other hand, a recent auction result for a similar coin to yours can be advantageous. In my experience, the first time that a particular coin type appears at auction after a long absence bidders are hesitant to make too strong a move; the gap between data points is too great and so unconfident bidders take their cue from one another. This can lead to somewhat lacklustre results. However, if a similar coin sells shortly afterwards, bidding can often be much stronger; this is because collectors can now refer to a recent result and feel comfortable paying a percentage over that result. As such it is can be sensible to consider consigning your coin if you see a similar piece appear in an upcoming auction. But bear in mind, the chance is also there that as the most motivated bidder now owns that piece, they will then stay their hand from bidding on your coin and the price may be less still than the previous result. In almost any case, a consignment to auction is a gamble which will inevitably pay off or underwhelm.

Auctions simply have no match in their reach to wide collector bases; they are purposefully designed to extract the highest price possible for your coins and indeed encourage this so as to maximise their own profits. As the most up-to-date means of tapping into the market, they also provide an opportunity to take advantage of bubbles and boosts and thus see sudden price growth. But, there is a reason why the quality of coins offered by auctioneers is steadily climbing – their BP is, too. The coins you sell at auction must have something special about them, some chance of attracting serious attention in order to sell for enough to justify paying the extra fees to the auction house. In cases where your coin has a standard enough price that most collectors or dealers could give you a relatively accurate indication of its value, you should consider an alternative route for sale. That being said, the 2020s has so far been a decade of change, and I have seen dealers and collectors alike despairing over the sudden inaccuracy of their valuations compared to the prices coins are achieving at auction. Research your coin, its chances at auction and the auction house itself, and then decide whether it is worth presenting it to the open market considering the BP and commission you will have to pay.

Selling. 3. Direct Sales

When selling through a numismatic professional – be it a dealer or auctioneer – you knowingly lose a percentage of your coin's total market value in the form of their profit margin or fees. If this loss is too unpalatable for you to bear, then your third main option is to try and sell your coins directly to collectors themselves. You can undertake this by offering coins to private clients, marketing online through your own website or an existing dealing platform, or bringing them in person to a coin show. Direct sales have the obvious advantage of cutting out the middle-men and securing the largest possible portion of your coin's value, but represent a different form of sacrifice: one of your time and effort. By directly selling coins you essentially put yourself on the same level as professional dealers, yet without the same expertise and platform they have taken the time to build. Before considering this approach, you must first consider the effort you must expend to market and list your coins versus the ease of using an already established professional entity or individual.

Generally, your direct sales will likely take place online or at numismatic conventions (unless you happen to own an antique shop or market stall). Of course, nothing is stopping dealers rather than collectors buying your coins when you offer them but the difference in these direct transactions is that regardless of who buys them, you set the price. Once you have bought coins that you think may be worth a premium, your first option is to contact specific collectors you know and personally offer them your material. This is the most preferable route of sale as it is the fastest and avoids the need to properly photograph and describe your coins. If this is not possible, then you can either offer your coins in person at a coin show or online. The former route is simple and has many advantages; it will allow collectors and dealers to examine and purchase your coins immediately and thus avoid any issues of postage or description. But this will involve booking a table at a convention at cost and will thus necessitate you having enough saleable material to make it worthwhile. This is an expenditure of time, effort and money that none but serious dealers and auctioneers generally bother with.

As such, the logical route for offering coins directly is online as this is where the majority of the market now resides. Not only does this option involve less time and dedication on your part but also significantly increases your audience. The benefit of the internet's presence in the numismatic market is its ability to connect collectors with the coins they seek, whereas for most of the history of coin collecting buyers would simply have to check auctions and coin shops, cross their fingers and hope. The first port of call for interested novices used to be searching the junk coin boxes of antique shops, yet nowadays it is to search online auction sites for the coins they like.

Should you choose the online route of direct sales, you can either use an existing sale platform, a dedicated coin dealing platform, or start your own website – each has its pros and cons, and most dealers use a combination of all three. Creating your own website means that you avoid the often fees that auctions and dealing platforms charge, and paves the way for you to build a following in the numismatic market. But it also raises the issue: how will collectors find your website amongst the hundreds of others? Most collectors will not shop and compare deals indefinitely, and so unless you are high up their list of visited websites it is more than likely that they will buy elsewhere and that your coins will remain unsold for some time. A successful coin trading website requires considerable marketing and advertising.

This is the main reason why those looking to sell coins directly turn to either a dedicated coin platform or another means of listing online – their collector bases are already set up for them, making the small usage fees worthwhile. In my experience, non coin-specific auction platforms usually feature several fake coins which can hurt buyer confidence - this limits the sums that collectors will pay as the average risk is perceived as too high. However, if your listing is moderately priced and inspires enough trust then you can find very competitive prices being paid for a particular type of coin: low-grade rarities. If you have a scarce variety or type which in good condition would be worth thousands, then collectors browsing non-expert sites are usually surprised to see them, whereas at major auction buyers will more commonly see finer specimens. This means that, when offered online, collectors with slightly shallower pockets who do not frequent major auctions can become excited by these rarities and throw more money at them than they should.

Meanwhile, dedicated dealer platforms such as VCoins have a better reputation for expertise and authenticity, so collectors are generally willing to pay greater sums on such websites, but you do lose the 'excitement' aspect – the collector base of these websites have higher standards and will generally be more clued in as to current market values.

Once again, it all comes down to the time and energy you want to put into your trading. Creating your own website will of course allow you to sell directly to buyers with no middle-man and at your own prices, but will take time and you will always be reliant on buyers finding your site. Most dealers begin using a pre-existing platform to build a collector following before launching their own website to ensure that it is worth the effort.

Whichever route you choose, there are some absolute truths of online listings that you should ensure you follow. First and foremost, remember: when selling online, the image of the coin is the most important part of your listing. Long gone are the days of the Victorian catalogues that describe coins as merely 'good' without any image, with the expectation that collectors will take the cataloguer's word for it. In today's grade- and quality-conscious market, you must take as clear a picture as possible of your coin or risk either buyer dissatisfaction or the loss of a potential premium for a well-preserved piece.

Along with the photograph, ensure you describe your coin to its maximum extent to show the market you have not simply pulled an image from elsewhere and are running some form of fraud. And finally, price your coins carefully. If you price your coins too low, you lose out on a potential margin and do not allow yourself wiggle room should collectors negotiate on price (which they almost always do). Being willing to discount your coins endears you to collectors and significantly raises the chance of repeat business. Meanwhile, if you price your coins too high you slam the door in the face of otherwise interested buyers and will swiftly tie up your cash flow. When offering coins directly, you must find a middle ground where you maintain a speedy flow of business yet still make enough to justify your trading.

Just as for direct purchases, when selling directly to collectors it is you who must introduce the expertise to the transaction. You have a duty of trust to describe your coins correctly and competently and to charge prices in line with expectations. The numismatic market is so saturated with fakes, damaged pieces and extortionate prices that many collectors are now highly distrustful; this means that just a few unscrupulous sales will be noticed and may permanently sour your reputation. Selling directly puts you in the market's public eye, and for collectors to be willing to pay you large sums for your coins, you need to generate trust and build relationships. Additionally, if you are unconfident in your ability to describe coins then TPG is an excellent tool for producing confidence in buyers around the world as it puts the onus of expertise on the grading companies.

If you choose to sell your coins directly, you can quite possibly find yourself making significantly higher returns than if you went to a dealer or an auction house. Selling your coins at your prices through your own website will eliminate all but the most trivial maintenance fees and give you the entirety of the return on your purchase. But remember, you will have poured so many of your hours and so much of your energy into the process that you must start calculating the cost of your time - you must decide on the extent to which numismatic trading should occupy your life. It is generally only professional dealers who offer coins at shows, host their own websites and actively pursue sale leads; this is a full-time job. If this is your passion, then there is no need to be daunted by this task, but if you have another means of income then to minimise your time expenditure you have the option of using a dealer or auctioneer. The existing collector bases and reputations of these professionals will likely help your cash flow move along much faster than through direct sales and require far less effort.

Selling. 4. Museums

In some specific instances there is an additional option for selling your coins, but in a manner that permanently banishes them from the numismatic market – a sale to a museum. This is a rare occurrence; as aforementioned, museums have little part to play in the coin trade itself, most institutions already boasting impressive reference collections of coins and other numismatic items (not to mention having limited funds). However, specifically in the United Kingdom, there are the laws discussed earlier pertaining to the discovery of coins or other treasure which, in some cases, will involve a museum purchasing artefacts outright.

Obviously, you cannot simply saunter up to a museum and slap a coin down on the counter, hoping for a quick sale. Instead, the treasure process is automatic when you first report a discovery of a coin or artefact through the Portable Antiquities Scheme. If you have found either a) two or more gold or silver coins buried together or b) an artefact made from precious metal - and your find is over 300 years old - then you must declare it within 14 days of discovery. The coroner will then hold an inquest to decide whether or not your find is treasure. If your find is declared to be treasure, it will then be assessed by independent experts to determine its value before it is taken to a Treasure Valuation Committee. The Committee will recommend a figure to the Secretary of State for Culture and your find will be offered to the museum nearest to the find spot. If they do not want it, it will be offered to other national museums. If no museum is interested in your find then it will be returned to you and its ownership will be split between you and the landowner. If, on the other hand, a museum wants it and the valuation is agreed, they will pay out the agreed amount which is usually split equally between you and the landowner.

Many finds that are declared treasure are hoards of unassuming coins, such as groupings of low-grade silver from the English Civil War or common Celtic pieces.

The advantage of a museum sale is that when selling to a dealer or through an auction, buyers will always pay less for a group of coins than they would have for the individual pieces. Museums and the Treasure Valuation Committee, on the other hand, will pay market price per coin which often lands you with a greater sum than you would have been paid were you to have marketed your finds to a collector or dealer.

Price advantage being as it may, the simple fact of it is that you do not have a choice in the matter when discovering potential treasure. If a museum wants your find, take solace in knowing that you will be receiving a fair market price for it. The penalties for not properly reporting treasure can be extremely severe. In recent news, two metal detectorists were reported to have discovered a magnificent hoard of Anglo-Saxon and Viking treasure in Leominster, England in June 2015 including jewellery, silver ingots and hundreds of valuable coins. Estimates put the total value of the hoard at between £3 million and £12 million. Unfortunately, these two detectorists were not satisfied with the UK's treasure process and instead decided to try and sell the treasure themselves. They were caught, and both received nearly a decade in prison apiece. Had they gone through the proper channels, they would have had to split the value of the find with the landowner – but even then, both would have taken home between £500,000 and £3 million each. Much of the hoard is still yet to be recovered.

'Two Emperors' Penny of King Alfred, 874-879, recovered from the Leominster hoard.

The Leominster case was an isolated incident, as the UK treasure act is very favourable in its granting fair market value for coins discovered on UK soil. However, this quirk of the UK's treasure act is sadly unique and most other European countries have far more severe and draconian measures in place for treasure. In these countries, coins and artefacts will be confiscated without any compensation even if they are discovered on private land. This has led to a thriving black market of antiquities coming out of Europe, meaning that coin collectors must exercise caution when buying ancient coins from these locations and without export paperwork.

Museums should not be considered an option for sale, but rather their scrutiny is a necessary stage of the finds process in the UK. On very isolated occasions museums will participate in auctions for coins such as in the case of the Coenwulf Mancus, but legislation is presently being introduced to try and stop such instances being necessary. For the most part museums are rarely involved in the numismatic market, but if these institutions decide that your find is of historical importance then you must surrender to them – and receive a handsome pay out in the process.

★ ★ ★

The sale of your coins is every bit as important as their purchase in the first place – perhaps even more so. If you have bought well then it is hard to go wrong when selling your coins, as the commoditisation of the numismatic market (particularly when using TPG) means that most avenues of sale will be likely to generate a profit. However, even if you have bought a coin at an aggressive price you have options available. You can calculate your chances of receiving a fair offer from a dealer or of a profitable sale at auction, and if neither are likely then you can consider direct sale options or otherwise wait and watch the market. Selling your coins and closing your financial position takes the same market and numismatic skill that you used to buy in the first place. Only through a sale can you determine just how successful your initial purchase was, and your performance in the numismatic market as a whole.

Heads or Tails?

Two and a half thousand years ago in ancient Lydia, the first *kapeloi* struck standard weight ingots of electrum between hammer and die and created the first coins. This seemed at the time to be convenience, a means of creating uniform pieces of precious metal for use in trade – but of course, we now know the shockwaves from this invention were far, far greater. Since these first Lydian 'Staters' came into being, coins have underpinned human society and allowed civilisation as we know it to come into being. Through the widespread exchange of stamped disks of precious metal, the perception of value and wealth began to transcend national borders and create a truly global trade. Coins allowed societies to rise and prosper, led wars to be fought and explorers to explore, all in the pursuit of the precious metals used to produce coins.

In the 17th century, society began to notice the limitations of this precious metal anchor to the financial market. Larger transactions began instead using banknotes or other forms of written exchange of assets that did not involve the physical transference of coins. Gradually, despite precious metals retaining their value, coins stopped being the sole indicator of wealth. Later on governments, in fear of the power they gave their people by allowing them to trade precious metal coins, reduced currencies worldwide to fiat money without intrinsic value – yet all the while allowing trade to continue and even increase. The idea that coins equal value is so burned into our collective consciousness that we no longer need our coins to actually have any value at all.

Still now, money continues to advance beyond its need for backing. Fiat money, both banknotes and coins, is in a gradual decline – especially in the wake of the Covid-19 pandemic. Online transactions and card payments dwarf the exchange of physical currency, and new and innovative forms of payments have come into being. The increasingly widespread use of cryptocurrency fully embodies the increasingly abstract concept of 'value' and reduced need for any physical asset; these online units are traded solely at the price the market is willing to pay, like any stock or share. Yet even with all these new forms of payment, rather than simply disappearing from sight and therefore from mind, coins have now shifted in the public consciousness from a day-to-day mark of small values to something far more significant. The high prices that coins can command among collectors are increasingly well known, and so in a sense coins have made a 180 degree turn from their original purpose; no longer representing standardised value, they now share the same status as a stock, share or unit of cryptocurrency – they are worth solely as much as the market will pay for them. This has been only emphasised by the growing presence of fractional ownership and NFTs within numismatics.

I began assembling this book in May 2020, and am now very glad I dragged my feet as much as I did! Writing in the period of 2020-2021 has allowed me to cover one of the most exciting and turbulent periods within the numismatic market experienced for decades. During this one short year I saw prices rise exponentially, unprecedented buyer and investment demand sweeping the trade and boosting auction results for previously unassuming types. I saw entirely new coins thought up, introduced, sold out and swiftly rise in price to ten times their original cost from the mint. Records were broken and billions of dollars changed hands for coins, in just one year.

Even without a desire to buy and sell coins yourself, the trade of coins worldwide is undeniably fascinating. The fact that these archaic metal disks can command such immense prices amongst collectors in regular times is surprising enough – and the period of 2020 to 2021 was no regular year. The absolute economic decline brought on by the Covid-19 pandemic saw businesses everywhere fail, jobs lost and the stock market taking a repeated beating. Nearly everywhere I turned, when I asked "how's business?" I was inevitably met with "not good". I have had to bite my tongue, as even during a global pandemic the numismatic market was beyond bustling, with investors and collectors taking this opportunity to put more of their capital into coins than perhaps ever before.

Coins are an easily tradable and trackable asset, their known production figures and the presence of independent assessment firms giving widespread consumer confidence and allowing them to act as commodities. But for many, the use of the word 'investing' within numismatics gives cause for immediate recoil. As mentioned, the market is split neatly down the middle between those academics who see numismatics as a purely bookish and archaeological pursuit and the businessmen who use coins as financial instruments. One cannot function properly without the other; the academics need the market value of coins to help pay for their studies and businessmen need the academics to properly catalogue and identify their coins for them. There will always be pure academics in the market who treat the prospect of investing in coins and turning a profit to be at best unreliable and at worst, vulgar, and in many ways their position is valid; you should first and foremost approach numismatics from a place of genuine interest and enthusiasm. However, it is never inappropriate to buy wisely in the hopes of a successful resale. As the 2020s so far have shown, there are constantly emerging opportunities to extract impressive profits within numismatics.

The 'Heads or Tails' decision you must make is to what extent you choose to act on the advice of this book. If you have decided to start your own collection or begin building your existing collection with a view to profit, there is no better undertaking to turn to first than extensive research. Do not make the mistake of assuming the market will be the same for all coins and proceed to buy indiscriminately; use all of the resources available to research the price history and past performance of one coin at a time, just as you would with a specific stock or share.

Remember that, despite moderate price standardisation, the subject of 'value' is near meaningless in coins. Its definition is traditionally seen as the most money a collector will pay for a coin, but if that collector then cannot resell it, was that then actually its real value? Imagine a coin is bought by a dealer for $50 then sold for $70. The buyer then consigns the coin to an auction with 10 per cent commission, where it sells for a hammer price of $100. This final buyer has paid $120 including Buyer's Premium, but the consignor will only get $90. So: is the coin worth $50, $70, $100, $120 or $90? And if that buyer at auction cannot sell it at the level he bought and must accept $80 for it, did he overpay? When buying and selling coins, always keep this factor in mind – that value is entirely arbitrary, an aspect that can be a double-edged sword depending on your skill and experience. On the one hand it is just this arbitrary value that allows dealers to extract a quick profit from a coin sold at auction, but also represents the reason why the coin you bought at auction for $1,000 might only resell for $500. The use of TPG has helped to effectively standardise prices, but coin values are not definitively found in a book or even from consulting past auction results – they are simply what they sell for when you decide to sell.

If this warning has not knocked your confidence and you do choose to make your foray into the market, it is worth following these five main principles of numismatic trading:

1. **Research.** You can never know too much about coins themselves or the market behind them. Read up extensively on your chosen area, always ensure you know exactly what it is you are buying, and never buy blind. Check auction records and dealers' prices when trying to establish what to pay for a coin; the bottom and middle tiers of the trade can be relatively safe but at the top, the market is delicate, often thin and must be approached with caution. Ensure you are confident in the coin you are buying and its resale potential.
2. **Skill.** Build your ability to determine a coin's authenticity and quality, the originality of its surfaces and the sharpness of its strike. Learn to identify damage in the form of cleaning, tooling or other post-strike alteration and to distinguish between an appealing piece and an unappealing one. When starting out (or if at any point unconfident), turn to TPG and buy only professionally assessed coins. Your coin's value will be entirely tied to its quality and can often spell the difference between hundreds and thousands of dollars.
3. **Buy the best.** Once you feel competent in recognising coin quality, buy the best coins you can and do the best buying you can. Use only reliable and trusted sources - or otherwise be entirely sure in your own skills - and aim for the finest coins with the best eye appeal at the top of your budget. If you buy the best, then when you come to resell you reopen bidding to all collectors who may already have their own example but want to upgrade.
4. **Manage your budget and store securely.** Remember that for the duration of your ownership, your coins will generate no income. Do

not buy so much that your cash flow is compromised, thus putting you in a weakened position and forcing you to sell prematurely. Coins also represent an easily portable form of wealth – ie they can be easily taken from you. Do not skimp on security measures and make sure that you are fully insured.

5. **Be ready to sell.** Weigh up your best options for sale, taking into consideration your coin type and the current market. Once you have chosen a route and feel that the time is right to sell, commit to your decision. Trust the market to find your coin's value level without placing hefty reserves. How your coins perform will tell you your current skill level and the strength of the market, and allow you to either repeat or improve on your method.

The numismatic heartbeat has continued unabated even through a major pandemic. This is no surprise; as part of human civilisation from almost its very roots, coins are not likely to disappear from the hearts of collectors anytime soon. Just like the collectors who accrue coins as children, leave collecting aside as they mature and return in their affluent years to collect once more, coins have been intrinsic to human society and their symbolism, history, beauty and popularity will keep them firmly in circulation - even when they disappear from our day to day lives. The legacy of coins in society lives on through the numismatic market, and the association of coins with treasure and value will hold fast forever.

Bibliography

Coins of England & The United Kingdom 2022: Pre-Decimal Edition, Spink & Son Ltd, London, 2021

Coins of England & The United Kingdom: Decimal Edition, Spink & Son Ltd, London, 2021

The Ascent of Money: A Financial History of the World, Niall Ferguson, 2008

A Report Containing an Essay for the Amendment of the Silver Coins, Charles Bill, London, 1695

An Historical Account of English Money, Stephen Martin-Leake Esq, London, 1745

The History of Money, Jack Weatherford, Crown Publications, 1998

The Engraved "Mature Head" Large Cent Design Model, Rex Goldbaum, Penny-Wise, July 2020

A Guidebook of United States Coins, Whitman Publishing, 75th edition, 2021

カネはやっぱり、アンティーク・コインにぶちこめ！―コイン長者になるための３３の法則 (After all, money is thrown into antique coins! - 33 Laws to Become a Coin Master), Masakazu Kaji, Toyo Keizai Inc., Tokyo, 2014

The Numismatic Chronicle and Journal of the Numismatic Society, volumes 9-10, Taylor & Walton, 1847

The Gold Sovereign Series, Michael A. Marsh with Steve Hill, Token Publishing, 2021

About the Author

Robert's first foray into numismatics began at the age of ten, when he opened a stall selling coins and fossils outside his home. Aged sixteen Robert also began numismatic consultation work, advising clients on the value of their coins and the best routes to buy and sell. He continued coin dealing throughout his study of Forensic Science and Archaeology at University College London. After graduation, Robert began work in auction production and coin cataloguing at the London and New York offices of Spink & Son Ltd. He then went on to work in Dallas, Texas as Senior Numismatist at Heritage Auctions, specialising in British coins. He now works for the London firm Sovereign Rarities Ltd. Robert currently writes the "NumisMarket" column for *Coin News* magazine covering the health of the numismatic market, and welcomes any and all numismatic enquiries.

Contact: **Robert@ECoinomics.co.uk**

Index

adjustment marks, 8, 38, **230-33**
advances, 137, 186, 281
alternative assets, 23, 128-29, 131, 180, 189, **203-8**
Alyattes, king of Lydia, 10, 11, 13
American Numismatic Association (ANA), 22, 223
ancient coins, 18, 34-35, 39, 41, 45, 71, 75, 86, 89, 168, 229-30, 246, 291
annealing marks, 231
art:
    numismatic, 17, **38**, 100,
    market, 94, 103, 120, 131, 133, 176, **204-5**
artificial toning, 65, 73, **247-48**
auction houses:
    overview, 21-22, 81, **103-5**, 111-12, 131
    buying from, 181, **263-66**
    selling to, 185-86, **278-85**
auction records, 28, **121-26**, 167, 219-22
Australia:
    market, 93, 141, 167, 183
    coins of, 92, 278-79
Avery, Henry (pirate), 57

bagmarks, 55
Bank of England, 14, 19
banknotes, 14-15, 19, 21, 74, 77, 250
Bermuda, coins of, 223-26
Bitcoin (BTC), 175
Boniface VIII, Pope, 18
books (numismatic), 21, 132, **215-18**
British Numismatic Trade Association (BNTA), 223
brockages, 43
Brutus, coins of, 12, 105-6, 152, **250-51**
bullion, 12, 26, 121, 131, 134-5, 138, 181, 190, **200-3**
buy and hold, 142-44
buyer's premium, 103, 178, 181, 186, 220, 265

Canada:
    coins of, 48, 71, 139, 141, 183, 240, 242
    market, 44, 93, 127
capital gains tax (CGT), 141, **186-87**, 193, 268
cars (as investments), 128, 132-33, **204-7**

cash flow, 101-2, **135-37**, 179-80, 288-89
centring, 39-40, 234-35
China:
    market, 31-32, 83, **93-96**, 139
    coins of, 11, 86, 95, 139, 248
Christie's, 102, 176
circulation damage, 55-56
circulation wear, 51-53
cleaning, 8, 53, 63, 65, 71, **242-43**, 248
Cameo, Deep/Ultra, 71
coin cabinets, 77
Coin Market Collapse, 1989, **22-4**, 29, 69, 76, 118, 128, 165
CoinArchives, 111, 121, **219-21**
collectors, 98-100
Commonwealth of England, coins of, 21, 64, 123, 252
Commonwealth of Nations, 92-93
Coutts Passion Index, 128-29, 132-33, **204-7**
Covid-19:
    pandemic, 102, 112, 161, 191, 193, 199, 201, 280
    bubble, 144, 161, 163, 261
crashes, 125, 128, 160, **163-68**
credit rating agencies, 78
Croesus, king of Lydia, 11
Crusades, 13
cryptocurrency, 175, 177, 189

dealers:
    overview, 22, 94, **100-102**
    buying from, 259-63
    selling to, 275-78
denominations, 8, 13, 62, 67, 85, 215, 250
devices, 8, 46, 54, 228, 239-41, 244
diamonds, 133
die polish lines, 239-40
die rust, 40, 235, **240-41**
dies, 8, **38-42**
Dinar (Islamic coin), 12, 229
dipping, 53-54, **248-49**
diversification:
    single market, 138-40
    multiple market, 140-42
double-striking, 234-35
Dow Jones, 2, 191
Durrant, Lieutenant-Colonel William, 49-50, 159

East Asian Markets (EAMs), 93-96
edge (coin):
    damage, 38, 55, 57, 230, **245-47**
    lettering/milling, 8, 9, 41, 57-58
    in forgeries, 253
Edward III, king of England, 62
electrum, 10-12
Elizabeth I, queen of England, 33, 45
engraving, 8, 22, 36, 38-39, 94, 229, 237
Enlightenment, Age of, 20-1
environmental damage, 59-60, 133
European Markets (EMs), **84-7**, 89-92
eye appeal, **63-68**, 84-85, 211, 214, 234, 247

Fatimid Caliphate, 89
Ferdinand I, Holy Roman Emperor, 18
fields, 8, 46, 54, 59, 71, 230, **238-45**
filing, 8, 57, 73, **246**
Financial Crisis of 2007-2008, 25, 267, 190-91
financial indexes, **128-29**, 132-33, 192-3, 203-5
financial markets, 188-94
Fischer, Gerhard, 168
forgeries, 168-71, **249-58**
fractional ownership, 174-77
France, coins of, 231
FTSE 100, 2, 129, 191-92

GB 200 Rare Coins Index, 129, 192
George II, king of Great Britain, 47, 56
graffiti, 58-59, 237
Great Britain:
    coins of:
    Coenwulf gold Mancus, 107, 170-71
    Henry III gold 20 Pence, 1257, 176
    Edward III gold Double Leopard, 1344, 62
    'Three Graces' pattern Crown, 1817, 38
    George IV proof Five Pounds, 1826, 143-44
    'Gothic' Crown, 1847, 38, 139
    'Una and the Lion' Five Pounds, 1839, 2, 3, 30, 38, 47, 95, **160-61**
    market, 26, 86, 107, 139, 141-2, 182, 187, 291
Great Recoinage of 1695, 14, 19
Greece, ancient, 8, 11, 16-17, 41, 46, 86
Greenspan, Alan, 159
Gresham's law, 19
Gross Domestic Product (GDP), 31, 44, 83-84, 87-8, 92, 96, 140-41

hairlines, 8, 239, **241-2**
hallmark, 8
hammered coins, 8, 28, **39-42**, 45, 57, 75, 170, 229-31, 234-41, 245-46
haymarks, 232-3
Henry VII, king of England, 46, 269
Henry VIII, king of England, 18, 37
Henry IV, king of France, 18
hoards, 34, 107, **169**, 290
'Hogge' money, 223-26

import duty, 182
Industrial Revolution, the, 20-21
industry professionals, 222-26
insurance, 183-84
internet:
    within numismatics, 24-25, 79, 118, 121-22, 158
    as a market participant, 110-12
    as a resource, 219-22
"irrational exuberance", 158-59

Jackman, Robert, 167
Japan:
    coins of, 139
    market, 31, 93-96, 99, 218
Joachim II Hector, Elector of Brandenburg, 105

Latin America, market, 83, **88-89**
legends, 8, 39, 42, 44, 221
liquidity, 24, 77, 80, 83-84, 112, **131-34**, 193, 201
loans, 137, 198
Louis XIV, king of France, 18
lustre, 8, 51, 59, **63-64**, 238-40, 244
Lydia, coins of, 10-11, 249

Madoff, Bernie, 167
margins, 111, 126, **134-35**, 193, 196, 202, 260, 268, 276-77
market bubbles, 23-24, 31, 94, 118, 143-44, 159-60, 164, 166, 218, 280
market inefficiencies, 156-63
matte/matt, 8, 46, 48, 71, 235, 239-42
Maximilian I, Holy Roman Emperor, 18
Medici Bank, 13
Merrill Lynch, 23
metal detecting, 59, 62, 86, 107, **168-69**, 176, 224, 278
Mexico, coin of, 30
milled coins, 8, 41, 46, 231
mint errors, 42-44, 91, 93, 236
mintmark, 7, 8, 52, 88
mints:

as market participants, 108-10
buying from, 266-71
mirrored (reflectivity), 46, 48, 63, 71, **239-40**
mirror marks (forgeries), 254-55
modern coins, 26, 32, 35, 41, 94, 108-10, **266-71**
moneyers, 9, 36, 40, 42, 234
mount marks, 58, 245-46
museums:
    as market participants, 105-7
    selling to, 289-91

New Zealand, 93, 183, 278-79
non-fungible tokens (NFTs), 176
Norway, coin of, 58
Numismatic Guaranty Company (NGC), **69-72**, 74, 79, 82, 91, 105, 117, 185, 220, 225, 251, 257
numismatic intrigue, 237
Numismatic Revolution, the, 18-22

obverse, 9
off-metal, 9
overdate, 9, 44

pattern coins, 9, 22, **44-48**, 71
Paul II, Pope, 18
Parr, Catherine, 18
PCGS 3000 (index), 128
piedfort, 9, 45-46
planchet, 8, 9, 36-38, 42, 56, 63, **229-32**
plugging, 57-58, **243-45**
Poland, market, 86-87
polishing, see *cleaning*
population reports, 72, 91, **126-28**
portability of coins, 132, 183, 197
Portable Antiquities Scheme (PAS), 225, 289
portrait, 9, 33, 66
presentation, 60-68
preservation, 49-60
price standardisation, 23, 78, 90, 111, 183, 206, 208, 281
production, 36-49
Professional Coin Grading Service (PCGS), 69, **71-72**, 74, 79, 82, 106, 117, 128, 175, 185, 220
proof coins, 9, 21, **46-48**, 71, 239
provenance, 32-36, 122-23, 257-58
Pyramid of Buyers, 151-56

rarity, **28-32**, 127, 221
real estate, 120, 136, 138, 165, 179, **194-99**
Renaissance, the, 18, 20, 33

reflectivity, see *mirrored*
repair, 54, **243-45**
reverse, 8
rim, 9, 57, 246
risk, 78, 120, 138, 145, 165, **171-73**
Rome, ancient, 8, 11, 16-17, 86, 199
Royal Canadian Numismatic Association (RCNA), 22
Royal Mint, the, 21, 25, 32, 38, 109, 268, 270
Russia, market, 83, 86-87

sales tax, 181-82
satellite markets (SMs), 87-89
Scandinavia, market, 86
Scientific Revolution, the, 21-21
scratches, 55-56, 73, 239, **241-42**
shares, 132, 136-37, 148, 165, 172, 174-75, 179, 192, 193, 202
Sheldon scale, 52, **69-71**, 75, 85
slab forgeries, 256-7
smoothing, 243-44
Sotheby's, 102, 117, 174
South Africa:
    coins of, 43, 141, 261-62
    market, 93, **165-67**
sovereign (coin), 46, 92, **141-42**, 187, 269, 278-79
Spain:
    coins of, 40, 95,
    price revolution, 14, 40
    market, 86, **88-89**
specimen coins, 9, **48**, 242, 262
speculation, 101, **145-48**, 164
stamps, 25-26, 44, 174, 204
Stanley Gibbons, 129, 174, 176
strike, 9, 39-41, 48, 75, **233-235**
supply and demand, **28-32**, 35, 67, 103, 148, 168, 173, 261, 270
surface alteration:
    natural, see *circulation wear*
    deliberate, 53-55, **241-45**
sweating, 54, 56

Tesla, 194
third-party grading (TPG):
    background, 69-72
    process, 72-74
    criticisms of, 74-77
    benefits of, 77-82
tone/patina, 9, 54, 64-65, 77, 233, 247-49
tooling, 59, 69, 244
transaction costs, 193, 201
Tyrant Collection, the, 29

United States:
  coins of,
    'Flowing Hair' Dollar, 1794, 155
    Proof Dollar, 1804, 2, 22, 47, 165, 191, 257
    'Morgan' Dollars, 51-52, 64
    $50 Panama, 1915, 145-48
    $20 Double Eagle, 1933, 117, 155, 174-75
    market, 22-24, 26, 31, 35, 44, 51-52, 87, **90-93**, 117, 123, 128, 132, 148, 165, 237
US Markets (UMs), 90-93

value investing, 148-50
value precedents, 124-26
varieties, 42-44, 90-93, **236-37**
value added tax (VAT), 141, 181-82, 200
VCoins, 271, 287
vogues, 31, 39, **162-64**, 167

Wall Street:
  in numismatics, 23
  Crash, 1929, 15, 117
whizzing, 59, 63, 73, 239, **244-45**
Wyon, William, 38
'wow' factor, 65-68

X-Ray fluorescence (XRF), 256

Yap, stone money of, 194-95

OFFERING THE BEST IN NUMISMATICS

SPINK
WHERE HISTORY IS VALUED

Henry III Gold Penny
Realised £648,000

The most valuable single coin find ever made in British soil

#SPINK_AUCTIONS

SPINK LONDON
Tel: +44 (0)20 7563 4000 | Email: concierge@spink.com
Southampton Row | WC1B 4ET | London

Follow us on social media

WWW.SPINK.COM

Trust Your Coins to the Experts

Founded in 1987, NGC is the world's largest third-party coin authentication, grading and encapsulation service. Collectors and dealers around the world trust NGC for its accurate and consistent grading, its commitment to impartiality and its industry-leading guarantee.

SERVING
UK COLLECTORS FROM
OUR OFFICE IN
BLOOMSBURY, LONDON

Contact
Service@NGCcoin.uk
for information.

Learn more at
NGCcoin.uk/about